The

AUTHENTIC LIBRETTOS

of the

ITALIAN OPERAS

The
AUTHENTIC
LIBRETTOS
of the
ITALIAN OPERAS

AÏDA

CAVALLERIA RUSTICANA

LA FORZA DEL DESTINO

LUCIA DI LAMMERMOOR

RIGOLETTO

BARBER OF SEVILLE

DON GIOVANNI

LA GIOCONDA

I PAGLIACCI

LA TRAVIATA

IL TROVATORE

*Complete with English and Italian Parallel Texts
and Music of the Principal Airs*

CROWN PUBLISHERS
NEW YORK

CONTENTS

CONTENTS

FOREWORD

The music is not everything in opera. Its full enjoyment can be achieved only with the knowledge of the words that are being sung—usually in a foreign language. In this series, the librettos are presented in the original language with an English line by line translation. Thus, it is possible to follow the song and to understand the meaning of the foreign words.

The natural grouping of Italian operas suggested itself as a logical volume in this Libretto series which was inaugurated with "The Authentic Librettos of the Wagner Operas."

It was in Italy that opera received its most enduring impetus. The Italian composers' "Musica Parlante" (Speaking Music) spread throughout the continent and made Italian opera supreme. And today undoubtedly more opera performances are given in Italian than in any other language.

But there is no one Italian composer who stands out as Wagner does among the Germans. Verdi, of course, is most important. He was prolific and his "Aïda" has the distinction of being first in number of performances by the Metropolitan. But only a few of his operas have retained their popularity.

The selection of the operas to be included in this volume was determined largely by importance and popularity as indicated by the number of performances at the Metropolitan Opera House in the past 56 years. The Puccini operas had to be omitted because of insurmountable copyright difficulties. Mozart's "Don Giovanni" may seem out of place among Italian operas. But since the libretto, by Lorenzo da Ponte, is in Italian and it is sung invariably in that language, it is included in this volume.

The record of performances of these operas at the Metropolitan Opera House, 1883-1938: Aïda, 284; I Pagliacci, 214; Cavalleria Rusticana, 187; La Traviata, 157; Rigoletto, 155; Il Trovatore, 127; Lucia di Lammermoor, 106; Barber of Seville, 96; La Gioconda, 94; Don Giovanni, 54; La Forza del Destino, 37.

RIGOLETTO

by

GIUSEPPE VERDI

THE STORY OF "RIGOLETTO"

RIGOLETTO, a hunchback buffoon, or jester to the libertine Duke of Mantua, and willing pander to his licentious habits, has by his ribald and unfeeling jests, together with his villanous connivance at the Duke's open disdain for all considerations of honor, rendered himself highly objectionable to the courtiers, particularly the Counts of Ceprano and Monterone, whose wife and daughter respectively have become victims to the unbridled passions of the Duke. Monterone, in indignation at the dishonor to which he is subjected, seeks the Duke's presence and boldly denounces his conduct, and that of his vile abettor, Rigoletto, who is inwardly terror-stricken by his vehement maledictions.

Rigoletto has a young and beautiful daughter, whom he conceals from public observation with the most jealous care; so strictly has she been guarded that she has not been allowed to leave her home, except to attend her religious observances at church. She, however, has not escaped the notice of the Duke, who has repeatedly observed her at her devotions, and contrived to track her to her humble habitation, where, by bribing her servant, he gains access to her. Representing himself to be a poor student deeply impressed with her attractions, he succeeds in inspiring her with reciprocal sentiments, never dreaming that it is the daughter of his buffoon he is thus beguiling.

The fact of the existence of a young and lovely woman in the dwelling of Rigoletto becoming known to the courtiers, they form a plot to abduct her therefrom by force and deliver her to the Duke. At a late hour in the evening they assemble (masked) in the neighborhood of Rigoletto's dwelling, and, under pretence that they are going to carry off the wife of Ceprano, whose house adjoins Rigoletto's, they induce him to assist. He is accordingly masked and bandaged, and is made to hold the ladder by which some of the party ascend to the window of his house, which they enter, and tear away the bewildered Gilda, whose mouth they cover, to prevent her giving any alarm, and carry her off triumphantly to the Ducal Palace.

The outwitted jester, finding himself deserted, immediately suspects that all is not right, and tearing off the bandage, perceives the scarf of his daughter, which has been dropped in the flight; he is instantly struck with the conviction that he has been robbed of his beloved Gilda, his only treasure, and that the curse of Count Monterone has already begun to work.

The courtiers relate to the Duke as a good joke how they have carried off the jester's *mistress*, but he knows full well from their description that it is Gilda they have abducted, and the unfortunate girl soon becomes a prey to his insatiate passions.

Rigoletto hastens to the palace, and demands his daughter from the courtiers, who treat him with contempt and derision, baffling all his endeavors to obtain access to the Duke. He is presently joined by his daughter, who has at length freed herself from the vicious attentions of the Duke, and after mutual condolence they quit the place, cursing the scene of their disgrace. Resolving to be revenged on the author of his daughter's and his own misery, Rigoletto hires a bravo named Sparafucile, for a stipulated sum, to assassinate the Duke, who is enticed by the blandishments of Maddelene, the sister of Sparafucile, to the bravo's house, a ruinous and lonely inn.

Gilda has been desired by her father to put on male attire and fly to Verona, but previous to starting, in order to extinguish the lingering affection which she still entertains for her unprincipled seducer, she is made an eye-witness, through crevices in the wall of the inn, of his inconstancy and perfidy. She overhears the sister of the bravo earnestly endeavoring to dissuade him from murdering the handsome guest; but he resolutely persists in his determination to fulfil his contract, unless some person should chance to come to the inn before midnight whom he might kill instead, and pass the body in a sack to Rigoletto as that of the murdered Duke. Upon hearing this Gilda at once resolves to save the life of the undeserving object of her affections by sacrificing her own. She knocks at the door of the inn, is admitted, and instantly stabbed by the cold-blooded assassin. Shortly after, Rigoletto appears, pays the bravo, and receives from him the sack containing (as he supposes) the body of the Duke; he proceeds to throw it into the river which runs at the back of the inn, but before he has time to accomplish it, he is astounded by the voice of the living Duke, which he hears at a short distance; he instantly suspects foul play, tears open the sack, and is horrified to find, instead of the dead body of the hated Duke, the dying form of his beloved daughter, who almost immediately expires. Overwhelmed with terror and anguish at the fulfilment of the dreaded malediction, he falls senseless on the body of his unfortunate daughter.

RIGOLETTO

ACT I.

SCENE I—Magnificent salon in the Ducal Palace, with opening in the back scene, through which other salons are seen, the whole brilliantly lighted for a Fête, which is at its height. Nobles and ladies in magnificent costumes moving in all directions. Pages passing to and fro. Music heard in the distance, and occasional bursts of merriment.

(Enter the DUKE and BORSA, from the back.)

Duke.

Beautiful as youthful is my unknown charmer,
And to the end I will pursue the adventure.

Borsa.

The maiden, you mean, whom you see at the church?

Duke.

For three months past, on every Sunday.

Borsa.

Know you where she lives?

Duke.

In a remote part of the city,
Where a mysterious man visits her nightly.

Borsa.

And do you not know who he is?
Is he her lover?

Duke.

I do not know.

(A group of ladies and gentlemen cross the stage.)

Borsa.

What beauty!—Do you not admire it?

Duke.

Ceprano's wife surpasses the handsomest of them.

Borsa.

Mind the Count does not hear you, Duke.
(Softly.)

Duke.

What care I for him?

Borsa.

It may get talked about.

ATTO I.

SCENA I—Sala magnifica ne. Palazzo Ducale, con porte nel fondo, che mettono ad altre sale, pure splendidamente illuminate; folla di cavalieri e dame in gran costume nel fondo delle sale; paggi che vanno e vengono. La festa è nel suo pieno. Musica interna da lontano e serosci di risa di tratto in tratto.

(Il DUCA e BORSA, che vengono da una porta del fondo.)

Duca.

Della mia bella incognita borghese,
Toccare il fin dell' avventura io voglio.

Borsa.

Di quella giovinche vedete al tempio?

Duca.

Da tre lune ogni festa.

Borsa.

La sua dimora?

Duca.

In un remoto calle;
Misterioso un uom v'entra ogni notte.

Borsa.

E sa colei chi sia
L'amante suo?

Duca.

Lo ignora.

(Un gruppo di dame e cavalieri attraversan la sala.)

Borsa.

Quante beltà!—Mirate.

Duca.

Le vince tutte di Cepran la sposa.

Borsa.

Non v'oda il Conte, o Duca—
(Piano.)

Duca.

A me che importa?

Borsa.

Dirlo ad altra ei potria—

Duke.

That would not much affect me.

Duca.

Nè sventura per me certo saria.

QUESTA O QUELLA——*'MID THE FAIR THRONG* Air (Duke)

Ques-ta o quel-la__ per me pa-ri so-no A quan-t'al-tre d'in-
'Mid the fair throng that spar-kles a-round me, Not one__ o'er my

tor-no,__ d'in-tor-no mi ve-do, Del mio co-re__
heart-no!__ not one o'er my heart holds sway; Though a sweet smile

__ l'im-pe-ro non ce-do__ Meg-lio ad u-na__
__ one mo-ment may charm me,__ A glance from some bright eye

__ che ad al-tra. bel-tà. La co-sto-ro av-ve-nen-za e qual
__ its spell drives a-way. All a-like may at-tract, each in

do-no Di che il fa-to ne in-fio-ra la
turn__ may please; Now with one I may tri-fle and

vi-ta;__ S'og-gi que-sta__ mi tor-na gra-di-ta, For-se un'
play,__ Then an-oth-er__ may sport with and tease—Yet all my

al-tra, for-se un' al-tra__ do-man lo sa-rà, un' al-
heart to en-slave their wiles dis-play,__ my heart to en-slave their wiles

-tra, for-se un' al-tra__ do-man lo sa-rà.
dis-play, their wiles dis-play,__ their wiles__ dis-play.

As a dove flies, alarmed, to seek shelter,
  Pursued by some vulture, to bear it aloft
    in flight,
Thus do I fly from constancy's fetter:
  E'en women's spells I shun—all their ef-
    forts I slight.
A husband that's jealous I scorn and de-
    spise,
  And I laugh at and heed not a lover's
    sighs;
If a fair one take my heart by surprise,
  I heed not scornful tongues or prying
    eyes.

(Enter COUNT CEPRANO, watching his wife, who is seen advancing from the distance, attended by a cavalier. Lords and ladies promenading at back.)

Duke
(meeting the COUNTESS, and addressing her with gallantry).

Are you already going, cruel one?

Countess.

I must obey my husband:
Ceprano desires me to leave.

Duke.

The light of your face
Sheds upon the court more lustre than the
  sun;
For your smile all alike must sigh;
For you love's flame doth all around con-
  sume;
Enslaved, enchanted, for you my heart is
  breaking.
    (Kissing her hand with warmth.)

Countess.

Be more circumspect.

Duke.

No! (Giving her his arm, and leading her off.)
(Enter RIGOLETTO, meeting the COUNT CEPRANO and nobles.)

Rigoletto.

What troubles your thoughts,
Signor Ceprano?

(COUNT shows impatience, and goes off after the DUKE.)

Rigoletto (to the Cavaliers).

He is out of temper, I see.

Chorus.

What sport!

Rigoletto.

Indeed!

La costanza tiranna del core
  Detestiamo qual morbo crudele,
  Sol chi vuole si serbi fedele;
  Non v' ha amor, se non v' è libertà.
De' mariti il geloso furore,
  Degli amanti le smanie derido,
  Anco d'Argo i cent' occhi disfide
  Se mi punge una qualche beltà.

(Entra il CONTE DI CEPRANO, che segue da lungi la sua sposa, seguita da altre cavaliere. Dame e signori entrano du varie parti.)

Duca
(alla SIGNORA DE CEPRANO, movendo ad incontrarla con molta galanterie).

Partite! Crudele!

Conte.

Seguire lo sposo.
M' è forza a Ceprano.

Duca.

Ma dee luminoso
In Corte tal astro qual sole brillar.
Per voi qui ciascuno dovrà palpitar.
Per voi già possente la fiamma d'amore
Inebria, conquide, distrugge il mio core.
  (Con enfasi baciandole la mano.)

Conte.

Calmatevi—

Duca.

No! (Ce da il braccio, ed esce con lei.)
Entra e RIGOLETTO, che s'incontra nel SIGNOR DI CEPRANO poi cortigiani.)

Rigoletto.

In testa che avete,
Signor di Ceprano?

(CEPRANO fa un gesto d'impazienza, e segue il DUCA.)

Rigoletto (ai Cortigiani).

Ei sbuffa, vedete?

Coro.

Che festa!

Rigoletto.

Oh sì—

Borsa.

  The Duke is having his diversion.

Rigoletto.

  Is it not always so? What is there new in
  it?

  Gambling and drinking, feasting and dancing,

  Fighting and banqueting, all come to him
  alike.

  Now 'gainst the Countess siege he is laying,
  Her husband's jealousy wholly deriding.

(Exit.)
(Enter MARULLO.)

Marullo (eagerly).

  Oh, such news! such news I have!

Chorus.

  What has happened? Tell us!

Marullo.

  You will be quite surprised.

Chorus.

  Narrate it! narrate it!

Marullo.

  Ah! ah! Rigoletto—

Chorus.

  What of him?

Marullo.

  A strange adventure.

Chorus.

  Has he lost his hump? Is he no longer
  deformed?

Marullo.

  Stranger much than that! The idiot has
  taken—

Chorus.

  Taken what?

Marullo.

  An inamorata!

Chorus.

  An inamorata!—Incredible.

Marullo.

  Into a Cupid the hunchback is transformed.

Chorus.

  Oh, what a Cupid!—What a comical
  Cupid!

(Enter the DUKE, followed by RIGOLETTO, and CEPRANO in
the background.)

Borsa.

  Il Duca quì pur si diverte.

Rigoletto.

  Così non è sempre? che nuove scoperte!
  Il giuoco ed il vino, le feste, la danza,
  Battaglie, conviti, ben tutto gli sta.
  Or della Contessa l'assedio egli avanza,
  E intanto il marito fremendo ne va.

(Esce.)

(Entra MARULLO.)

Marullo (premuroso).

  Gran nuova! gran nuova!

Coro.

  Che avvenne? parlate!

Marullo.

  Stupir ne dovrete—

Coro.

  Narrate, narrate—

Marullo.

  Ah! ah!—Rigoletto—

Coro.

  Ebben?

Marullo.

  Caso enorme!—

Coro.

  Perduto ha la gobba? non è più difforme?

Marullo.

  Più strana è la cosa!—Il pazzo possiede—

Coro.

  Infine?

Marullo.

  Un' amante!

Coro.

  Amante! Chi il crede?

Marullo.

  Il gobbo in Cupido or s' è trasformato!—

Coro.

  Quel mostro Cupido!—Cupido beato!—

(Entra il DUCA, seguito da RIGOLETTO, indi CEPRANO.)

Duke   (to RIGOLETTO).

What a troublesome fellow is that Ceprano!

But his wife—to my mind she's an angel!

Rigoletto.

Then carry her off.

Duke.

That is easily said—but how to do it?

Rigoletto.

Do it to-night.

Duke.

You do not consider the Count.

Rigoletto.

Can you not put him in prison?

Duke.

Ah! no.

Rigoletto.

Then why not banish him?

Duke.

Buffoon, I dare not.

Rigoletto.

His head, then.
     (Making signs of cutting it off.)

Ceprano   (coming forward).

(Black-hearted villain!)

Duke.

Is this the head you speak of?
  (Placing his hand on the shoulder of the COUNT.)

Rigoletto   (laughing).

Of what value is such a head as that?

Ceprano.

Miscreant!
     (Furiously, and drawing his sword.)

Duke.

Forbear.   (To CEPRANO.)

Rigoletto.

He only makes me laugh.

Chorus.

He is frantic with rage.
     (Among themselves.)

Duke.

Buffoon, come hither.
     (To RIGOLETTO.)

You always carry your jokes too far;—

The anger you provoke may one day on
   your head alight.

Rigoletto.

Who can hurt me?—I have no fear.

Duca   (a RIGOLETTO).

Ah, quanto Ceprano, importuno niun v' è.

La cara sua posa è un angiol per me!

Rigoletto.

Rapitela.

Duca.

E detto; ma il farlo?

Rigoletto.

Stassera.

Duca.

Nè pensi tu al Conte?

Rigoletto.

Non c' è la prigione?

Duca.

Ah, no.

Rigoletto.

Ebben—s'esilia.

Duca.

Nemmeno, buffone.

Rigoletto.

Adunque la testa—
     (Indicando di farla tagliare.)

Ceprano.

(Oh, l'anima nera!)

Duca.

Che di' questa testa?—
  (Battendo colla mano una spalla al Conte.)

Rigoletto.

Che far di tal testa?—A cosa ella vale?

Ceprano.

Marrano.
     (Infuriato, battendo la spada.)

Duca.

Fermate—   (A CEPRANO.)

Rigoletto.

Da rider mi fa.

Coro.

In furia è montato!
     (Tra loro.)

Duca.

Buffone, vien quà.
     (A RIGOLETTO.)

Ah! sempre tu spingi lo scherzo all' estremo.

Quell' ira che sfida colpir ti potrà.

Rigoletto.

Che coglier mi puote? Di loro non temo;

The Duke's protégé no one dares to injure! | Del Duca un protetto nessun toccherà

Ceprano
(aside to Courtiers).
Vengeance on the buffoon!

Ceprano
(ai Cortigiani, a parte).
Vendetta del pazzo—

Chorus.
And who amongst us
Has not some wrong to be avenged!

Coro.
Contr' esso un rancore
Pei tristi suoi modi, di noi chi non ha?

Ceprano.
And they shall be avenged!

Ceprano.
Vendetta.

Chorus.
But how?

Coro.
Ma come?

Ceprano.
To-morrow, let all who have the courage,
By my side, and armed, appear.

Ceprano.
Domani, chi ha core,
Sia in armi da me.

Chorus.
Be it so.

Tutti.
Sì.

Ceprano.
At night.

Ceprano.
A notte.

Chorus.
Agreed.
(Groups of Dancers appear.)
All here is joyful—all here is festive;
To pleasure all here invites;
Oh, look around, and in all faces see
The reign of voluptuous delights.

Tutti.
Sarà.
(La folla de' danzatori invade la sala.)
Tutto è gioja, tutto è festa,
Tutto invitaci a goder!
Oh, guardate, non par questa,
Or la reggia del piacer!

Count Monterone
(from without).
I will speak to him.
(Enter COUNT MONTERONE.)

Conte di Monterone
(dall intorno).
Ch' io gli parli.
(Entra il CONTE DI MONTERONE.)

Duke.
No.

Duca.
No.

Monterone.
But I will.

Monterone.
Il voglio.

Chorus.
Monterone!

Tutti.
Monterone!

Monterone
(looking scornfully at the DUKE).
Yes, Monterone—against crimes like thine
There is yet one to raise a voice.

Monterone
(fissando il DUCA con nobile orgoglio).
Sì Monteron—la voce mia qual tuono
Vi scuoterà dovunque—

Rigoletto
(to the DUKE, mimicking the voice of MONTERONE).
I will speak to him.
(With mock gravity.)
Against us you have conspired, signor,
And we, in our clemency, have pardoned
   you.
'Tis madness in all seasons to come here,
Wailing about the honor of your daughter.

Rigoletto
(al DUCA, contraffacendo la voce di MONTERONE).
Ch' io gli parli.
(Si avanza con ridicola gravita.)
Voi congiuraste contro noi, signore,
E noi, clementi in vero, perdonammo—
Qual vi piglia or delirio—a tutte l'ore
Di vostra figlia reclamar l'onore?

Monterone (looking scornfully at RIGOLETTO).

Despicable buffoon!—
(To DUKE.)
Ah! thus will I
Thy vile orgies ever disturb. In all places
Shall my weeping voice attend you,
While unavenged shall remain
The gross insult on my family inflicted.
And if to the hangman you consign me,
As a spirit will I again visit thee,
Till the vengeance of God and man o'er-
whelm thee.

Duke.

No more of this—arrest him.

Rigoletto.

He is mad!

Chorus.

What ravings!

Monterone.

Oh! on both of ye be my malediction!
(To the DUKE and RIGOLETTO.)
Vile is he who hounds the dying lion,
But viler thou, O Duke, and thy serpent
there,
Who the anguish of a parent can deride!
A parent's curse be on ye both!

Rigoletto.

(What do I hear? Oh, horror!)
(Greatly agitated.)

All (except RIGOLETTO).

Audaciously thou hast this fête disturbed,
By an infernal spirit hither led.
Vain are thy words—deaf to them our ears.
Go, tremble, old man, at the sovereign anger
Thou hast provoked. No hope for thee re-
mains;
Fatal will this day prove to thee.

MONTERONE is marched off between halberdiers—the others
follow the DUKE.)

SCENE II—The extremity of a street that has no thor-
oughfare. On the left a house of retired appearance, within
a court-yard, from which there is a doorway into the
street. In the court-yard are seen a tall tree and a marble
seat. At the top of the wall, a terrace, supported by arches,
and reached by a flight of steps in front. On the right of
the passage is the highest wall of the garden, and the gable
end of the palace of CEPRANO. It is night.

(Enter RIGOLETTO, enveloped in a cloak, followed by SPAR-
AFUCILE, who has a long sword under his cloak.)

Rigoletto.

(How fearfully that man cursed me!)

Monterone (guardando RIGOLETTO con ira sprezzante).

Novello insulto!—
(Al DUCA.)
Ah, sì a turbare
Sarò vestr' orgie—verrò a gridare,
Fino a che vegga restarsi inulto
Di mia famiglia l'atroce insulto;
E se al carnefice pur mi darete
Spettro terribile mi rivedrete,
Portante in mano il teschio mio,
Vendetta chiedere al mondo e a Dio.

Duca.

Non più, arrestatelo.

Rigoletto.

E matto!

Coro.

Quai detti!

Monterone.

Oh, siate entrambi voi maledetti.
(Al DUCA e RIGOLETTO.)
Slanciare il cane al leon morente
E vile, o Duca—e tu serpente,
(A RIGOLETTO.)
Tu che d'un padre rida al dolore,
Sii maledetto!

Rigoletto.

(Che sento? orrore!)
(Colpito.)

Tutti (meno RIGOLETTO).

Oh, tu che la festa audace hai turbito,
Da un genio d'inferno quì fosti guidato;
E vano ogni detto, di quà t'allontana—
Va, trema, o vegliardo, dell' ira sovrana—
Tu l' hai provocata, più spheme non v' è.
Un' ora fatale fu questa per te.

(MONTERONE parte fra due alabardieri; tutti glī altr
seguirono il DUCA in altra stanza.)

SCENA II—L'estremita più deserta d'una Via Cieca. A
sinistra, una casa di discreta apparenza, con una piccola
corte circondato da muro. Nella corte un grosso ed alto
albero ed un sedile di marmo; nel muro una porta che mette
ella strada; sopra il muro un terrazzo practicabile, sostenuto
da arcate. La porta del primo piano dà su detto terrazzo,
a cui si ascende per una scala di fronte. A destra, della
via è il muro altissimo del giardino, e un fiance del Palazzo
di CEPRANO. E notte.
(RIGOLETTO chiuso nel suo mantello. SPARAFUCILE lo
segue, portando sotto il mantello una lunga spada.)

Rigoletto.

(Quel vecchio maledivami!)

Sparafucile.

    Signor—

Rigoletto.

    Go: I have no need of you.

Sparafucile.

    Be that as it may, you have before you
    A man who knows how to use a sword.

Rigoletto.

    A robber?

Sparafucile.

    No— a man who, for a trifle,
    Will from a rival free you;—
    And have you not one?

Rigoletto.

    Who is he?

Sparafucile.

    Have you not a mistress here?

Rigoletto.

    (What do I hear?) What would it cost me
    To rid me of a signor?

Sparafucile.

    More than for a lesser man.

Rigoletto.

    When must it be paid?

Sparafucile.

    One-half beforehand,
    The other when the deed is done.

Rigoletto.

    (O demon!) And how can you
    Be sure of success?

Sparafucile.

    In the street sometimes they fall.
    At other times in my own house;—
    I waylay my man at night—
    A single blow, and he is dead.

Rigoletto.

    And how in your own house?

Sparafucile.

    All the easier—
    I have a sister there who helps.
    She dances in the streets—she is handsome—
    Those I want she decoys—and then—

Rigoletto.

    I comprehend

Sparafucile.

    Signor?

Rigoletto.

    Va non ho niente.

Sparafucile.

    Nè il chiesi—a voi presente
    Un uom di spada sta.

Rigoletto.

    Un ladro?

Sparafucile.

    Un uom che libera
    Per poco da un rivale,
    E voi ne avete—

Rigoletto.

    Quale?

Sparafucile.

    La vostra donna è là.

Rigoletto.

    (Che sento?) E quanto spendero
    Per un signor dovrei?

Sparafucile.

    Prezzo maggior vorrei—

Rigoletto.

    Com' usasi pagar?

Sparafucile.

    Una metà s'anticipa,
    Il resto si da poì—

Rigoletto.

    (Dimonio!) E come puoi
    Tanto securo oprar?

Sparafucile.

    Soglio in cittade uccidere,
    Oppure nel mio tetto.
    L'uomo di sera aspetto—
    Une stoccata, e muor.

Rigoletto.

    E come in casa?

Sparafucile.

    E facile—
    M'ainta mia sorella—
    Per lè vie danza—è bella—
    Chi voglio attira—e allor—

Rigoletto.

    Comprendo—

Sparafucile.

There is nothing to fear;
My trusty weapon never betrays me.
(Showing his sword.)
Can I serve you?

Rigoletto.

No; not at present.

Sparafucile.

The worse for you.

Rigoletto.

Your name?

Sparafucile.

Sparafucile is my name.

Rigoletto.

A foreigner?

Sparafucile.

From Burgundy.
(About to go.)

Rigoletto.

Where are you to be found?

Sparafucile.

Hereabouts, every night.

Rigoletto.

Go. (Exit SPARAFUCILE.)
How like are we!—the tongue my weapon,
the dagger his!
To make others laugh is my vocation—his
to make them weep!
How that old man cursed me!
O man!—O human nature!
What scoundrels dost thou make of us!
O rage! To be deformed—the buffoon to
have no play!
Whether one will or not, to be obliged to
laugh!
Tears, the common solace of humanity,
Are to me prohibited!
Youthful, joyous, high-born, handsome,
An imperious master gives the word—
"Amuse me, buffoon,"—and I must obey.
Perdition! How do I not despise ye all,
Ye sycophants—ye hollow courtiers!
If I am deformed, 'tis ye have made me so;
But a changed man will I now become.

Sparafucile.

Senza strepito—
E questo il mio stromento.
(Mostra la spada.)
Vi serve?

Rigoletto.

No—al momento—

Sparafucile.

Peggio per voi—

Rigoletto.

Chi sa?

Sparafucile.

Sparafucile mi nomino—

Rigoletto.

Straniero?—

Sparafucile.

Borgognone—
(Per andarsene.)

Rigoletto.

E dove all' occasione?—

Sparafucile.

Quì sempre a sera.

Rigoletto.

Va. (SPARAFUCILE parte.)
Pari siamo!—Io la lingua, egli ha il pug-
nale;
L'uomo son io che ride, ei quel che spegne!
Quel vecchio maledivami!
O uomini!—o natura!
Vi! scellerato mi faceste voi!
Oh rabbia!—esser difforme!—esser buffone!
Non dover, non poter altro che ridere!
Il retaggio d'ogni uom m' è tolto—il pianto!
Questo padrone mio,
Giovin, giocondo, si possente, bello
Sonnecchiando mi dice;
Fa ch'io rida, buffone.
Forzarmi deggio, e farlo! Oh, dannazione!
Odio a voi, cortigiani schernitori!
Quanta in mordervi ho gioia!
Se iniquo so, per cangion vostra e solo—
Ma il altr' uom quì mi cangio!
Quel vecchio malediami! Tal pensiero
Perchè conturba ognor la mente mia?

That old man cursed me! Why does that curse

Thus ever haunt my harassed mind?

What have I to fear? Ah, no, this is mere folly!

(Opens a door with a key, and enters the yard.)

(Enter GILDA, coming from the house, and throwing herself into her father's arms.)

Rigoletto.

My daughter!

Gilda.

My dear father!

Rigoletto.

Only when near to thee

Does my oppressed heart know joy.

Gilda.

Oh, what affection!

Rigoletto.

My only life art thou!

What other earthly happiness have I?

           (Sighing.)

Gilda.

Why do you sigh? What ails you?

Open your mind to your poor daughter.

If any secret you have, to her confide it;

And do about her family inform her.

Rigoletto.

Thou hast not any.

Gilda.

What is your real name?

Rigoletto.

What matters it to thee?

Gilda.

If you are not willing

Of your family to speak—

Rigoletto.

Do you ever go out?

           (Interrupting her.)

Gilda.

Only when I go to church.

Rigoletto.

In that thou dost right.

Gilda.

If of yourself you will not speak,

At least tell me something of my mother.

Mi coglierà sventura? Ah no, è follia.

(Apre con chiave, ad entra nel cortile.)

(Entra GILDA, ch'esce dalla casa e segetta nelle sue braccia.

Rigoletto.

Figlia!

Gilda.

Mio padre!

Rigoletto.

A te dapresso

Trova sol gioia il core oppresso.

Gilda.

Oh, quanto amore!

Rigoletto.

Mia vita sei!

Senza te in terra qual bene avrei?

           (Sospira.)

Gilda.

Voi sospirate!—che v'ange tanto?

Lo dite a questa povera figlia—

Se v' ha mistero—per lei sia franto—

Ch'ella conosca la sua famiglia.

Rigoletto.

Tu non ne hai—

Gilda.

Qual nome avete?

Rigoletto.

A te che importa?

Gilda.

Se non volete

Di voi parlarmi—

Rigoletto.

Non uscir mai.

           (Interrompendola.)

Gilda.

Non vo che al tempio.

Rigoletto.

Or ben tu fai.

Gilda.

Se non di voi, almen chi sia.

Fate ch'io sappia la madre mia.

DEH NON PARLARE —— *SPEAK NOT OF ONE* Air (Rigoletto)

Deh non par-la-re al mi-se-ro Del suo per-du-to be — ne;
Speak not of one, whose loss to thee, *All earth can boast could ne'er re-store;*

El - la sen - tia, quell' an - ge-lo, Pie - tà del - le mie
Her an-gel form me-thinks I see, *Who loved me, though de-form'd and*

pe - ne; So - lo, dif-for-me, po-ve-ro, Per com-pas-sion mi a-
poor. — *Pi - ty,* *O Gil-da;* *spare me!* *Ask it, my child, no*

mò. Ah! mo - ri - a, mo - ri - a, le zol - le co-pra-no Lie-vi quel ca-po a-
more. Ah! she died;— *may earth* *rest light-ly on — her; To me she's lost for-*

ma-to; So-la or tu re - sti, So-la or tu res-ti al mi - se - ro;—
ev - er. Thou art my on - ly hope, *Thou art my on - ly hope, my child!*

Di - o, sii rin - gra - zia - to, si rin-gra - zia-to.
Fa - ther of all!— oh! bless her with Thy mer - cy mild!

Gilda.

Alas! what anguish! such bitter grief
What language can express!
Father, dear father, calm yourself,
Or my heart will surely break.
To me your name pray tell;
The grief that saddens you impart.

Rigoletto.

'Twere useless myself to discover;
Suffice it that thy father I am.
Some in the world there are who fear me,
In others, perhaps, envy I excite;
But one there is who has cursed me!

Gilda.

Quanto dolor! che spremere
Sì amaro pianto può?
Padre, non più, calmatevi—
Mi lacera tal vista—
Il nome vostro ditemi,
Il duol che sì v'attrista—

Rigoletto.

A che nomarmi? è inutile!
Padre ti sono, e basti—
Me forse al mondo temono,
D' alcuno ho forse gli asti:
Altri mi maledicono—

Gilda.

　Country, family, friends,
　Possess you none of them?

Rigoletto.

　Country, family, friends, say'st thou?
　Thou art my country, family, and friends!
　The whole universe thou art to me!
　　　　　(Passionately.)

Gilda.

　Ah! if happier I could render you,
　What joy to my heart it would bring!
　Three months full it is since hither I came,
　And nothing yet have I of the city seen.
　With your permission I should like to see it.

Rigoletto.

　Never! never! Hast thou ever left the
　　house?

Gilda.

　No.

Rigoletto.

　That's well.

Gilda.

　(What have I said?)

Rigoletto.

　I'll take care thou shalt not!
　(She might be followed—stolen from me!
　To dishonor the daughter of a buffoon
　Would here be laughed at. Horror!) Ho,
　　there!
　　　　　(Turning towards the house.)

　　　(Enter Giovanna, from the house.)

Giovanna.

　Signor?

Rigoletto.

　Has any one seen me come hither?
　Mind—speak the truth.

Giovanna.

　Oh, no—no one.

Rigoletto.

　That is well. The gate that to the bastion
　　leads—
　Is that always closed?

Giovanna.

　It is, and shall be.

Gilda.

　Patria, parenti, amici,
　Voi dunque non avete?

Rigoletto.

　Patria! parenti! dici?
　Culto, famiglia, patria,
　Il mio universo è in te!
　　　　　(Con effusione.)

Gilda.

　Ah! se può lieto rendervi,
　Gioia è la vita a me!
　Già da tre lune son quì venuta,
　Nè la cittade ho ancor veduta;
　Se il concedete, farlo or potrei—

Rigoletto.

　Mai! mai! uscita, dimmi, unqua sei?

Gilda.

　No.

Rigoletto.

　Guai!

Gilda.

　(Che dissi?)

Rigoletto.

　Ben te ne guarda!
　Potrian seguirla, rapirla ancora!
　Qui d'un buffone si disonora
　La figlia, e ridesi—Orror! Olà?
　　　　　(Verso la casa.)

　　　(Entra Giovanna, dalla casa.)

Giovanna.

　Signor?

Rigoletto.

　Venendo, mi vide alcuno?
　Bada, di' il vero—

Giovanna.

　Ah, no, nessuno.

Rigoletto.

　Sta ben—la porta che dà al bastione
　E sempre chiusa?

Giovanna.

　Lo fu e sarà.

VEGLIA O DONNA——*SAFELY GUARD THIS TENDER BLOSSOM* Duet (Rigoletto and Gilda)

RIGOLETTO

Ve-glia, o don-na, ques-to fio - re, Che a te pu - ro con-fi-
Safe - ly guard this ten - der blos - som, Which to thee I am con-

da - i; Ve-gli at - ten - ta e non sia ma - i Che s'of-
fid - ing, In her guile - less heart and bos - om May no

fu - schi il suo can-dor. Tu dei ven - ti dal fu - ro - re Ch'al-tri
thought of ill be - tide; From the arts of vice pro - tect her, May its

fio - ri han-no pie - ga - to,. Lo di - fen - di, e im-ma-co-
snares be laid in vain; Her fa - ther will from thee ex-

la - te Lo ri - do - na al ge - ni - tor, Quan-to af - fet - to! qua-li
pect her Pure re - stored to him a - gain. Ah! such fear for me re-

GILDA

cu - re! Che te - me - te, pa - dre mi - o? Las - sù in
veal - ing, Fa - ther dear, why thus dis - play? One from

cie - lo, pres-so Di - o Ve-glia un an - giol pro-tet - tor. Da noi
whom there's no con - ceal - ing Guides me ev - er on my way. From on

sto - glie le sven - tu - re Di mia ma - dre il prie-go san - to Non fia
high my moth-er's spir - it Leads me on with ten-der care; While this

mai dis-vel-to o fran - to Ques-to a voi di - let - to fior.
heart bears life with - in it, 'Twill de - fy each art - ful snare.

(The DUKE, in disguise, is seen to arrive in the street.)

Rigoletto.

There is some one outside.

(RIGOLETTO comes through the garden-gate, and looks about the street; while doing so, the DUKE stealthily glides in, and hides himself behind a tree, throwing a purse to GIOVANNA.)

Gilda.

Oh, Heavens!

He is always suspicious.

Rigoletto   (returning to GILDA.)

Does any one ever follow you to church?

Gilda.

No.

Duke.

(Rigoletto.)

Rigoletto.

Should any one knock,

On no account admit him.

Giovanna.

Not even the Duke?

Rigoletto.

Above all others keep him out. Daughter, adieu!

Duke.

(His daughter!)

Gilda.

Adieu, dear father.

(They embrace, and RIGOLETTO departs, closing the door after him.)

Gilda   (in the yard).

Giovanna, I am struck with remorse.

Giovanna.

What about, pray?

Gilda.

I did not tell him of the youth who follows me to church.

Giovanna.

Why should you tell him? Do you hate the youth,

And would you thus dismiss him?

Gilda.

No, no! his looks are pleasing to me.

Giovanna.

And he has the appearance of a wealthy signor.

Gilda.

Neither signor nor wealth do I wish to have;

(Entra il DUCA, in costume borghese, della strada.)

Rigoletto.

Alcuno è fuori—

(Apre la porta della corte e, mentre esce a guardar sulla strada, il DUCA guizza furtivo nella corte, e si nasconde dietro l'albero; gettando a GIOVANNA una borsa la fa tacere.)

Gilda.

Cielo!

Sempre novel sospetto—

Rigoletto   (a GILDA, tornando).

Vi seguiva alla chiesa mai nessuno?

Gilda.

Mai.

Duca.

(Rigoletto.)

Rigoletto.

Se talor quì picchiano

Guardatevi d'aprire—

Giovanna.

Nemmeno al Duca?

Rigoletto.

Meno che a tutti a lui. Mia figlia, addio.

Duca.

(Sua figlia!)

Gilda.

Addio, mio padre.

(S'abbraciano, e RIGOLETTO parte, chiudendosi dietro la porta.)

Gilda   (nella corte).

Giovanna, ho dei rimorsi—

Giovanna.

E perchè mai?

Gilda.

Tacqui che un giovin ne sequiva al tempio.

Giovanna.

Perchè ciò dirgli?—l'odiate dunque

Cotesto giovin, voi?

Gilda.

No, no, chè troppo è bello, e spira amore—

Giovanna.

E magnanimo sembra e gran signore.

Gilda.

Signor nè principe—io lo vorrei:

The poorer he prove, the more shall I love him.

Sleeping or waking, my thoughts are all of him,

And my heart longs to tell him I lo—

Duke

(suddenly coming forward, motioning GIOVANNA to retire, and kneeling at the feet of GILDA).

I love thee!

The words repeat! Such delicious accents

Open to me a heaven of enjoyment.

Gilda.

Giovanna? Alas, no one answers me!

There's no one here! Oh, heavens, I'm alone!

Duke.

No! I am here; and to thee I respond—

Against all the world I will protect thee!

Gilda.

Why thus address yourself to me?

Duke.

Whate'er your state, to me it matters not—

I love thee!

Gilda.

Oh, go away.

Dyke.

Go away! No, not yet!

If love's fire within us both be lighted,

Inseparable we should henceforth be;

O maiden bright, thy lot with mine unite!

Sento che povero—più l'amerei.

Sognando o vigile—sempre lo chiamo,

E l'alma in estasi—gli dice t'a—

Duca

(esce improvviso, fa cenno a GIOVANNA d'andarsene, e in ginocchiandosi a' pied di GILDA termina la frase).

T'amo!

T'amo, ripetilo—si caro accento,

Un puro schiudimi—ciel di contento!

Gilda.

Giovanna? Ahi, misera! non v' è più alcuno

Che quì rispondami! Oh Dio! nessuno!

Duca.

Son io coll' anima—che ti rispondo—

Ah, que che s'amano—son tutto un mondo!

Gilda.

Chi mai, chi giungere—vi fece a me?

Duca.

S'angelo o demone—che importa a te?

Io t'amo—

Gilda.

Uscitene.

Duca.

Uscire! adesso!

Ora che accendene—un fuoco istesso!

Ah, inseparabile—d'amore, il dio

Stringeva, o vergine—tuo fato al mio!

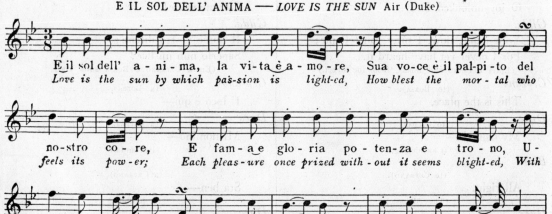

E IL SOL DELL' ANIMA — *LOVE IS THE SUN* Air (Duke)

E il sol dell' a - ni - ma, la vi - ta e a - mo - re, Sua vo - ce è il pal - pi - to del
Love is the sun by which pas - sion is light - ed, How blest the mor - tal who

no - stro co - re, E fam - a e glo - ria po - ten - za e tro - no, U -
feels its pow - er; Each pleas - ure once prized with - out it seems blight - ed, With

ma - ne, fra - gi - li qui co - se so - no: U - na pur av - ve - ne,
it we heed not what fate may show - er. Feel - ing ce - les - tial,

Gilda.

(Ah! how these words my ears delight!
His tones, how tender—and how pure his
    love!)

Duke.

That you love me—oh, the words repeat—

Gilda.

You have heard.

Duke.

O joy unlooked for!

Gilda.

Your name, now, I pray you tell me;
For I never yet have heard it.

(Enter CEPRANO and BORSA, from the street.)

Ceprano (to BORSA).

This is the place.

Duke (to GILDA).

My name is—

(Considering.)

Borsa (to CEPRANO).

All right.

(They depart.)

Duke.

Walter Maldè.
I am a student—a poor student.

Gilda.

(Ah de' miei vergini—sogni son queste—
Le voci tenere—si care a me!)

Duca.

Che m'ami—deh! ripetimi—

Gilda.

L'udiste.

Duca.

'Oh, me felice!

Gilda.

Il nome vostro ditemi;
Saperlo non mi lice?

(Entra CEPRANO e BORSA sulla via.)

Ceprano (a BORSA).

Il loco è quì—

Duca (a GILDA).

Mi nomino—

(Pensando.)

Borsa (a CEPRANO).

Sta ben—

(E partono.)

Duca.

Gaultier Maldé.
Studento sono, povero.

Giovanna. (In alarm.)

I hear footsteps outside.

Gilda.

Perhaps it is my father.

Duke.

Ah! could I the traitor catch
Who thus presumes to interrupt
The joy I have in being with thee!

Gilda (to GIOVANNA).

(Quickly away!
To the bastion conduct him—go!)

Duke.

First say that you love me?

Gilda.

And you?

Duke.

With my whole heart I swear it.

Gilda.

No more, no more, at once depart.

Both.

Farewell, my hope, my soul, farewell;
For thee alone henceforth I'll live;
Farewell! Immutable as Fate
Shall be my love and truth to thee.

(Exit the DUKE, escorted by GIOVANNA, GILDA following his steps with her eyes.)

Gilda (alone).

Walter Maldè! What a romantic name!
Already is it on my heart engraven!

Giovanna. (Spaventata.)

Rumor di passi è furore.

Gilda.

Forse mio padre.

Duca.

Ah! cogliere
Potessi il traditore
Che sì mi sturba!

Gilda (a GIOVANNA)

(Adducilo
Di quà al bastione, ite!)

Duca.

Di m'amerai tu?

Gilda.

E voi?

Duca.

L'intera vita, poi.

Gilda.

Non più, non più, partite.

A 2.

Addio, speranza ed anima
Sol tu sari per me.
Addio, vivrà immutabile
L'affretto mio per te.

(Parte il DUCA scortato da GIOVANNA, GILDA resta fissando è partito.)

Gilda (sola).

Gualtier Maldé! nome di lui si amato.
Scolpiciti nel core innamorato!

CARO NOME CHE IL MIO COR — *DEAR NAME WITHIN THIS BREAST*   Air (Gilda)

Ca-ro no-me che il mio cor Fes-ti pri-mo pal-pi-
Dear name, with-in this breast, Thy mem-'ry will re-

tar, Le de-li-zie dell' a-mor Mi dèi sem-pre ram-men-
main; My love, for thee con-fess'd, No pow-er can re-

tar! Col pen-sier il mio de-sir A te sem-pre vo-le-
strain. Ah! yes, 'tis bliss to own The joy that fills my-

ra, E fin l'ul - ti - mo   so - spir, Ca - ro no - me, tuo___ sa -
heart; 'Twill beat for thee a - lone; Till death 'twill ne'er   de -

rà.   Col pen - sier il mio de - sir   A te sem - pre vo - le - rà.___
part!   'Twill___ beat for thee a - lone;   Ah! till death 'twill ne'er de - part!

                          E fin l'ul - ti - mo___   mi - o___ so -
                          'Twill beat, 'twill beat for   thee a - ...

spir, Ca - ro no - _____ me, tuo sa - rà.
lone, Ah!___ till death _____ 'twill ne'er de - part.

(She ascends the terrace, with a lantern ,in her hand.)

(Enter MARULLO, CEPRANO, and BORSA, accompanied by courtiers, in masks, and armed.)

Borsa.

Look there!

(Pointing towards GILDA.)

Ceprano.

Ah! there she is—

Chorus.

Oh! how beautiful she is!

Marullo.

A fairy or an angel!

Chorus.

Can that the mistress be
Of Rigoletto?

(They all laugh.)
(Enter RIGOLETTO, absorbed in thought.)

Rigoletto.

(Laughing! what can it mean?)

Borsa.

Silence, to our work; we've no time for
laughing.

Rigoletto.

(Ah, how fiercely that old man cursed me!)
Who is there?

(San al terrazzo con una lanterna, che tono entra in casa.)

(Entrano MARULLO, CEPRANO, e BORSA, cortigiani, armati e mascherati, dalla via.)

Borsa.

E là.

(Indicanda GILDA.)

Ceprano.

Miratela—

Coro.

Oh! quanto è bella!

Marullo.

Par fata od angiol!

Coro.

L'amante è quella
Di Rigoletto?

(Entra RIGOLETTO, concentrato.)

Rigoletto.

(Riedo! perche?)

Borsa.

Silenzio, all' opra, badate a me.

Rigoletto.

(Ah da quel vecchio fui maledetto!)
Chi è là?

Borsa (to his companions).

Be silent, 'tis Rigoletto.

Ceprano.

A double capture! We can also slay him.

Borsa.

No; to-morrow it will make more sport.

Marullo.

But now everything is ready.

Rigoletto.

(Who is speaking there?)

Marullo.

Is't you, Rigoletto—say.

Rigoletto (considerably agitated).

Who goes there?

Marullo.

You will not betray us—I am—

Rigoletto.

Who?

Marullo.

Marullo.

Rigoletto.

In the dead of night for good you are not
here.

Marullo.

'Tis a ridiculous frolic brings us here;
Ceprano's wife we mean to carry off.

Rigoletto.

(Once more do I breathe.) But how do you
enter?

Marullo (to CEPRANO).

Hand here the keys!
(To RIGOLETTO.)
Doubt us not;
We are not to be foiled in a stratagem.
(Handing him the keys taken from CEPRANO.)
Here are the keys.

Rigoletto (feeling the keys).

I feel that this is his crest.
(Ah! then all my terrors have been need-
less!)
(He breathes more freely.)
Yonder is his palace—I will go with you.

Marullo.

We are all disguised.

Borsa (ai compagni).

Tacete, c' è Rigoletto.

Ceprano.

Vittoria doppia! L'uccideremo.

Borsa.

No: chè domani più rideremo.

Marullo.

Or tutto aggiusto.

Rigoletto.

(Chi parla quà?)

Marullo.

Ehi, Rigoletto?—di

Rigoletto (con voce terribile).

Chi va là?

Marullo.

Eh, non mangiarci—son—

Rigoletto.

Chi?

Marullo.

Marullo.

Rigoletto.

In tanto bugo lo squardo è nullo.

Marullo.

Quì ne condusse ridevol cosa;
Tòrre a Ceprano vogliam la sposa.

Rigoletto.

(Ohimè, respiro.) Ma come entrare?

Marullo (a CEPRANO).

La vostra chiave?
(A RIGOLETTO.)
Non dubitare;
Non de mancarci lo stratagemma.
(Gli dà chiave avuta da CEPRANO.)
Ecco le chiavi.

Rigoletto (palpandole).

Sento il suo stemma.
(Ah, terror vano fu dunque il mio!)

(Respirando.)
N' è là palazzo—con vio son io.

Marullo.

Siam mascherati.

Rigoletto.

Then so will I be;

Give me here a mask.

Marullo.

Well, here is one.

You shall hold the ladder.

(Puts a mask on the face of RIGOLETTO, fastens it by a handkerchief across his eyes, and places him at a ladder, against the terrace wall, to keep it steady.)

Rigoletto.

How very dark it has become!

Marullo.

The bandage renders him both blind and deaf.

(To his companions.)

All.

Silence! silence! while vengeance we seek;

In his own trap now let him be caught;

The jester who constantly makes us his sport,

Shall now, in his turn, our laughter provoke.

Hush! be quiet! his mistress we'll seize,

And, to-morrow, at court have our laugh.

(Some ascend to the terrace, force a window, by which they enter, and descend to the door, which they open to others, who enter and drag out GILDA. She has her mouth gagged with a handkerchief. While being dragged across the stage, a scarf falls from her.)

Gilda.

Help! help! Father, dear, help!

Chorus.

Victory!

Gilda.

Help! help!

(At a distance.)

Rigoletto.

Is it not yet done? What a capital joke!

(Putting his hands to his face.)

Why, my eyes are bandaged!

(He snatches off the bandage and mask, and, by the light of the lantern, recognizes the scarf, and sees the door open; he rushes in, and drags out GIOVANNA, greatly frightened; he fixes his eyes upon her in stupefaction, tears his hair in agony, and, after many ineffectual efforts to speak, exclaims:)

Ah! this is the Malediction!

(Swoons.)

END OF ACT I.

Rigoletto.

Ch' io pur mi mascheri;

A me una larva?

Marullo.

Sì pronta è già.

Terrai la scala.

(Gli mette una maschera, e nello stesso tempo lo benda con un fazzoletto, e lo pone a reggere una scala, che avranna appostata al terrazzo.)

Rigoletto.

Fitta è la tenebra!

Marullo.

La benda cieco e sordo il fa.

(A compagni.)

Tutti.

Zitti, zitti, moviamo a vendetta,

Ne sia còlto, or che meno l'aspetta.

Derisorë sì audace constante

A sua volta schernito sarà!

Cheti, cheti, rubiamgli l'amante,

E la Corte doman riderà.

(Alcuni salgono al terrazzo, rompon la porta del primo piano, scendono, aprono ad altri ch'entrano dalla strada, e riescono, trascinando GILDA, la quale avrà la bocca chiusa da un fazzoletto. Nel traversare la scena ella perde una sciarpa.)

Gilda.

Soccorso, padre mio—

Coro.

Vittoria!

Gilda.

Aita!

(Più lontano.)

Rigoletto.

Non han finito ancor! qual derisione!

(Si tocca gli occhi.)

Sono bendato!

(Si strappa impetuosamente la benda e la maschera, ed al chiarore d'una lanterna scordata riconosce la sciarpa; vede la porta aperta, entra, ne trae GIOVANNA spaventata; la fissa con istapore, si strappa i capelli senza poter gridare; finalmente, dopo molti sforzi, esclama:)

Ah!—la Maledizione!

FINE DELL' ATTO PRIMO

ACT II.

SCENE I—Salon in the DUKE's Palace. Large folding-doors in back-scene, and smaller ones on each side, above which hang portraits of the DUKE and the DUCHESS. A table covered with velvet, handsome chairs, and other appropriate furniture.

(Enter the DUKE, by centre doorway, much agitated.)

Duke.

She has been stolen from me!

But how, and by whom? Oh, heavens!

Thus to lose her at the very moment

When my passion most demanded her!

The door was wide open—the house deserted!

Whither can the dear angel have flown!

She who first within this wandering heart

The joys of a true love hath awakened—

She so pure that, by her modest bearing,

To truthfulness I feel me now inclined.

She has been stolen from me! But, to do it,

Who has dared! On him shall vengeance alight!

Grief for my beloved one vengeance demands!

ATTO II.

SCENA I—Salotto nel Palazzo DUCALE. Vi sono due porte laterali, una maggiore nel fondó che si chiude. A' suoi lati pendono i ritrati, in tutta figura, a sinistra, del DUCA, a destra della sua sposa. V' ha un seggiolone presso una tavola coperta di velluto, ed altri mobili.

(Entra il DUCA, dal mezzo, agitato.)

Duca.

Ella mia fu rapita!

E quando, o ciel?—ne' brevi istanti, prima.

Che un mio presagio interno

Sull' orma corsa ancora mi spingesse!

Schiuso era l'uscio! la magion deserta!

E dove ora sarà quell' angiol caro!

Colei che potè prima in questo core

Destar la fiamma di costanti affetti?

Colei sì pura, al cui modesto accento

Quasi tratto a virtù talor mi credo!

Ella mi fu rapita!

E chi l'ardiva?—ma ne avro vendetta:

Lo chiede il pianto della mia diletta.

PARMI VEDER LE LAGRIME — *DEAR MAID, EACH TEAR* Air (Duke)

Par - mi ve - der le la - gri - me Scor - ren - ti da___ quel ci - glio,
Dear maid, each tear of thine that falls, Each sad sigh that bos - om heav - ing,

Quand - do fra il dub - bio e l'an - sia Del su - bi - to pe -
Pin - ing with - in some dark walls, Fills me____ with pain and

reg - lio, Dell' a - mor no - stro me - mo - re, Dell' a - mor no - stre
griev - ing. Ah! vain - ly didst thou cry to me, Ah!___ vain - ly didst thou .

me - mo - re, Il suo Gual - tier chia - mò. Ned ei pe - tea soc -
cry___ to me, "Help me, dear Wal - ter, help!" I then, a - las! was

cor - rer - ti,   Ca - ra   fan - ciul - la a - ma - ta;
far   a - way,   No   aid   could I___   af - ford   thee;

Ei   che vor - ria   coll' a - ni - ma___   Far - ti quag - giù be -
Yet, could my life   thy   woes   re - pay,___   Glad - ly ex - changed it

a - ta;   Ei che le sfe - rea   gl'an - ge - li,   Ei___ che le sfe - rea
should be.   Not e'en the an - gels'   blest   a - bode   Could peace to   me re -

gl'an - ge - li Per te non in - vi - diò,   Ei che le
store,___   to   me re - store, from thee   a - part;   Could peace to

sfe - re;   Le sfe - rea gl'an - ge - li Per te, per   te___ Le sfe - rea
me re - store: Not e'en the an - gels' blest a - bode___ Could peace   to

gl'an - ge - li Per te___   non in - vi - diò,   non in - vi - diò.
me re - store, Could peace___   to   me re - store,   from thee a - part.

(Enter MARULLO, CEPRANO, BORSA, and other courtiers.)	(Entrano MARULLO, CEPRANO, BORSA, ed altri cortigiani.)
All.	*Tutti.*
Oh, Duke! oh, Duke!	Duca, Duca!
Duke.	*Duca.*
What news?	Ebben?
All.	*Tutti.*
From Rigoletto	L'amante
We have carried off his mistress.	Fu rapita a Rigoletto.
Duke.	*Duca.*
Capital! Where is she?	Bella! e d'onde?
All.	*Tutti.*
In your palace.	Dal suo tetto.
Duke.	*Duca.*
Ah, ah! tell me how 'twas done?	Ah, ah; dite, come fu?

SCORRENDO UNITI — *AS WE WITH GLEE* (Chorus)

Scor-ren - dou - ni - ti re - mo - ta
As we with glee on mis - chief bent last

vi - a Bre - v'o - ra do - po ca - du - to il
night roved, When hush'd in peace - ful sleep the world seem'd

dì,__ Co - me pre - vi - sto ben s'e - ra in pri - a, Ra - ra bel -
bu - ried, The one we sought we met, a - lone, mis - trust - ing, Be - side the

tà ci si sco - prì, ci si sco - prì. E - ra l'a -
house in which we guess'd the bird was caged. The charm - ing

man - te di Ri - go - let - to Che, vis - ta ap -
fair was Ri - go - let - to's mis - tress; But she af -

pe - na, si di - le - guò.__ Già di ra - pir - la s'a - vea il pro -
fright - ed to her home then ran;__ The jest - er then ap - pear'd, with whom we

get - to, Quan - do il buf - fon ver noi spun - tò, ver noi spun -
sport - ed: "Give us thy aid, Ce - pra - no's wife to steal a -

tò; Che di Ce - pra - no noi la Con - tes - sa Ra - pir vo -
way!" The trap he fell in; oh, sport worth tell - ing! A ban - dage

les - si - mo, stol - to, cre - de; La sca - la quin - di all' uo - po
then we placed be - fore his eyes; A lad - der quick - ly placed to the

mes - sa, Ben - da - to, ei stes - so fer - ma te -
win - dow, We bade him stand by, and firm - ly

nè, La sca - la quin - di ei stes - so, ei stes - so fer - ma, fer - ma te - nè.
hold. Ah, yes, he firm - ly held the lad - der; the lad - der firm - ly held.

All.

In haste we mounted, and searched the chambers,
And with the lady away we sped;
But when he'd found out the trick we'd played him,
He raved for vengeance upon our heads.

Duke.

(What do I hear? Of my own charmer they are speaking!
I have yet a chance of regaining her.)
But where is the poor creature to be found?
(To the Chorus.)

All.

All proper care we have taken of her.

Tutti.

Salimmo, e rapida la giovinetta,
Ci venne, fatte quinci asportar.
Quand' ei s'accorse della vendetta
Restò scornato ad imprecar.

Duca.

(Che sento?—è dessa la mia diletta!
Ah, tutto il cielo non mi rapì!)
Ma dove or trovasi, la poveretta?
(Al Coro.)

Tutti.

Fu da noi stessi addotta or qui.

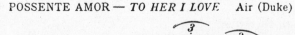

POSSENTE AMOR — *TO HER I LOVE* Air (Duke)

Pos - sen - te a - mor mi chia - ma, Vo - lar io deg - gio a
To her I love with rap - ture, I must with speed flee a -

le - i; Il ser - to mio da - rei___ Per__ con - so - lar__ quel
way;___ All thought of her base cap - ture I'll gen - tly soothe a -

cor.   Il ser - to mio da - rei _____ Per con - so - lar quel
way;   All thought of her base cap - ture I'll gen - tly soothe a -

cor.   Ah! sap - pi al - fin chi l'a - ma Co - no - sca al - fin chi
way.   From her my name and sta - tion I can - not now con -

so - no, Ap - pren - do ch'an - co in tro - no Ha deg - li schia - vi A -
ceal, ___ Yet, free from ob - ser - va - tion, I may my love re -

mor;   Ap - - pren - do ch'an - co in tro - no, ch'an - co in
veal;   I _____ may ___ my ___ love re - veal ___ I ___ may my

tro - no Ha deg - li schia - vi,   Ha ___ deg - li schia - vi A - mor.
love,   yes, my love to her ___ re - veal,   My ___ love to her may re - veal.

(What new thought now has seized him—	(O qual pensiero l'agita
A sudden change has just come o'er him.)	Come congiò d' umor!)
Marullo.	*Marullo.*
Unlucky Rigoletto!—	Povero Rigoletto!—
Chorus.	*Coro.*
Here he comes—be silent, all.	Ei vien—silenzio.
(Enter RIGOLETTO.)	(Entra RIGOLETTO.)
All.	*Tutti.*
Good morning to you, Rigoletto.	Buon giorno, Rigoletto—
Rigoletto.	*Rigoletto.*
(They are all of them in the plot.)	(Han tutti fatto il colpo!)
Ceprano.	*Ceprano.*
What news do you bring,	Ch' hai di nuovo,
Buffoon?	Buffon?
Rigoletto.	*Rigoletto.*
More than ever	Che dell' usato
Are you wearisome to me.	Più noioso voi siete.
All.	*Tutti.*
Ah! ah! ah!	Ah! ah! ah!

Rigoletto.

(Whither can they have carried her?)
(Looking about anxiously.)

All.

(See how uneasy he appears!)

Rigoletto (sardonically).

Happy I am
To see that no hurt you have taken
From the cold air of last night.

Marullo.

Last night, said you?

Rigoletto.

Yes—Ah! 'twas a capital trick.

Marullo.

I was asleep, all night.

Rigoletto.

Oh! you were asleep! then I have been
    dreaming!

(He is about to go, when, seeing a handkerchief on the table, he anxiously examines the cipher on it.)

All.

(See how everything he scrutinizes!)

Rigoletto.

(It is not hers.)
(Throwing it down.)
Is the Duke still sleeping?

All.

Yes, he is still sleeping!
(Enter a Page of the Duchess.)

Page.

The Duchess desires to speak to her lord.

Ceprano.

He sleeps.

Page.

Was he not here but lately?

Borsa.

He has gone hunting.

Page.

Without his suite! without arms!

All.

Canst thou not understand,
That for a short time he cannot be seen?

Rigoletto
(who has been anxiously listening, suddenly rushes amongst them, and exclaims:)

Ah! she is here, then. She is with the Duke!

All.

Who?

Rigoletto.

(Dove l'avran nascosta?)
(Spiando inquieto dovunque.)

Tutti.

(Guardate com' è inquieto!)

Rigoletto.

Son felice
Che nulla a voi nuocesse
L'aria di questa notte.

Marullo.

Questa notte!

Rigoletto.

Sì—Ah! fu il bel colpo!

Marullo.

S' ho dormito sempre!

Rigoletto.

Ah! voi dormiste! avrò dunque sognato!

(S'allontana, e vendendo un fazzoletto sopra una tavola ne osserva inquieto la cifra.)

Tutti.

(Ve' come tutto osserva!)

Rigoletto.

(Non è il suo.)
(Gettandolo.)
Dorme il Duca tuttor?

Tutti.

Sì, dorme ancora.
(Entra un Paggio della Duchessa.)

Paggio.

Al suo sposo parlar vuol la Duchessa.

Ceprano.

Dorme.

Paggio.

Quì or or con voi non era?

Borsa.

E a caccia.

Paggio.

Senza paggi! senz' armi!

Tutti.

E non capisci
Che vedere per ora non può alcuno?

Rigoletto
(che a parte e stato attentissimo al dialogo, balzande improvviso tra loro prorompe).

Ah, ell' è quì dunque! Ell' è col Duca!

Tutti.

Chi?

Rigoletto.

    The maiden whom last night
    From my house you forced away.

All.

    You must be mad.

Rigoletto.

    But I will have her back—she must be here.

All.

    If your mistress you have lost, elsewhere
    Seek for her.

Rigoletto.

    I will have back my daughter!

All.

    His daughter, says he?

Rigoletto.

    Yes, she is my daughter; you will not now
    O'er such a victory exult.
    She is here, I will have her, give her back
      to me!

(He rushes towards the door in the centre, but the courtiers bar his progress.)

    Minions, sycophants, panders, thieves,
    At what price have you my daughter sold?
    Your sordid souls no crime intimidates,
    But priceless is a daughter to her father.
    Restore her, or, though unarmed I am,
    Fearfully shall this hand assail ye;
    Naught on earth can a father dismay,
    When the honor of his child he doth defend!
    Assassins, open that door, and let me pass.

(He again attempts to pass the door, but is restrained by the courtiers; he struggles with them for a while and then sinks exhausted to the ground.)

    Ah! come ye thus all against me!

        (Weeping.)

    Well, see; I weep! Marullo—Signor,
    In heart and mien thou seemest gentle,—
    Tell me where they have my daughter hidden!
    Is she here? Tell me truly! Silent! Why?
    O, my lords, I pray you to have pity on me—
    To an old man give back his daughter!
    To restore her will you nothing cost,
    While to me my child is all the world.

(Enter GILDA, through the doorway on the left. She rushes into the arms of her father.)

Gilda.

    O, my father!

Rigoletto.

    Le giovin che stanotte
    A mio tetto rapisti—

Tutti.

    Tu deliri!

Rigoletto.

    Ma la saprò riprender—Ella è qui.

Tutti.

    Se l'amante perdesti, la ricerca
    Altrove.

Rigoletto.

    Io vo' mia figlia!

Tutti.

    La sua figlia!

Rigoletto.

    Sì, la mia figlia—D'unta tal vittoria—
    Che? adesso non ridete?
    Ella è là, la vogl' io, la renderete.

(Corre verso la porta di mezzo, ma i cortigiani gli attraversano il passaggio.)

    Cortigiani, vil razza dannata,
    Per qual prezzo vendeste il mio bene?
    A voi nulla per l'oro sconviene,
    Ma mia figlia è impagabil tesor.
    La rendete—o se pur disarmata
    Questa man per voi fora cruenta;
    Nulla in terra più l'uomo paventa,
    Se dei figli difende l'onor.
    Quella porta, assassina, m'aprite:

(Si getta ancor sulla porta che gli è nuovamente contesa dai gentiluomini; lotta alquanto, poi torna spossato sul davanti del teatro.)

    Ah! voi tutti a me contro venite!

        (Piange.)

    Ebben piango—Marullo—signore,
    Tu ch' hai l'alma gentil come il core,
    Dimmi or tu, dove l'hanno nascosta?
    E là? E vero? tu taci? perchè?
    Miei signori—Perdono, pietate;
    Al vegliardo la figlia ridate;
    Ridornarla a voi nulla ora costa,
    Tutto il mondo è tal figlia per me.

(Entra GILDA, ch'esce dalla stranza a sinistra, e si getta nelle paterne braccia.)

Gilda.

    Mio padre!

Rigoletto.

O God! my own Gilda!
Signors, in her you behold
My whole family. Have no further fear,
My angel child! It was a joke—was it not
so?   (To the courtiers.)
I wept, but now I laugh. Yet thou—why
weepest thou?

Gilda.

For shame, father! I have been maltreated!

Rigoletto.

Heaven! what say'st thou?

Gilda

What I have to say no one else must hear.

Rigoletto
(turning towards the courtiers, imperatively).

Away, away! all of ye!
And if your Duke should hither dare approach,
Tell him not to enter—for I am here.
          (Falling into a chair.)

All.

(With children and madmen
It is sometimes well to simulate;
Therefore will we depart; but what he does
We will not fail unseen to watch.)
(Exeunt through doorway in front, closing it after them.

Rigoletto.

Now speak—we are alone.

Gilda.

(Heaven, now grant me courage!)
Whene'er to church I went,
There my prayers to say,
A youth of handsome mien
Before me always stood.
Although our lips were silent,
Our hearts discoursed through our eyes
Stealthily, in night's darkness,
While alone, he came to me:
"A student poor am I,"
Plaintively he said to me;
And with ardent sighings
His love for me protested.
Then he left me; and my heart
To hope's bright visions opened,
When men ferocious and unlook'd-for
Tore me from our home away.

Rigoletto.

Dio! mia Gilda!
Signori, in essa è tutta
La mia famiglia. Non temer più nulla,
Angelo mio—fu scherzo non è vero?
          (Ai cortigiani.)
Io che pur piansi or rido—E tu a che piangi?

Gilda.

Ah! l'onta, padre mio!

Rigoletto.

Cielo! che dici?

Gilda.

Arrossir voglio innanzi a voi soltanto.

Rigoletto
(trivolto ai cortigiani, con imperioso modo.)

Ite di quà, voi tutti—
Se il Duca vostro d'appressarsi osasse,
Che non entri gli dite, e ch' io ci sono
          (Si abbandona sul seggiolone.)

Tutti.

(Co' fanciulli e coi dementi
Spesso giova il simular.
Partiam pur, ma quel ch' ei tenti
Non lasciamo d'osservar.)
          (Escon dal mezzo e chindon la porta.)

Rigoletto.

Parla—siam soli.

Gilda.

(Ciel, dammi corraggio!)
Tutte le feste al tempio
Mentre pregava Iddio,
Bello e fatale un giovane
S'offerse àl guardo mio—
Se i labbri nostri tacquero,
Dagli occhi il cor parlò.
Furtivo fra le tenebre
Sol iera a me giungeva;
Sono studente, povero,
Commosso mi diceva.
E con ardente palpito
Amor mi protestò.
Parti—i! mio core aprivasi
A speme più gradita,
Quando improvvisi apparvere
Color che m' han rapita.

And hither forcibly brought me,
To my ruin and dismay.

Rigoletto.

Stop—say no more, my angel—
(I know all! Avenging Heaven,
Upon my head falls the infamy
I have of thee invoked!) O God!
That she might be exalted,
How miserably have I fallen!
Ah! often near the altar
The scaffold should be reared;
But now all is out of order,
And e'en the altar desecrated.
Weep, my child, and let thy tears
Within thy father's bosom fall.

Gilda.

Father, like an angel you speak to me
These words of consolation.

Rigoletto.

What must be done I will quickly dispose
of,
And then for ever will we quit this fatal
place.

Gilda.

Yes!

Rigoletto.

How changed in one short day may be our
destiny!

(Enter a Herald and the COUNT MONTERONE, who is
marched across the back of the stage, between guards.)

Herald.

Make way; he is ordered to the prison of
Castiglion.

(To the guards.)

Monterone.

Since in vain thou hast by me been cursed,

(Stopping before the portrait.)

The wrath of neither heaven nor earth can
reach thee,
And happy wilt thou yet live, O Duke!

(Exit, between the guards.)

Rigoletto.

No, old man, not so—thou shalt be avenged!
Yes, vengeance, dire vengeance, awaits thee!
The one hope of my soul is thee to punish!
And the hour of retribution is nigh
That to thee shall prove fatal.

E a forza quì m'addussero
Nell' ansia più crudel.

Rigoletto.

Non dir; non più, mio angelo.
(T'intendo, avverso ciel!
Solo per me l'infamia
A te chiedeva, o Dio!
Ch' ella potesse ascendere
Quanto caduto er' io;
Ah! presso del patibolo
Bisogna ben l'altare!
Ma tutto ora scompare;
L'altar si roversciò!)
Piangi, fanciulla, e scorrere
Fa il pianto sul mio cor.

Gilda.

Padre, in voi parla un angelo
Per me consolator.

Rigoletto.

Compiuto pur quanto a fare mi resta,
Lasciare potremo quest' aura funesta.

Gilda.

Sì.

Rigoletto.

(E tutto un sol giorno cangiare potè!)

(Entra un Usciere ed il CONTE DI MONTERONE, che dalla
destra attraversa il fondo della sala fra gli alabardieri.)

Usciere.

Schiudete—ire al carcere Castiglion dee.

(Alle guardie.)

Monterone.

Poichè fosti invano da me maledetto,

(Fermandosi verso il ritratto.)

Nè un fulmine o un ferro colpiva il tuo
petto,
Felice per anco, o Duca, vivrai—

(Esce fra le guardie dal mezzo.)

Rigoletto.

No, vecchio, t'inganni—un vindice avrai.
Sì, vendetta, tremenda vendetta
Di quest' anima è solo desio—
Di punirti giè—l'ora s'affretta,
Che fatale per te tuonerà.

Like thunder from the heavens hurled,
Shall fall the blow of the despised buffoon.

Gilda.

O father dear, what joy ferocious
I see your flashing eyes light up!
Ah! pardon him, as we ourselves
The pardon of heaven hope to gain.
(I dare not say how much I love him,
And pity him who none for me hath shown!)

(Exeunt, through centre door.)

END OF THE SECOND ACT.

ACT III.

SCENE I—A desolate place on the banks of the Mincio. On the right, with its front to the audience, a house, two stories high, in a very dilapidated state, which is nevertheless used as an inn. The doors and walls are so full of crevices, that whatever is going on within can be seen from without. In front, the road and the river. In the distance, the city of Mantua. It is night.

(GILDA and RIGOLETTO discovered, in apparent altercation, SPARAFUCILE seen in the house, cleaning his belt, unconscious of what is going on outside.)

Rigoletto.

Yet you love him?

Gilda.

I cannot help it.

Rigoletto.

Surely
This madness ere now you should have conquered.

Gilda.

Yet I love him!

Rigoletto.

How weak is the heart of woman!
Her vile seducer she'd forgive—
But avenged thou shalt be, my Gilda.

Gilda.

Have pity on him, dear father!

Rigoletto.

If of his treachery I convince you,
Will you then from your heart discard him?

Gilda.

I do not know;—but he to me is true.

Rigoletto.

He!

Come fulmin scagliato da Dio
Il buffone colpirti saprà.

Gilda.

O, mio padre, qual gioja feroce,
Balenarvi negli occhi vegg' io!
Perdonate—a noi pure una voce
Di perdono dal cielo verrà.
(Mi tradiva, pur l'amo, gran Dio,
Per l'ingrato ti chiedo pietà!)

(Escon dal mezzo.)

FINE DELL' ATTO SECONDO.

ATTO III.

SCENA I—Deserta sponda del Mincio. A sinistra è una casa in due piani, mezzo diroccata, la cui fronte, volta allo spettatore, lascia vedere per una grande arcata l'interno d'una rustica osteria; il muro poi n' è sì pien di fessure, che dal di fuori si può facilmente scorgere quanto avviene nell' interno. Al di là del fiume è Mantova. E notte.

(GILDA e RIGOLETTO inquieto, sono sulla strada. SPARAFU-CILE nell' interno dell' osteria, seduto presso una tavola sta ripulendo il suo cinturone, senza nulla intenders di quanto accade al di fuori.)

Rigoletto.

E l'ami?

Gilda.

Sempre.

Rigoletto.

Pure
Tempo a guarirne t' ho lasciato.

Gilda.

Io l'amo.

Rigoletto.

Povero cor di donna! Ah, il vile infame!
Ma avrai vendetta, o Gilda—

Gilda.

Pietà, mio padre—

Rigoletto.

E se tu certa fossi
Ch' ei ti tradisse, l'ameresti ancora?

Gilda.

Nol so, ma pur m'adora.

Rigoletto.

Egli!

Gilda.

Yes.

Rigoletto.

Well, then, this way come, and see.

(He conducts her to one of the crevices in the wall, and motions her to look through.)

Gilda.

A man, surely,

I see!

Rigoletto.

Wait a little longer.

(Enter the DUKE, dressed as a private soldier, through a door on the left, opening into the ground-floor room.)

Gilda.

Ah, my father!

(Surprised.)

Duke.

Two things I want, and quickly.

(To SPARAFUCILE.)

Sparafucile.

What are they?

Duke.

A room and some wine.

Rigoletto.

(His usual custom, no doubt.)

Sparafucile.

(Oh! the fine gentleman!)

(Goes off into an adjoining room.)

Gilda.

Sì.

Rigoletto.

Ebbene, osserva dunque.

(La conduce presso una delle fezzure del muro, ed ella vi guarda.)

Gilda.

Un uomo

Vedo.

Rigoletto.

Per poco attendi.

(Entra il Duca, in assisa di semplice officiale di cavalleria, nella sala terrena per un aporta a sinistra.)

Gilda.

Ah, padre mio!

(Trasalendo.)

Duca.

Due cose, e tosto—

(A SPARAFUCILE.)

Sparafucile.

Quali?

Duca.

Una stanza e del vino—

Rigoletto.

(Son questi i suoi costumi!)

Sparafucile.

(Oh, il bel zerbino!)

(Parte nella vicina stanza.)

LA DONNA E MOBILE — *HOW FICKLE WOMEN ARE* Air (Duke)

La don-na è mo-bi-le Qual piu-ma il ven-to, Mu-ta d'ac-
How fick-le wo-men are, Fleet-ing as fall-ing star, Chan-ging for

cen-to; E di pen-sie-ro. Sem-pre un a-ma-bi-le
ev-er; Con-stant, ah! nev-er; Like feath-ers fly-ing,

Leg-gia-dro vi-so In pian-to o in ri-so, E men-zo-
On the wind hie-ing Ev-er in mo-tion, Like waves of

gne - ro   La_ don-na è - mo - bil   Qual piu-ma al ven - to,
o - cean.   Yet_ there's no   feel - ing   Love's pleas-ure   steal - ing,

Mu - ta_d'ac - cen - to___   e_ di pen - sier,   Their
Like   that   of   seal - ing Their   lips_ with   a   kiss!

e_ di pen - sier!   e, _____   e_ di pen - sier!
lips_ with   a   kiss!   Their _____   lips with a_ kiss!

(Re-enter SPARAFUCILE, with a bottle of wine and two glasses, which he places on the table, and then twice strikes the ceiling with the hilt of his sword. At this signal, MADDELENE, a smiling lass, in Gipsy costume, descends by a ladder. The DUKE approaches to embrace her, but she repulses him. Meanwhile SPARAFUCILE goes out into the road, and says to RIGOLETTO:)

Your man is there! Is he to live or die?

Rigoletto.

Wait awhile; and then my pleasure you shall
learn.

(SPARAFUCILE goes off between the house and the river, GILDA and RIGOLETTO remaining in the road.)

Duke.

One day, if I remember rightly,
O beauty bright, I thee encountered,
And ever since I've sought thee out,
Till here at last I've found thee;
Ah! now believe me, while I swear,
That henceforth this heart will thee adore.

Maddelene.

Ah, ah! and since then twenty others
Are by you quite as much remembered,
(To give the gentleman his due, though,
He has a cavalier-like bearing.)

Duke.

Yes; a bad one I am!

(Attempts to kiss her.)

Maddelene.

Leave me alone,
Stupid, do.

Luke.

Eh! what a fuss!

(Rientra SPARAFUCILE, con una bottiglia di vino e due bicchieri, che depone sulla tavola, quindi batte col pomo della sua lunga spada due colpi al soffitto. A quel segnale, una ridente GIOVANE, in costume di Zingara, scenda a salti la scala. Il DUCA corre per abbracciarla, ma ella gli sfugge. Frattanto SPARAFUCILE, uscito sulla via, dice a parte a RIGOLETTO:)

E là il vostr' uomo—viver dee o morire?

Rigoletto.

Più tardi tornero l'opra a compire.

(SPARAFUCILE si allontana dietro la casa lungo il flume, GILDA e RIGOLETTO sulla via.)

Duca.

Un dì, se ben rammentomi,
O, bella, t'incontrai,
Mi piacque di te chiedere,
E intesi che quì stai.
Or sappi, che d'allora
Sol te quest' alma adora.

Maddalena.

Ah, ah!—e vent' altre appresso
Le scorda forse adesso?
(Ha un' aria il signorino
Da vero libertino.)

Duca.

Sì; un mostro son!

(Per abbracciarla.)

Maddalena.

Lasciatemi,
Stordito.

Duca.

Ih! che fracasso!

Maddelene.

Be quiet, will you?

Duke.

If you'll be gentle,
And not make so much resistance.
When the joys of love await us,
Virtue need not be so prudish.
(Taking her hand.)
How beautiful and white your hand is.

Maddelene.

You're pleased to joke me, signor.

Duke.

No, no.

Maddelene.

I know I'm ugly.

Duke.

Embrace me.

Maddelene.

Thou'rt drunk!

Duke.

With love of thee I may be.
(Laughing.)

Maddelene.

Signor, these words unmeaning
Why to me address?

Duke.

No, no—I will marry you.

Maddelene.

Your word of honor, then, give me.

Duke.

Most lovely of your sex art thou!
(Ironically.)

Rigoletto.

Well! have you now heard enough?
(To GILDA, who has seen and heard all that has passed.)

Gilda.

Oh! the wicked traitor!

Duke.

Ah! of Venus the fairest daughter,
The slave of your charms here behold;
One word from thy beautiful lips
My suffering alone can assuage;
Come, and my fond heart relieve
Of its anxious palpitations.

Maddelene.

Ah, ah! with all my heart I laugh
At stories which so little cost;

Maddalena.

Stia saggio.

Duca.

E tu sii docile,
Non farmi tanto chiasso.
Ogni saggezza chiudesi
Nel guadio e nell' amore.
(Le prende la mano.)
La bella mano candida!

Maddalena.

Scherzate voi, signore.

Duca.

No, no.

Maddalena.

Son brutta.

Duca.

Abbracciami.

Maddalena.

Ebro.

Duca.

D'amore ardente.
(Ridendo.)

Maddalena.

Signor, l'indifferente,
Vi piace canzonar?

Duca.

No, no—ti vo' sposar.

Maddalena.

Ne voglio la parola.

Duca.

Amabile figliuola!
(Ironico.)

Rigoletto.

Ebben?—ti basta ancor?
(A GILDA, che avrà tutto osservato ed inteso.)

Gilda.

Iniquo traditor!

Duca.

Bella figlia dell' amore,
Schiavo son de' vezzi tuoi;
Con un detto sol tu puoi
Le mie pene consolar.
Vieni, e senti del mio core
Il frequente palpitar.

Maddalena.

Ah! ah! rido bèn di core,
Chè tai baie costan poco;

Your jokes I prize, you may believe me,
At just as much as they are worth.
Accustomed am I, my gallant signor,
To badinage as good as this.

Gilda.

Ah! thus to me of love he spoke,
Thus the wretch hath me betrayed;
Unhappy me!—forlorn, deserted,
With anguish how my heart doth ache!
Oh! what a weak credulity
In such a libertine to trust!

Rigoletto.

Be silent;—now to grieve is useless;
That he deceived thee thus thou see'st;
Be silent, and on me depend
Vengeance eternal to insure;
Prompt as dreadful shall it be—
Like thunder on his head 'twill fall!
Hear me;—at once to the house return,
What gold you may require there obtain;
A horse provide, and the apparel of a youth;
Then to Verona hasten,
Where to-morrow I will join thee.

Gilda.

Come now with me.

Rigoletto.

Impossible.

Gilda.

I tremble.

Rigoletto.

Go.

(Exit GILDA.)

(RIGOLETTO goes behind the house, and returns in conversation with SPARAFUCILE. During the scene between them the DUKE and MADDELINE remain seated in the inn, talking, laughing, and drinking.)

Rigoletto.

Twenty crown-pieces, say you?—Here are
  ten;
When the deed is done, ten more you shall
  have.
Is he still here?

Sparafucile.

Yes.

Rigoletto.

At the hour of midnight.
I shall return.

Quanto valga il vostro giuoco,
Mel credete, so apprezzar.
Sono avvezza, bel signore,
Ad un simile schervar.

Gilda.

Ah! così parlar d'amore
A me pur l'infame ho udito!
Infelice cor tradito,
Per angoscia non scoppiar.
Perchè o credulo mio core,
Un tal uom dovevi amar!

Rigoletto.

Taci, il piangere non vale;

(A GILDA.)

Ch' ei mentiva or sei secura—
Taci, e mia sarà la cura
La vendetta, d'affrettar.
Pronta fia, sarà fatale;
Io saprollo fulminar.
M'odi, ritorna a casa—
Oro prendi, un destriero,
Una veste viril che t'apprestai,
E per Verona parti—
Sarrovvi io pur domani—

Gilda.

Or venite.

Rigoletto.

Impossibil.

Gilda.

Tremo.

Rigoletto.

Va.

(GILDA parte.)

(RIGOLETTO va dietro la casa, e ritorna parlando con SPARAFUCILE e contandogli della monete. Durante questa scena e la sequente il DUCA e MADDALENA stanno fra loro parlando, ridendo, bevendo.)

Rigoletto.

Venti scudi hai tu detto? Eccone dieci;
E dopo l'opera il resto.
Ei quì rimane?

Sparafucile.

Sì.

Rigoletto.

Alla mezzanotte
Ritornerò.

Sparafucile.

You need not hurry.

Alone into the river I can cast him.

Rigoletto.

No, no,—I wish to throw him in myself.

Sparafucile.

Well, so let it be.   But what is his name?

Rigoletto.

Perhaps of both you'd like to know the names?

His name is *Crime,* and mine is *Punishment.*

(Exit—the darkness increases, distant thunder heard.)

Sparafucile.

A storm in the distance is arising;

Darker the night is becoming.

Duke.

Maddelene!

(Attempting to take hold of her.)

Maddelene.

Desist—my brother comes.

(Repelling him.)

Duke.

Well, what matters his coming?

(Thunder.)

Maddelene.

It thunders.

(Enter SPARAFUCILE.)

Sparafucile.

And rain is coming.

Duke.

So much the better;

I will lodge here—in the stable you may sleep—

Or in the regions below—or where you please.

Sparafucile.

Thank you.

Maddelene.   (Aside to the DUKE.)

(Ah, no—depart.)

Duke   (to MADDELENE).

In such weather as this?

Sparafucile   (to MADDELENE).

Twenty crowns of gold, remember.

Signor,

To offer you my room I shall be happy:

At once I'll show you to it, if you please.

(He takes a light, and goes toward the staircase.)

Sparafucile.

Non cale,

A gettarlo nel fiume basto io solo.

Rigoletto.

No, no,—il vo' far io stesso.

Sparafucile.

Sia—il suo nome?

Rigoletto.

Vuoi saper anco il mio?

Egli è *Delitto, Punizion* son io.

(Parte—Il cielo ci oscura e tuona.)

Sparafucile.

La tempesta è vicina.

Più scura fia la notte.

Duca.

Maddalena!

(Per prenderla.)

Maddalena.

Aspettate—mio fratello viene.

(Sfuggendogli.)

Duca.

Che importa?

(S' ode il tuona.)

Maddalena.

Tuona.

(Entra SPARAFUCILE.)

Sparafucile

E pioverà tra poco.

Duca.

Tanto meglio.

Io qui mi tratterò—tu dormirai

In scuderia—all' inferno—ove vorrai.

Sparafucile.

Grazie.

Maddalena.   (Piano al DUCA.)

(Ah, no—partite.)

Duca   (a MADDALENA).

(Con tal tempo?)

Sparafucile   (piano a MADDALENA).

Son venti scudi d'ore.

Ben felice.   (Al DUCA.)

D' offrivi la mia stanza—se a voi piace

Tosto a vederla andiamo.

(Prende una lume, e s' avvia per la scala.)

Duke.

    With all my heart—be quick, let me see it.

    (Whispers to MADDELENE, and follows SPARAFUCILE.)

Maddelene.

    (Poor young man! so much, too, the gentleman!

    O God!—what a fearful night is coming!)
               (Thunder.)

Duke
    (observing that the window has no shutters).

    If here you sleep, plenty of air you get.

    Well, good night!

Sparafucile.

    May God protect you, signor.

Duke.

    Quickly I shall be asleep, so weary am I.

    (He lays down his hat and sword, throws himself on the bed, and in a short time falls asleep. MADDELENE, below, stands by the table. SPARAFUCILE finishes the contents of the bottle left by the DUKE. Both remain silent for awhile, and apparently in deep thought.)

Maddelene.

    What pleasing manners the young man has!

Sparafucile.

    Oh, truly; but twenty crowns I'm to have.

Maddelene.

    Only twenty! too little! much more he's worth!

Sparafucile.

    Go—and, if he sleeps, his sword bring hither.

Maddelene
    (ascending, and contemplating him while sleeping).

    It is a sin to kill so nice a youth!

    (She takes up the DUKE's sword, and begins to descend.)

    (Enter GILDA, approaching by the passage, in the attire of a youth, with whip and spurs; she advances slowly towards the house; SPARAFUCILE continues drinking. It lightens and thunders.)

Gilda.

    Ah! my reason seems quite to desert me!

    Love overcomes me! O father, pardon!
               (Thunder.)

    What a night of horrors! How will it end?

Maddelene.

    Brother!

    (Having descended, she deposits the DUKE's sword on the table.)

Gilda.

    Who speaks?

    (Looking through the crevices.)

Duca.

    Ebben sono con te—presto, vediamo.

    (Dice una parola all' orecchio di MADDALENA e segue SPARAFUCILE.)

Maddalena.

    (Povero giovin!—grazioso tanto!

    Dio!—qual mai notte è questa!)
               (Tuona.)

Duca
    (vedendone il balcone senza imposte).

    Si dorme all' aria aperta? bene, bene—

    Buona notte.

Sparafucile.

    Signor, vi guardi Iddio.

Duca.

    Breve sonno dormiam—stanco son io.

    (Depone il capello, la spada, e si stende, sul letto, dove in breve addormentasi. MADDALENA frattanto siede presso la tavola. SPARAFUCILE beve dalla bottiglia lasciata dal DUCA—Rimangono ambidue taciturni per qualche istante, e preoccupati da gravi pensieri.)

Maddalena.

    E amabile invero cotal giovinotto.

Sparafucile.

    Oh sì—venti scudi ne dà di prodotto.

Maddalena.

    Sol venti!—son pochi—valeva di più.

Sparafucile.

    La spada, s' ei dorme, va, portami giù.

Maddalena
    (sale, e contemplando il dormente).

    Peccato! è pur bello!

    (Prende la spadà del DUCA, e scende.)

    (Entra GILDA, che comparisce nel fondo della via in costume virile, con stivali e speroni, e lentamente si avanza verso l' osteria, mentre SPARAFUCILE continua a beve. Spess lampi e tuoni.)

Gilda.

    Ah, più non ragiono!

    Amor mi trascina!—mio padre, perdono!
               (Tuona.)

    Qual notte d' orrore! Gran Dio, che accadrà.

Maddalena.

    Fratello!

    (Sara discesa, ed avrà posata la spada del DUCA sulla tavola.)

Gilda.

    Chi parla?

    (Osserva pella fessura.)

Sparafucile.
To the devil be gone!
(Seeking something in a cupboard.)
Maddelene.
Handsome as an Apollo is this youth—
I love him—he loves me—so slay him not.

Gilda.
Oh, heavens!   (Listening.)
Sparafucile.
Mend the holes in that sack.
Maddelene.
Why?
Sparafucile.
Thy beautiful Apollo I must kill,
And into the river cast.
Gilda.
O hellhound!
Maddelene.
The promised money you may yet obtain
And spare his life.
Sparafucile.
I think that difficult.
Maddelene.
Listen, and hear how easy my project.
Ten crowns already from the hunchback
Thou hast received.   In a little time
Hither with the other ten he will come;
Kill him, and then the twenty thou wilt
have.
Sparafucile.
Kill the hunchback!   What dost thou sug-
gest?
For a thief, or a swindler, do you take me?
Did I ever a client betray?   No!
The man who pays me faithful ever finds
me!
Gilda.
What do I hear?   My father!
Maddelene.
Ah, mercy on him!
Sparafucile.
He must die!
Maddelene.
I'll give him a hint to fly.
(About to go.)

Sparafucile.
Al diavol ten va.
(Frugando in un credenzone.)
Maddalena.
Somiglia un Apollo quel giovine—io l'amo—
Ei m'ama—riposi—nè più l'uccidiamo.

Gilda.
Oh, cielo!   (Ascoltando.)
Sparafucile.
Rattoppa puel sacco—
Maddalena.
Perche?
Sparafucile.
Entr' esso il tuo Apollo, sgozzato da me,
Gettar dovro al fiume.
Gilda.
L'inferno qui vedo!
Maddalena.
Eppure il danaro salvarti scommetto,
Serbandolo in vita.
Sparafucile.
Difficile il credo.
Maddalena.
M'ascolta—anzi facil ti svelo un progetto.
De' scudi, già dieci dal gobbo ne avesti;
Venire cogli altri più tardi il vedrai—
Uccidilo, e venti allora ne avrai,
Così tutto il prezzo goder si potrà.

Sparafucile.
Uccider quel gobbo!—che diavol dicesti!
Un ladro son forse?   Son forse un bandito?
Qual altro cliente da me fu tradito?
Mi paga quest' uomo—fedele m' avrà.

Gilda.
Che sento! mio padre!
Maddalena.
Ah, grazia per esso.
Sparafucile.
E d'uopo ch' ei muoia—
Maddalena.
Fuggire il fo adesso.
(Va per salire.)

Gilda.

O kind-hearted woman!

Sparafucile.

The reward we shall lose.

Maddelene.

That's true.

Sparafucile.

Let me do it.

Maddelene.

He must be saved.

Sparafucile.

Should any other before midnight arrive,

Him I will slay instead of him now here.

Maddelene.

The night is dark, through the sky the
thunder roars,

No one at such a time this place will pass.

Gilda.

Oh, what a temptation—for th' ingrate to
die!

And for thee, father! O heaven, guide me!

(The clock strikes the half-hour.)

Sparafucile.

There is still half an hour.

Maddelene.

Brother, wait.

(Weeping.)

Gilda.

What! that woman weep, and I not help
him!

Ah! although to my love truthless he be,

My life for his shall be the sacrifice!

(Knocks at the door.)

Maddelene.

Who knocks?

Sparafucile.

'Tis the wind.

Maddelene.

Some one knocks, I'm sure.

Sparafucile.

It is strange.

Maddelene.

Who's there?

Gilda.

Have pity on a stranger;

A lodging grant him for this bitter night.

Gilda.

Oh, buona figliuola!

Sparafucile.

Gli scudi perdiamo.

Maddalena.

E ver!

Sparafucile.

Lascia fare—

Maddalena.

Salvarlo dobbiamo.

Sparafucile.

Se pria ch' abbia il mezzo la notte toccate

Alcuno qui giunga, per esso morrà.

Maddalena.

E buia la notte, il ciel troppo irato,

Nessuno a quest' ora di qui passerà.

Gilda.

Oh, qual tantazione! morir per l'ingrato!

Morire! e mio padre! Oh, cielo pietà!

(Battono le undici e mezzo.)

Sparafucile.

Ancor c' è mezz' ora.

Maddalena.

Attendi, fratello.

(Piangendo.)

Gilda.

Che! piange tal donna! Nè a lui darò aita

Ah, s' egli al mio amore divenne rubello

Io vo' per la sua gettar la mia vita.

(Picchia alla porta.)

Maddalena.

Si picchia?

Sparafucile.

Fu il vento—

Maddalena.

Si picchia, ti dico.

Sparafucile.

E strano!

Maddalena.

Chi è?

Gilda.

Pietà d'un mendico;

Asil per la notte a lui concedete.

Maddelene.

A long night 'twill be for him!

Sparafucile.

Wait awhile.

(He searches the cupboard for something.)

Gilda.

Ah! so near to death, and yet so young!

Oh! for these wretches God's pardon I ask;

Forgive, O father, thine unhappy child!

And happy live the man I die to save!

Maddelene.

Now hasten, quick, the fatal deed enact;

To save one life another I yield up.

Sparafucile.

Well, I am ready the issue to abide,

I care not so that the reward I get.

(He goes behind the doorway with a dagger. MADDELENE opens the door, and then runs forward, to close that in front. GILDA enters and SPARAFUCILE closes the door. All the rest is buried in silence and darkness.)

(Enter RIGOLETTO, enveloped in a cloak; he advances from the road to the front of the scene. The violence of the storm has abated, the lightning and thunder still continuing occasionally.)

Rigoletto.

At last the hour of my revenge is nigh;

Full thirty days and nights for this I've waited,

My soul with tears of blood consuming,

Under the guise of a buffoon. That door

(Examining the house.)

Is shut! 'Tis not yet the hour—I must wait.

What a night of foul mystery is this!

The heavens in a tempest,

On the earth a homicide!

Oh, how truly great do I now feel!

'Tis midnight!

(The clock strikes twelve.)

(Enter SPARAFUCILE, from the house.)

Sparafucile.

Who is there?

Rigoletto.

It is I.

(About to enter.)

Sparafucile.

Wait where you are.

(Re-enters the house, and returns, dragging a sack.)

Your man is here disposed of.

Rigoletto.

O joy—a light!

Maddalena.

Fia lunga tal notte!

Sparafucile.

Alquanto attendete.

(Va a cercare nel credenzone.)

Gilda.

Ah, presso alla morte, sì giovane, sono!

Oh cielo, pegli empi ti chiedo perdono.

Perdona tu, o padre, a questa infelice!

Sia l' uomo felice—ch' or vado a salvar.

Maddalena.

Su, spicciati, presto, fa l'opra compita;

Anelo una vita—con altra salvar.

Sparafucile.

Ebbene—son pronto, quell' uscio dischiudi;

Piucch' altro li scudi—mi preme salvar.

(Va a postarsi con un pugnale dietro la porta. MADDALENA apre, poi corre a chiudere la grande arcata di fronte. Mentre entra GILDA, dietro a cui SPARAFUCILE chiude la porta, e tutto resta sepolto nel silenzio e nel buoi.)

(Entra RIGOLETTO, solo, si avanza dal fondo della scena chiuso nel suo mantello. La violenza del temporale è diminuita, nè più si vede e sente che qualche lampo e tuono.)

Rigoletto.

Della vendetta olfin giunge l'istante!

Da trenta di l'aspetto

Di vivo sangue a lagrime piangendo

Sotto la larva del buffon—Quest' uscio!

(Esaminando la casa.)

E chiuso! Ah, non è tempo ancor! S'attenda.

Qual notte di mistero!

Una tempesto in cielo!

In terra un omicidio!

Oh, come invero qui grande mi sento!

Mezza notte!

(Suona mezza notte.)

(Entra SPARAFUCILE, dalla casa.)

Sparafucile.

Chi è là?

Rigoletto.

Son io.

(Per entrare.)

Sparafucile.

Sostate.

(Rientra, e torna, trascinando un sacco.)

E qui spento il vostr' uomo—

Rigoletto.

Oh, gioja! un lume!

Sparafucile.

A light? No—first the money.

(RIGOLETTO hands him a purse.)

Sparafucile.

Let us into the river cast him.

Rigoletto.

No! alone I'll do it.

Sparafucile.

As you please; but this place is not the best;

Higher up, the stream is deeper. Be quick,

That no one may observe you. Good night.

(He re-enters the house.)

Rigoletto.

Here he is!—dead. I should like to see him!

But what matters? 'Tis done! Here are his spurs.

Now will the world again look well with me!

Here is the buffoon, and here his master!

At my feet he lies. It is he! It is he!

Now hath my grief its just revenge attained!

In the sea shall be his sepulchre,

This sack his winding-sheet!

(He tries to drag the sack towards the river, when he is surprised at hearing the voice of the DUKE, who passes along the background.)

What voice is that! Or is it an illusion?

No! no! it is he! it is he himself!

(Greatly alarmed.)

The Malediction! Oh, there! demon of hell!

(Nearing the house with the sack.)

But who, instead of him, can be in the sack!

(Tearing open the sack.)

I tremble. It is a human body!

(Lightning.)

My daughter! O God, my daughter!

Ah, no! it is impossible;

Towards Verona she journeyeth;

A dreadful vision this must be.

(Kneeling down.)

O my Gilda! Tell me who this has done?

The assassin to me reveal! Ho! who's here?

(Knocking violently at the door.)

No one! Oh, my daughter!

Sparafucile.

Un lume? No, il danaro.

(RIGOLETTO gli dà una borsa.)

Sparafucile.

Lesti all' onda il gettiam—

Rigoletto.

No—basto io solo.

Sparafucile.

Come pi piace—Qui men atto è il sito—

Più avanti è più profondo il gorgo—Presto

Che alcun non vi sorprenda—Buono notte.

(Rientra in casa.)

Rigoletto.

Egli è là! morto! O sì—vorrei vederlo!

Ma che importa! è ben desso! Ecco i suo sproni!

Ora mi guardo, o mondo—

Quest' è un buffone, ed un potente è questo!

Ei sta sotto a' miei piedi. E desso! E desso!

E giunta alfin la tua vendetta, o duolo!

Sia l'onda a lui sepolcro,

Un sacco il suo lenzuolo!

(Fa per trascinare il sacco verso la sponda, quando è sorpreso dalla lontana voce del DUCA, che nel fondo attraversa la scena.)

Qual voce! illusion notturna è questa!

No! no! egli è desso! è desso!

Maledizione! Olà—dimon bandito?

(Trasalendo verso la casa.)

Chi è mai, chi è qui in sua voce;

(Taglio il sacco.)

Io tremo—E umano corpo!

(Lampeggia.)

Mia figlia! Dio! mia figlia!

Ah no—è impossibil! per Verona è in via!

Fu vision! E dessa!

(Inginocchiandosi.)

Oh, mia Gilda! fanciulla a me rispondi!

L' assassino mi svela—Olà? Nessuno!

(Picchia disperatamente alla casa.)

Nessun! mia figlia—

Gilda.

Who calls on me?

Rigoletto.

She speaks! she moves! she lives! Oh,
    heaven!
Ah! my only worldly solace,
Look on me; dost thou not know me?

Gilda.

Father!

Rigoletto.

Unveil this mystery! Art thou wounded?

Gilda.

The sword pierced me here.
                (Points to her breast.)

Rigoletto.

Who was it stabbed you?

Gilda.

I have deceived you! I am guilty!
Too much I loved him—now I die for him!

Rigoletto.

(O awful fate, by my hand hath she fallen,
Of my righteous vengeance the sole victim.)
Angel dear, look on me, to me listen;
Speak, oh, speak to me, my darling daughter!

Gilda.

More I cannot say; pardon me and him!
O my father, bless your dying daughter.

Gilda.

Chi mi chiama?

Rigoletto.

Ella parla! si move! è viva! oh Dio!
Ah! mio ben solo in terra;
Mi guarda—mi conosci—

Gilda.

Ah, padre mio—

Rigoletto.

Qual mistero! che fu! sei tu ferita?

Gilda.

L'acciar qui mi piagò—
                (Indicando il core.)

Rigoletto.

Chi t' ha colpita?

Gilda.

V' ho ingannata—colpevole fui;
L'amai troppo—ora muoio per lui!

Rigoletto.

(Dio tremendo! ella stesso fu côlta
Dallo stral di mia giusta vendetta!)
Angiol caro; mi guarda, m'ascolta.
Parla; parlami, figlia diletta!

Gilda.

Ah! ch'io tacchia! a me—a lui perdonate;
Benedite alla figlia, o mio padre.

LASSU IN CIELO — *IN HEAV'N ABOVE* Duet (Rigoletto and Gilda)

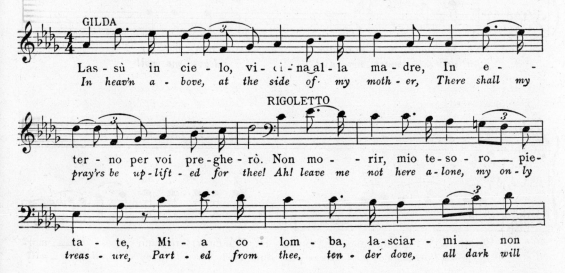

GILDA

Las - sù in cie - lo, vi - ci - na al - la ma - dre, In e -
In heav'n a - bove, at the side of my moth - er, There shall my

RIGOLETTO

ter - no per voi pre - ghe - rò. Non mo - rir, mio te - so - ro__ pie -
pray'rs be up - lift - ed for thee! Ah! leave me not here a - lone, my on - ly

ta - te, Mi - a co - lom - ba, la - sciar - mi__ non
treas - ure, Part - ed from thee, ten - der dove, all dark will

GILDA

Las - sù in cie - lo, vi - ci - na al - la
In heav'n a - bove at the side of my

RIG.

dêi, no' la - sciar - mi non dêi
be. all dark. all dark will be!

ma - dre In e - ter - no per voi pre - ghe -
moth - er, There shall my pray'rs be up - lift - ed for

Oh mia fi - glia!
Oh, stay, dear child!

rò, Pre - ghe - rò, Per voi pre - ghe -
thee! There I will pray, I will pray for

No, la - sciar - mi non dêi non mo - rir
Ah, no, thou must not die! leave me not!

rò
thee.

Se t'in - vo - li - qui sol qui sol — ri - mar - rei, Non mo - ri - re o qui te - co — mor -
Ah! do not leave me here a - lone, — my — child. Part - ed from thee, my child, all dark — will

Non più A lui per-do-na-te, mio pa-dre, Ad-
And when I'm gone, give him par-don, my fa - ther! Then

ró! O mia fi - glia! o mia Gil-da! no, la-sciar-mi non
bel Oh! stay, my child! Oh! my Gil-da! Leave me not here a -

di - - o! las - sù in ciel, las - sù in
fare - - well! In heav'n a - bove, In heav'n a -

dêi, non mo - rir,
lone! do not die!

ciel Pre - ghe - rò, per voi, pre - ghe -
bove, There shall my pray'rs be raised___ for

No, la-sciar-mi non dêi, non mo - rir,
Leave me' not here a - lone! do not die!

RIG.

Gil-da! mia Gil-da! È mor - ta! Ah! la ma - le - di - zio - ne!
Gil-da! my Gil-da! All's dark, now! Ah! yes, his curse is on___ me!

(Falling and tearing his hair over the corpse of his daughter.) | (Strappendosi e capelli, cade sul cadavere della figlia.)

END OF THE OPERA.

IL TROVATORE
(THE TROUBADOUR)

by

GIUSEPPE VERDI

THE STORY OF "IL TROVATORE"

THE old Count di Luna, now deceased, had two sons, not much apart in age. One night, while they were both yet in their infancy and under the care of a nurse, an old gipsy-woman — a tribe which, at that dark age, was universally believed to be closely allied to evil spirits, and possessing great magic powers — was discovered by the servants near the cradle of the youngest of the two children, to whose chamber she had stealthily gained access, while the nurse was asleep. The gipsy was quickly and violently expelled from the castle, but from that day the child's health began to fail. No remedies proving of avail, the old gipsy was suspected of having bewitched the child. Search was instituted, the woman taken prisoner, and, agreeably to the barbarous modes of punishment of the times, burned alive. A daughter of the gipsy, with her child in her arms, witnessed the execution. To her the unhappy victim of superstition bequeathed the task of vengeance. During the night following the young gipsy managed to steal the youngest child of the Count from the castle. She hurried with it to the stake, where the flames were still raging over the remains of her ill-fated mother. Arrived there, and almost out of her senses by the vivid recollection of the horrible scene she had just witnessed, she, by a fatal mistake, hurled her own child into the flames instead of the young Count. She discovered her error too late. But still she was not to be baffled in her dark designs. She fled, taking the child with her, joined her tribe, and brought him up — Manrico, the Troubadour — as her own son, trusting the secret of his parentage to no one, and waiting for a favorable moment to make him the tool of her vengeance against his own kindred.

In the meanwhile the old Count died, leaving the oldest son sole heir of his title and possessions, but doubting, up to his last moment, the death of his last born, although a heap of infant's bones, found among the ashes around the stake, seemed to be proof conclusive.

After this preliminary knowledge we now come to the actual business of the piece.

Manrico, grown up a valiant and daring knight, well skilled in arms, and of high mind and bearing, entered the contest at a tourney disguised, won all the honors, and was crowned victor by the hands of the Duchess Leonora, lady attendant on the Queen. From this moment dated a passionate love, shared by both. The Troubadour made his feelings known by nightly serenades performed below the window of the Duchess.

Unhappily, the Count di Luna (brother to Manrico, although this was unknown to both of them) was also smitten with a deep passion for the Duchess. One night, while the Count was lingering in the gardens attached to the Royal palaces, he suddenly heard the voice of the Troubadour in a thicket close by. Presently a door in the palace buildings opened, the Duchess stole out, and mistaking the Count for his sweet-voiced rival, she hastened towards him. Manrico stepping out from the foliage, she saw her mistake and sought his protection. Hard words passed between the two rivals. The Troubadour unmasked himself, revealing to his antagonist the features of one whose life had been forfeited to the laws by some act of violence against the existing government. The two knights retired with drawn swords to a more secluded spot, leaving the Duchess insensible on the ground.

The duel — this we learn from a conversation between Azucena and her supposed son, at the beginning of the second act — quickly terminated in favor of the Troubadour. The latter had already lifted his sword, to pierce the heart of his adversary, when he felt the influence of some secret power suspending the intended motion. A voice from heaven seemed to say to him, "Spare thy foe." Manrico, obeying reluctantly, retired. Joining the army, opposing his country's forces, he was left for dead on the battle-field of Pelilla. His mother sought him out by night, intending to give him fit burial. She discovered that life was not yet extinct, and had him removed to one of the mountain resorts of her tribe, and there restored him to health. Thus we find him at the beginning of Act Second, yet feeble and suffering.

His Prince, having heard of Manrico's being still alive, despatched a messenger to his retreat, bidding him to repair to the fortress of Castellar and to defend it against the forces of the Count di Luna. At the same time he communicated to him that the Duchess Leonora, believing in the current reports of his death, was about to take the veil that very evening, at a convent in the neighborhood of Castellar. Upon receipt of this message Manrico at once departed, and arrived at the convent just in time to rescue Leonora, who was about to be carried off forcibly by the Count di Luna and his followers. The Troubadour conducted the Duchess to Castellar, which place was immediately enclosed and besieged by the Count di Luna's troops.

Azucena, following Manrico (to whom she had become unconsciously attached) to Castellar, had ventured too far in the lines of the enemy, was taken prisoner and led before the Count, charged with being a spy. Here it happened that an old servant of the house of Luna, Ferrando, recognized her features. The gipsy, frightened and confounded by this unexpected discovery, called for her son Manrico to protect her. This only added to the Count's wrath, who gave orders to have her burned immediately in face of the castle.

The Troubadour, in the meanwhile, was making preparations to celebrate his union with Leonora on the morrow, when he was informed by the sentinels that a gipsy woman was about to be burned alive in front of the enemy's camp. Quickly recognizing the form of his mother, he gathered a squad of his troops around him and sallied out to rescue his ill-fated mother. But fortune was against him; his forces were repulsed and himself taken.

The Count di Luna, after storming the fortress of Castellar on the day following — but without finding a trace of Leonora — took his prisoners to the capital of the province. Here, on the eve before the day fixed for the execution of son and mother, Leonora suddenly appeared before the Count, offering him her hand in exchange for the life of Manrico. The Count consents, and Leonora is admitted into the dungeon, to restore Manrico to liberty. Before she enters, however, she takes poison, which she carried concealed in a ring on her finger. Manrico refuses to accept of his liberty, accusing the Duchess of basely betraying his affections. During this delay the poison begins to take its effect. Manrico discovers the extent of her sacrifice too late. The Count enters, understands at a glance what has happened, and orders Manrico to be beheaded immediately. While his order is being obeyed, he rouses the gipsy from the stupor in which she has been lying, motionless, in a corner of the dungeon. He drags her to the window, showing her the execution of her supposed son. Then the gipsy triumphantly divulges her secret. "Manrico is thy brother!" exclaims she to the horror-stricken Count, and with a "Mother! thou art avenged," she falls lifeless.

IL TROVATORE

(THE TROUBADOUR)

ACT I.	ATTO I.
THE DUEL.	IL DUELLO.

SCENE I—Vestibule in the palace of Aliaferia, with side door conducting to the apartments of COUNT DI LUNA. FERRANDO and servants of the COUNT reclining near the door. Armed men are seen walking in the background.

Ferrando
(to the servants, who are falling asleep).

Arouse ye! arouse ye! The Count's approach
Must find us watchful:
Ye know 'tis his wont
Under the casement of his beloved one
To pass whole nights unsleeping.

Servants.
'Tis the venom of jealous doubt
That has entered his bosom.

Ferrando.
This minstrel knight, who in the garden
Sings with his lute at midnight,
Seems a rival not idly dreaded.

Servants.
Pray dispel from our eyelids
The sleep that on us falls,
By now relating the truthful tale
Of Garzia, late brother to Count Luna.

Ferrando.
Be it so;
Come close around me here.
(The servants cluster around him.)

Soldiers.
We're ready.

Servants.
We hear thee.
(All surround FERRANDO.)

Ferrando.
With two sons, heirs of fortune and affection,

SCENA I—Atrio nel palazzo dell' Aliaferia; porta da un lato, che mette agli appartamenti del CONTE DI LUNA. FERRANDO, e molti famigliari del Conte, che giacciono presso la porta, alcuni uomini d'arme che passeggiano in fondo.

Ferrando
(parla ai famigliari).

All' erta, all' erta! Il Conte
N' è d'uopo attender vigilando; ed egli
Talor, presso i veroni
Della sua cara, intere
Passa le notti.

Famigliari.
Gelosia le fiere
Serpi gli avventa in petto!

Ferrando.
Nel Trovator, che dai giardini muove
Notturno il canto, d'un rivale a dritto
Ei teme.

Famigliari.
Dalle gravi
Palpêbre il sonno a discacciar, la vera
Storia ci narra di Garzia, germano
Al nostro Conte.

Ferrando.
La dirò: venite
Intorno a me.
(Famigliari eseguiscono accostandosi pur essi.)

Arme.
Noi pure—

Famigliari.
Udite, udite.
(Tutti accerchiano FERRANDO.)

Ferrando.
Di due figli vivea, padre beato,
Il buon Conte di Luna

Lived the Count in enjoyment;
Watching the younger for his safe protec-
tion
The good nurse found employment.
One morning, as the dawn's first rays were
shining,
From her pillow she rose,—
Who was found, think ye, near the child
reclining?

Chorus.
Who? Pray tell us! speak, disclose!

Fida nutrice del secondo nato
Dormia presso la cuna
Sul romper dell' aurora un bel mattino
Ella dischiude i rai,
E chi trova d'accanto a quel bambino?

Coro.
Chi?—Favèlla—chi mai?

ABBIETTA ZINGARA — *SAT THERE A GIPSY HAG*   Ballad (Ferrando)

Ab-biet-ta Zin-ga-ra fo-sca ve-gliarda! Cin-ge-vai sim-bo-li
Sat there a gip-sy-hag, witch-like ap-pearing; Of her dark mys-te-ries

di-ma-li-ar-da; e sul fan-ciul-lo con vi-so ar-ci-gno,
strange sym-bols wear-ing. O'er the babe sleep-ing with fierce looks bend-ing,

l'oc-chioaf-fig-ge-a tor-vo, san-gui-gno! D'or-ror com-
Gazed she up-on him, black deeds in-tend-ing! Hor-ror pro-

pre-sa com-pre-saè la nu-tri-ce a-cu-to un gri-do
found seized the nurse at that dark vi-sion; Sharp cries of ter-ror

un gri-do all'au-ra scio-glie, ed ec-co, in me-no che lab-bro il
soon rent the air a-bove her, And swift-ly as thought flies, with speed-y de-

di-ce, i ser-vi, i ser-vi ac-cor-ro-no, i servi ac-cor-ro-no in quel-la so-glie;
ci-sion, The serv-ants, the serv-ants all a-larm'd, the servants round a-bout the threshold hov-er;

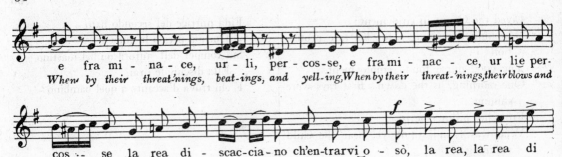

e fra mi - na - ce, ur - li, per - cos - se, e fra mi - nac - ce, ur lie per-
When by their threat-'nings, beat-ings, and yell-ing,When by their threat-'nings,their blows and

cos - - se la rea di - scac-cia-no ch'en-trar-vi o - sò, la rea, la rea di -
cos - - se la rea di-scac-cia-no ch'en-trar-vi o - sò, la rea, la rea di -
yell - ing, The dark in - trud - er was soon ex - pell'd, the guilt - y wretch was

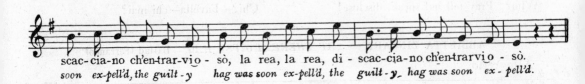

scac-cia-no ch'en-trar-vio - sò, la rea, la rea, di - scac-cia-no ch'en-trarvi o - sò.
soon ex-pell'd, the guilt - y hag was soon ex-pell'd, the guilt - y hag was soon ex - pell'd.

Chorus.

'Twas just resentment their bosoms swell-
   ing;
For her offences was she expelled.

Ferrando.

She declared that to read the stars prevailing
   At his birth, was her mission.
'Twas falsehood! Soon they found the child
   was failing,
   And in wasting condition;
With features pale and wan, languid, weak
   and weary.
Coming darkness appalled him,
The days passed slowly in lamentations
   dreary;
   The hag's dark spell enthralled him!
      (All appear horrified.)
Sought they the gipsy on all sides turning,
Seized, and condemned her to death by
   burning.
One child, accursed, left she remaining,
Quick to avenge her, no means disdaining.
Thus she accomplished her dark retribution!
Lost was the young child; search unavailing;
But on the site of the hag's execution
They found, 'mid the embers (a scene of
   horror
Their eyes assailing), of a young infant,
Alas! the bones half consumed and burning.

Coro.

Giusto quei petti sdegno commosse;
L'infame vecchia lo provocò!

rando.

Asserì che tirar del fanciullino
   L'oroscopo volea—
Bugiarda!—Lenta febbre del meschino
   La salute struggea!
Coverto di pallor, languido, affranto
   Ei tremava la sera,
Il dì traeva in lamentevol pianto—
   Ammaliato egli era!
      (Il coro inorridisce.)
La fattuchiera perseguitata
Fù presa, e al rogo fù condannata;
Ma rimanea la maledetta
Figlia, ministra di ria vendetta!—
Compì quest' empia nefando eccesso!—
Sparve il bambino—e si rinvenne
Mal spenta brage, nel sito stesso
Ov' arsa un giorno la strega venne!—
E d'un bambino—ohimè!—l' ossame
Bruciato a mezzo, fumante ancor!

Chorus.

Ah! fiend inhuman! such deeds revolting
My soul with horror and hatred fill!

Some of Chorus.

The father?

Ferrando.

Few his days, and filled with sorrow;
Yet a secret presentiment at heart made
    him still hopeful;
It told him his son was living;
And on his dying bed he claimed of the
    Count, our master,
His solemn promise, a careful search to in-
    stigate.
Ah! how vainly!

Chorus of Soldiers.

But what of her?
No tidings as yet you've heard?

Ferrando.

No word hath reached us! Oh, heaven grant
That haply we may meet one day!

Chorus of Servants

And were it so, would'st thou know her?

Ferrando.

Yes, by counting the years
That have vanished, I should know her.

Chorus of Soldiers.

Be that
The moment, down near her mother
In perdition to send her!

Ferrando.

To perdition? 'Tis believed, that on this
    earth
She's doomed to wander—she, the soul-ac-
    cursed, the witch infernal.
And when the skies are darkened,
In forms oft-changing have some beheld her.

Chorus.

'Tis true!

Some of Chorus.

They say some have seen her o'er housetops
    careering!

Coro.

Oh, scellerata!—oh, donna infame!
Del par m'investe odio ed orror.

Alcuni.

E il padre?

Ferrando.

Brevi e tristi giorni visse;
Pure ignoto del cor presentimento
Gli diceva, che spento
Non era il figlio; ed a morir vicino
Bramò che il signor nostro a lui giurasse
Di non cessar le indagini—ah!—fur vane!

Arme.

E di colei non s'ebbe
Contezza mai?

Ferrando.

Nulla contezza—Oh! dato
Mi fosse rintracciarla
Un dì!

Famigliari.

Ma ravvisarla potresti?

Ferrando.

Calcolando
Gli anni trascorsi—lo potrei.

Arme.

Sarebbe
Tempo presso la madre
All' inferno spedirla.

Ferrando.

All' inferno?—E credenza, che dimori
Ancor nel mondo l'anima perduta
Dell' empia strega, e quando il cielo è nero
In varie forme altrui si mostri.

Coro.

E vero!

Alcuni.

Sull' orlo dei tetti alcun l' ha veduta!

Others.

> Transformed to a bird, or a vampire appearing!

Still Others.

> Sometimes like a raven, or owl, shrilly crying,
> From daylight and thunder she's seen madly flying!

Ferrando.

> The Count's faithful servant, the old witch assaulting,
> Soon died in an access of terror revolting!
> (All manifest great terror.)
> She came to his chamber, an owl's form assuming,
> The silence disturbing, the darkness illuming;
> She gazed on him fiercely with eyes brightly flaming;
> With loud cries of anguish the still air was rent!
> That moment the bell struck, midnight proclaiming.
> (A bell suddenly strikes the hour of midnight.)

Chorus.

> Ah! maledictions fall on the witch of infernal descent!

(The servants hasten towards the door. The soldiers retire in the background.)

SCENE II—Gardens of the Palace; on one side a flight of marble steps, leading to the apartments. Thick clouds conceal the moon.

(Enter LEONORA and INEZ.)

Inez.

> What still detains thee? late 'tis growing;
> Come then; already her Highness has called thee;
> Did'st hear her?

Leonora.

> Another night goes by,
> Yet him I behold not!

Inez.

> Peril tends the flame
> That thou dost nourish.
> Oh, tell me, prithee, how the spark
> First was kindled in thy bosom?

Altri.

> In upupa o strige talora si muta!

Altri.

> In corvo tal' altra; più spesso in civetta,
> Sull' alba fuggente al par di saetta!

Ferrando.

> Mori di paura un servo del conte,
> Che avea della zingara percossa la fronte!
> (Tutti si pingono, di superstizzoso terrore.)
> Apparve a costui d' un gufo in sembianza
> Nell' alta quiete di tacita stanza!—
> Con occhi lucenti guardava—guardava,
> Il cielo attristando con urlo feral!
> Allor mezzanotte appunto suonava—
> (Suona mezzanotte.)

Tutti.

> Ah! sia maledetta la strega infernal!
> (Con subito soprasalto.)

(Odonzi alcuni tocchi di tamburo. Gli uomini d'arme accorrono in fondo; i famigliari traggonsi verso la porta.)

SCENA II—Giardini del palazzo; sulla destra narmora scalinata che mette negli appartamenti. La notte è inoltrata, ed dense nubi cuoprono la luna.

(Entra LEONORA ed INEZ.)

Ines.

> Che più t'arresti?—l'ora è tarda; vieni,
> Di te la regal donna
> Chiese, l'udisti.

Leonora.

> Un' altra notte ancora
> Senza vederlo!

Ines.

> Perigliosa fiamma
> Tu nutri!—Oh, come, dove
> La primieri favilla
> In te s'apprese?

Leonora.

At the Tournay.   He entered;
Dark were his vestments and his crest;
His shield and banner no devices bearing;
An unknown Knight he came,
And in the lists bore away all the honors;
   mine was the hand
That crowned his brow as victor.   Soon, a
   civil war outbreaking,
He disappeared.   Ah! like a golden vision
Fled his dear image!   One other moment,
Long after this,—but then—

Inez.

What chanced then?

Leonora.

Now hear!

Leonora.

Ne' tornei.   V'apparvo
Bruno le vesti ed il cimier, lo scudo
Bruno e di stemma ignudo,
Sconosciuto guerrier, che dell' agone
Gli onori ottente—Al vincitor sul crine
Il serto io posi—Civil guerra intanto
Arse—nol vidi piú!—come d'aurato
Sogno fuggente imago!—ed era volta
Lunga stagion—ma poi—

Ines.

Che avvenne?

Leonora.

Ascolta!

TACEA LA NOTTE PLACIDA — *THE NIGHT, CALMLY AND PEACEFULLY*   **Air (Leonora)**

Words, like the prayers, a humble heart
Outpours to heaven when lonely,
In which one well-known name was oft
Repeated; 'twas mine, mine only!
Reaching in haste the balcony,
I saw him standing before me!
Joy, such as only angels know,
With glowing thrill came o'er me!
To heart, and eyes, with rapture filled,
The earth like heaven appeared.

Inez.

What thou relatest sadly disturbs me,
Filling my bosom with terror.

Leonora.

'Tis idle!

Inez.

Doubtings and dark forebodings arise within
    me,
Concerning this Knight's strange move-
    ments!
Try to forget him!

Leonora.

What saidst thou! No more, then!

Inez.

Heed friendly counsel; heed it,
I pray; heed it!

Leonora.

To forget him! Ah, thou art speaking
    words
Which the soul can ne'er comprehend.

Versi di prece, ed umile,
Qual d'uom che prega Iddio;
In quella ripeteasi
Un nome—il nome mio!
Corsi al veron sollecita—
Egli era, egli era desso!—
Gioja provai che agli angeli
Solo è provar concesso!—
Al core, al guardo estatico
La terra un ciel sembrò!

Ines.

Quanto narrasti di turbamento
M' ha piena l'anima!—Io tremo—

Leonora.

Invano!

Ines.

Dubbio, ma tristo presentimento
In me risveglia quest' uomo arcano!
Tenta obliarlo—

Leonora.

Che dici!—Oh, basti!

Ines.

Cedi al consiglio dell' amistà--
Cedi—

Leonora.

Obliarlo!—Ah! tu parlasti
Detto, che intendere l'alma non sà.

DI TALE AMOR — *OF LOVE LIKE THIS, HOW VAINLY* . Air (Leonora)

cor,___ il_ cor si - ne - bri - ò. Il mio des - ti - no com - pir - ed
heart,___ the_ heart with rap-ture glows. My fate would not com - plet - ed

si, non puo che a lui d'ap - pres - - so, S'io non vi - vrò per es - - be, If he were not be - side___ me; Were life with him de - nied___

so, Per es - so, per es - so, per es-so,_ mo - ri - rò!_ S'i-o non vi-vrò per
me, Then wel - come, then wel - come, then wel-come death's re - pose. Yes, were life with him de -

es - so, per es-so io mo - ri - rò, Ah! sì per es - so,_ mo - ri -
nied_ me, I'd wel - come death's re - pose, ah! yes, for him, in_ death re -

rò!_ per_ es - so mo-ri - rò, mo - - - - ri - rò!
pose, in_ death would I re - pose, I'd___ re-pose.

Inez (aside).

No cause for sad repentance
May coming time disclose!

(They ascend to the apartments.)
(Enter the COUNT.)

Count.

Night reigns in silence! Her Highness, no doubt,
Is now immersed in peaceful slumber;
Not yet sleeps her companion—Oh! Leonora,
Thou art still wakeful; the tremulous light
Now shining from thy casement tells me
Of thy nocturnal vigils—
Ah! how this amorous passion
Thrills each nerve within me!—I must now behold thee,
And thou shalt hear me! Loved one! To us belongs
This blissful moment—

(Blinded by passion, he approaches the steps, but suddenly pauses, on hearing the sound of a lute.)

The Troubadour! I tremble!

Ines (da se).

Non debba mai pentirsi
Chi tanto un giorno amo!

(Ascendono agli appartamenti.)
(Entra il CONTE.)

Conte.

Tace la notte! Immersa
Nel sonno è, certo, la regal signora;
Ma veglia la sua dama—Oh! Leonora,
Tu desta sei; mel dice
Da quel verone tremolante un raggio
Della notturna lampa—
Ah!—l'amorosa vampa
M'arde ogni fibra!—Ch'io ti vegga è d'uopo,
Che tu m'intenda—Vengo—A noi supremo
E tal momento—

(Cieco d'amore avviasi alla gradinata; odonsi gli accordi d'un liuto; egli si arresta.)

Il Trovator!—Io fremo.

DESERTO SULLA TERRA — *LONELY ON EARTH ABIDING*   Romanza (Manrico)

Count.

  Oh, accents! I shudder!

Manrico.

  But that fond treasure gaining,

  Its faith and love obtaining,

  High o'er all kings would soar,

  The happy Troubadour!

Count.

  Oh, accents! Oh, jealous anger!

  'Tis no error—she approaches!

      (Wraps himself in his mantle.)

        (Enter LEONORA.)

Leonora

     (hastening towards the COUNT).

  Oh, my beloved!

Count.

  What now?

Leonora.

  More late than usual

  Is thy coming; each moment have I counted

  With heart and pulses beating!—At length

  'Tis love filled with pity that brings thee

    to these loving arms.

Voice of the Troubadour.

  Deceiver!

(The moon emerging from the clouds reveals the figure of
a masked cavalier.)

      (Enter MANRICO.)

Leonora

(recognizing each and falling at the feet of MANRICO).

  That voice!—Ah, darkness and unrest

Conte.

  Oh, detti! Io fremo!

Manrico.

  Ma s'ei quel cor possiede,

  Bello di casta fede,

  E d'ogni re maggior

  Il Trovator!

Conte.

  Oh detti, oh gelosia!—

  Non m'inganno—Ella scende;

      (Si avvolge nel suo mantello.)

        (Entra LEONORA.)

Leonora

     (correndo verso il CONTE).

  Anima mia!

Conte.

  (Che far!)

Leonora.

  Più dell' usato

  E tarda l'ora; io ne contai gl'istanti

  Coi palpiti del core!—Alfin ti guida

  Pietoso amor tra queste braccia—

Le Voce del Trovatore.

  Infida.

(La luna mostrasi dai nugoli, e lascia scorgere una persona
di cui la visiera nasconde il volto.)

      (Entra MANRICO.)

Leonora.

(Riconoscendo entrandi, e gettandosi ai piedi di MANRICO.)

  Qual voce!—Ah, dalle tenebre

My eager steps misguided!
'Twas thee, I thought, my words addressed!
In thee, not him, confided.
To thee my soul expandeth!
No other bliss demandeth!
I love thee, ah, believe me,
With lasting, boundless love!

Count.

And dar'st thou?

Manrico
(raising LEONORA).
Enough, forgive me!

Count.

With rage my heart doth move!
If thou'rt not base, reveal thyself!

Leonora.

Alas!

Count.

Thy name declaring—

Leonora.

Oh, speak, I pray!
(Aside to MANRICO).

Manrico.

Behold me, then,
Manrico!

Count.

Thou?—wherefore?
Rash traitor! bold and daring!
Urgel's accomplice, the laws have condemned
    thee.
And dar'st thou thus return
Within these royal portals?

Manrico.

What stays thee? Go call the guards, to
    aid thee;
Seize me, thy rival,
And to the headsman's gleaming axe
Consign me.

Count.

Thy fatal hour.
Perchance, already is at hand!
Oh, insensate! Come then—

Leonora.

Stay thee!

Tratta in errore io fui!
A te credei rivolgere
L'accento, e non a lui—
A te, che l'alma mia
Sol chiede, sol desia—
Io t'amo, il giuro, io t'amo
D' immenso eterno amor!

Conte.

Ed osi?—

Manrico
(sollevandola).
(Ah, più non bramo!)

Conte.

Avvampo di furor!
Se un vil non sei, discovriti.

Leonora.

(Ohimè!)

Conte.

Palesa il nome—

Leonora.

Deh, per pietà!—
(Sommessamente a MANRICO.)

Manrico.

Ravvisami,
Manrico io son.

Conte.

Tu!—Come!
Insano, temerario!
D'Urgel seguace, a morte
Proscritto, ardisci volgerti
A queste regie porte?—

Manrico.

Che tardi?—or via le guardie
Appella, ed il rivale
Al ferro del carnefice
Consegna.

Conte.

Il tuo fatale
Istante assai più prossimo
E, dissennato!—Vieni—

Leonora.

Conte!—

Count.

To my rage thou'rt victim doomed,
And fate wills I must slay thee.

Leonora.

One moment stay thee!

Count.

Follow me.

Manrico.

Lead on!

Leonora.

(What must I do?—
A single cry from me
May cause his ruin!)   Hear me.

Count.

No!
Fires of jealous, despised affection
In my heart are fiercely raging!
Wretch! thy blood for this foul defection
Soon shall flow, its pains assuaging!

(To LEONORA.)

Thou hast dared me, thy passion revealing!
He thou lovest in death shall lie,
Thy fond words his fate now sealing,
By this hand he's doomed to die!

Leonora.

One short moment thy fury restraining,
Let thine anger give way to reason;
I, alone, thy base passion disdaining,
Roused thy hateful charge of treason!
Let thy vengeance on me then descending,
Who have scorned thee, and still can defy,—
Strike thy dagger in this heart offending,
From thy love that dared to fly.

Manrico.

Vainly anger his proud heart is moving,
He shall soon fall by death inglorious;
Haply he who inspires thee with loving
Is by thy love made ever victorious.

(To the COUNT.)

Thy dark fate is already decided,
Doomed to perish, thy last hour is nigh!
Heart and life to my hand are confided,
Heaven condemns thee, and thou shalt die!

(The two rivals retire with drawn swords. LEONORA falls senseless.)

END OF FIRST ACT.

Conte.

Al mio sdegno vittíma
E forza ch' io ti sveni—

Leonora.

Oh ciel!—t'arresta—

Conte.

Seguimi—

Manrico.

Andiam—

Leonora.

Che mai farò?—
Un sol mio grido perdere
Lo puote!)—M'odi—

Conte.

No.
Di geloso amor sprezzato
Arde in me tremendo foco!
Il tuo sangue, o sciagurato,
Ad estinguerlo fia poco!

(A LEONORA.)

Dirgli, o folle—io t'amo—ardisti—
Ei più vivere non può—
Un accento proferisti,
Che a morir lo condannò!

Leonora.

Un istante almen dia loco
Il tuo sdegno alla ragione—
Io, sol io di tanto foco
Son, pur troppo, la cagione!
Piombi, ah! piombi il tuo furore
Sulla rea che t'oltraggiò—
Vibra il ferro in questo core,
Che te amar non vuol, non può.

Manrico.

Del superbo vana è l'ira;
Ei cadrà da me trafitto.
Ii mortal che amor t'inspira,
Dall' amor fu reso invitto.
La tua sorte è già compita—

(Al CONTE.)

L'ora omai per te suonò!
Il tuo core e la tua vita
Il destino a me serbò!

(I due rivali si allontanano con le spade sguainate; LEONORA cade priva di sentimento.)

FINE DELL' ATTO PRIMO.

ACT II.

THE GIPSY.

SCENE I—A ruined house at the foot of a mountain in Biscay; the interior is partly exposed to view; within, a great fire is lighted. Day begins to dawn.

(AZUCENA is seated near the fire. MANRICO, enveloped in his mantle, is lying upon a mattress; his helmet is at his feet; in his hand he holds a sword, which he regards fixedly. A band of gipsies are sitting in scattered groups around them.)

Gipsies.

See, how the shadows of night are flying!

Morn breaketh, heaven's glorious arch unveiling;

Like a young widow, who, weary of sighing,

Lays by her garments of sorrow and wailing.

Rouse up to labor! Take each his hammer!

Who makes the gipsy's a life with pleasure laden?

The gipsy maiden.

(They take up the implements of labor, and strike with their hammers upon anvils, in regular measure.)

Men

(resting awhile from their labor, they address the women).

Fill me a bumper; both arm and hand

New strength and courage draw from flowing beakers.

(The women pour out wine for them in rustic cups.)

All.

See how the sunlight, radiantly glowing,

Borrows new beams from our wine-cups o'erflowing!

Resume our labor! Take each his hammer!

Who makes the gipsy's a life with pleasure laden?

The gipsy maiden!

Azucena

(as she begins to sing, the gipsies gather about her).

ATTO II.

LA GITANA.

SCENA I—Un diruto abituro sulle falde d'un Monte della Biscaglia—nel fondo, quasi tutto aperto, arde un gran fuoco I primi albori.

(AZUCENA siede presso il fuoco—MANRICO, le sta disteso accanio sopra una coltrice, ed avviluppato nel suo mantello; ha l'elmo ai piedi, e fra le mani la spada, su cui figge immobilmente lo sguardo—Una banda di Zingari è sparso all'intorno.)

Zingari.

Vedi! le fosche notturne spoglie

De' cieli sveste l'immensa volta;

Sembra una vedova che alfin si toglie

I bruni panni ond' era involta.

All' opra, all' opra. Dagli, martella.

Chi del gitano i giorni abbella?

La zingarella.

(Danno di piglio ai loro ferri di mestiere—al misurato tempestar dei martelli cadenti sulle incudini, ou uomini, ou donne, e tutti in un tempo in fine intuonano la cantilena seguente.)

Uomini

(alle donne, sostando un poco dal lavoro).

Versami un tratto: lena e coraggio

Il corpo e l'anima traggon dal bere.

(Le donne mescono ad essi in rozze coppe.)

Tutti.

Oh, guarda, guarda! del sole un raggio

Brilla più vivido nel ${tuo \atop mio}$ bicchiere—

All' opra, all' opra—Dagli, martella—

Quale a ${voi \atop noi}$ splende propizia stella?—

La zingarella.

Azucena

(canta: gli zingari le si fanno allato).

STRIDE LA VAMPA — *UPWARD THE FLAMES ROLL* Air (Azucena)

re a quel fuo- - co- Lie- -ta in sem-bian- -za! Ur-
to the burn- -ing with- - seem-ing glad- -ness; Loud

-li-di gio-ja- D'in- tor-no ec-cheg-gia-no- Cin-ta di-
cries of- plea-sure from- all sides re-ech-o-ing! By- guards sur-

sgher- ri- Don- na s'a-van- za! Si- nis-tra splen- -
round-ed- forth comes a- wo- man! While, -o'er them shin -

de Sui- vol-ti or-ri- bi-le, La 'te-tra fiam- ma che
ing, with- wild, un- earth - ly glare, Dark wreaths of flame curl- as-

s'al- za, Che s'al- za al ciel!- che- s'al-za al ciel!
cend-ing, as- cend-ing to heav'n,- roll- up to heav'n!

Upward the flames roll! on comes the victim still;	Stride la vampa!—giunge la vittima
Robed in dark garments, ungirt, unsandalled,	Nero-vestita—discinta e scalza!
Fierce cries of vengeance from that dark crowd arise;	Grido feroce—di morte levasi;
Echo repeats them from mountain to mountain.	L'eco il repete—di balza in balza!
O'er them reflecting, with wild, unearthly glare,	Sinistra splende—su' volti orribili
Dark wreaths of flame curl, ascending to heaven.	La tetra fiamma che s' alza al ciel!

Gipsies.

 Thine is a mournful song!

Azucena.

 Yes, sad indeed,

 As is the mournful story,

 From which it draws its dreary burthen.

  (Turns her face to Manrico and murmurs)

 Avenge thou me!

Zingari.

 Mesta è la tua canzon!

Azucena.

 Del pari mesta

 Che la storia funesta

 Da cui tragge argomento!

 (Rivolge il capo dalla parte di Manrico, e mormora cupa-mente)

 Mi vendica—mi vendica!

Manrico.

    (Again those mysterious words!)

Elderly Gipsy.

    Companions, day advances;

    'Tis time to seek for food; let us descend

    To the towns that lie beneath us.

Manrico.

    Come on, then!

              (Putting away their tools.)

Women.

    Come on, then!

(Commence descending promiscuously; their song is heard growing fainter in the distance.)

Gipsies.

    Who makes the gipsy's a life with pleasure
        laden?

    The gipsy maiden!

Manrico

            (rising).

    All have left us; ah, now relate

    That dark mournful story!

Azucena.

    Thou dost not know it as yet?

    Thou wert but still young, when,

    Spurred on by ambition, far away

    Thou didst wander!—My mother's final
        doom

    This tale relateth. She was charged

    With fearful crimes by a haughty noble,

    Whose failing infant she was accused of
        charming!

    Doomed to the stake, she perished

    Where this fire is burning!

Manrico.

    Ah, fate unhappy!

      (Drawing back with horror from the fire).

Azucena.

    In fetters, they led her onward to meet her
        dark fate impending;

    With babe in hand, I followed sadly, with
        tears descending.

    In vain tried I to approach her, through
        crowds that round her were pressing;

    In vain did she attempt to stay, to leave
        with me her blessing.

    Goaded by spears and lances, with oaths and
        jeers assaulted,

Manrico.

    (L'arcana parola ognor!)

Vecchio Zingara.

    Compagni, avanza il giorno;

    A procacciarci un pan, sù, sù!—scendiamo

    Per le propinque ville.

Uomini.

    Andiamo.

    (Ripongona sollecitamente nei sacchi i loro arnesi.)

Donne.

    Andiamo.

(Tutti scendono alla rinfusa giù per la china; tratto tratto e sempre a maggior distanza, odesi il loro canto.)

Zingari.

    Chi del gitano i giorni abbella?

    La zingarella!

Manrico

            (sorgendo).

    Soli or siamo; deh narra

    Quella storia funesta.

Azucena.

    E tu la ignori,

    Tu pur!—Ma giovinetto i passi tuoi

    D'ambizïon lo sprone

    Lungi traca!—Dell' ava il fine acerbo

    E quella storia—La incolpò superbo

    Conte di malefizio, onde apparia

    Côlto un bambin suo figlio—Essa bruciata

    Fù dov' arde or quel foco!

Manrico.

    Ahi! sciagurata!

      (Rifuggendo con raccapriccio dalla fiamma.)

Azucena.

    Condotta ell' era in ceppi al suo destin
        tremendo

    Col figlio—teco in braccio io la seguia pian-
        gendo:

    Infino ad essa un varco tentai, ma invano,
        aprirmi—

    Invan tentò la misera fermarsi, e benedirmi!

    Che, fra bestemmie oscene, pungendola coi
        ferri

    Al rogo la cacciavano gli scellerati sgherri!

The guards pursued her ruthlessly, 'till at the stake they halted.

At length, with broken accents, "Avenge thou me," she cried!

Those dying words will ever within my heart abide.

Manrico.

Didst thou avenge her?

Azucena.

The Count's young child, ere the day was ended,

I stole and brought him hither; the flames still to heaven ascended!

Manrico.

The flames?—Oh, heav'n—thou couldst not—

Azucena.

Sadly the child began weeping;

Rent was my heart with his sorrow, o'er me pity was creeping,

When quickly, my mind disordered, saw what like dreams came o'er me.

Deadly shapes and phantoms brought the dark scene before me;

The guardsmen, this place of torture, the mother pale, confounded,

Barefoot, ungirdled, the outcry of anguish,

That cry within me resounded: "Avenge thou me!"

All heedless, my hand extended held fast the victim pale;

The flames rolled expectant; in I hurled him!

Calmed was the fatal madness, fled was the horrid vision;

The fire still glowed in silence, gorged with its foul commission!

Gazing around in sadness, I saw the infant cherished

Of that vile Count approaching!

Manrico.

Ah, what say'st thou?

Azucena.

My child had perished,

My child through me had perished!

Allor, con tronc.. accent, mi vendica! es. clamò—

Quel detto un eco eterno in questo cor lasciò.

Manrico.

La vendicasti?

Azucena.

Il figlio giunsi a rapir del Conte;

Lo trascinai quì meco—le fiamme ardean già pronte.

Manrico.

Le fiamme?—oh ciel!—tu forse?—

Azucena.

Ei distruggeasi in pianto—

Io mi sentiva il cor dilaniato, infranto!—

Quand'ecco agli egri spirti, come in un sogno, apparva.

La vision ferale di spaventose larve!—

Gli sgnerri ed il supplizio!—la madre smorta in volto—

Scalza, discinta!—il grido, il noto grido ascolto—

Mi vendica!—La mano convulsa tendo stringo

La vittima—nel foco la traggo, la sos pingo!—

Cessa il fatal delirio—

L'orrida scena fugge—

La fiamma sol divampa,

E la sua preda strugge!

Pur volgo intorno il guardo,

E innanzi a me vegg' io

Dell' empio Conte il figlio!—

Manrico.

Ah! come?

Azucena.

Il figlio mio,

Mio figlio avea bruciato!

Manrico.

Horrid crime!

Azucena.

Once more my thin locks with horror rise
up, unsoothed by time!

(AZUCENA falls fainting on her seat; MANRICO is struck
dumb with surprise and horror.)

Manrico.

I'm not thy son, then? tell me, who am I,
I pray thee?

Azucena

(hastily, as if to repair an involuntary admission).

Mine art thou ever.

Manrico.

Thy words denied it.

Azucena.

It may be; what wouldst thou?

When wandering thoughts such terrible
scenes encounter!

The mind, disordered, heeds not all the follies

Unguarded lips may utter.   Mother tender
and true.

Hast thou not found me ever?

Manrico.

Can I disown it?

Azucena.

To me thy life's protection

Thou owest.   At midnight, on the field of
battle

At Petilla, where reports declared thou hadst
fallen,

Did I not come to give thee fit burial?

In thy breast, my cares revived the vital
spark,

But there the affection fond, maternal,
stayed not.

How many hours did I tend thee, healing
thy wounds

So ghastly and numerous?

Manrico   (with noble pride).

Wounds obtained on that dark morning;

My breast alone received them! 'Mid all
the thousands that disbanded,

I alone faced the foe, still firm, unyielding.

The vile de Luna then

Manrico.

Che dici quale orror!

Azucena.

Sul capo mio le chiome sento drizzarsi ancor!

(AZUCENA ricade trambasciata sul proprio seggio: MAN-
RICO ammutisce, colpito d'orrore e di sorpresa—Momenti di
silenzio.)

Manrico.

Non son tuo figlio?—E chi son io, chi dunque?

Azucena

(con sollecitudine di chi cerca emendare involontario fallo)

Tu sei mio figlio!

Manrico.

Eppur dicesti—

Azucena.

Ah!—forse—

Che vuoi!—Quando al pensier s'affaccia il
truce

Caso, lo spirto intenebrato pone

Stolto parole sul mio labbro—Madre,

Tenera madre non m'avesti ognora?

Manrico.

Potrei negarlo?—

Azucena.

A me, se vivi ancora,

Nol dêi? Notturna, nei pugnati campi

Di Petilla, ove spento

Fama ti disse, a darti

Sepoltura non mossi?   La fuggente

Aura vital non iscovri, nel seno

Non l'arrestò materno affetto?—E quanta

Cure non spesi a risanar le tante ferite!

Manrico   (con nobile orgoglio).

Che portai quel di fatale—

Ma tutte qui, nel petto?—Io sol, fra mille

Già sbandati, al nemico

Volgendo ancor la faccia!—Il rio de Luna

Sù me piombò col suo drappello; io caddi,

Charged me with his troops o'erwhelming;
 I faltered and fell,
Yet brave and unconquered!

Azucena.

Such were the thanks
Which the villain did repay thee,
For sparing his base life in that combat at
 night!
What then did blind thee?
Was it a strange compassion?

Manrico.

Oh, mother! I cannot tell thee! I know
not!

Però da forte io caddi!

Azucena.

Ecco mercede
Ai giorni, che l'infame
Nel singolar certame
Ebbe salvi da te?—qual t'acciecava
Strana pietà per esso?

Manrico.

Oh madre!—non saprei dirlo a me stesso!

MAL REGGENDO — *ILL SUSTAINING* Air (Manrico)

Mal reg-gen-do all' a-spro as-sal-to Ei già toc-co il
Ill sus-tain-ing the fu-rious en-coun-ter, At my mer-cy he

suo-lo a-ve-a: Ba-le-na-va il col-po in al-to
fell un-de-fend-ed: Bright-ly gleam-ing, my sword was up-lift-ed

agitato e cupo

Che tra-fig-ger-lo, tra-fig-ger-lo, do-ve-a.— Quan-do ar-res-ta, quan-do ar-
Soon to strike his heart, to pierce his heart in-tend-ed. When some se-cret pow'r, some

res-ta un mo-to ar-ca-no Nel di-scen-der, nel di-scen-der ques-ta ma-no— Le mie
pow'r the blow sus-pend-ing, Firm-ly held my arm, with-held my arm de-scend-ing; Thro' each

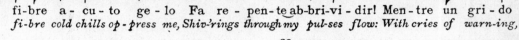

fi-bre a-cu-to ge-lo Fa re-pen-te ab-bri-vi-dir! Men-tre un gri-do
fi-bre cold chills op-press me, Shiv-'rings through my pul-ses flow: With cries of warn-ing,

cresc. *ff* *pp*

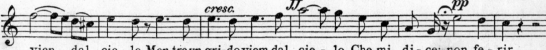

vien dal cie-lo, Men-tre un gri-do viem dal cie-lo, Che mi di-ce: non fe-rir.
Heav'n ad-dress'd me, with a loud commanding cry, Heav'n thus ad-dress'd me."Spare thy foe!

Azucena.

But within that soul ungrateful
Not one word from heaven hath resounded!
Oh! if with that villain hateful
Thou in fight shouldst be confounded,
Haste to accomplish (Heaven doth will it)
What I command thee, hear and fulfil it!
To the handle send this weapon
Through the monster's cruel heart.
(The prolonged note of a horn is heard.)

Manrico.

Ruiz sends hither th' accustomed courier,
Haply—
(Sounds his horn in reply.)

Azucena.

Avenge thou me!
(Remains in thought and seemingly unconscious of what is passing.)
(Enter a Messenger.)

Manrico
(to the Messenger).

Approach this way. Proceed
And tell me what news thou bringest.

Messenger.

The scroll I bring here will tell thee all.
(Presenting a letter.)

Manrico
(reads).

"Within our power is Castellor;
By the order of our prince thou must watch
o'er
And defend it. Wherever this may reach
thee,
Come in haste. Kept in error still by thy
reported death,
This very evening Leonora will assume the
nun's dark veil within the neighboring
convent."
Just heaven, forbid it!
(With exclamations of sorrow.)

Azucena
(starting).

What dost thou?

Manrico
(to the Messenger).

Hence quickly down to the valley
Without delay, a steed provide me.

Messenger.

Be it so.

Azucena.

Ma nell' alma dell' ingrato
Non parlò del cielo il detto!
Oh! se ancor ti spinge il fato
A pugnar col maledetto,
Compi, o figlio, qual d'un Dio,
Compi allora il cenno mio:
Sino all' elsa questa lama
Vibra, immergi all' empio in cor.
(Odesi un prolungato suono di corno.)

Manrico.

L'usato messo Ruiz invia!—
Forse—
(Dà fiato anch' esso al corno che tiene ad armacollo.)

Azucena.

Mi vendica!
(Resta concentrata, quasi inconsapevole di ciò che succede.
(Entra il Messo.)

Manrico
(al Messo).

Inoltra il piè.
Guerresco evento, dimmi, seguia?

Messo.

Risponda il foglio che reco a te.
(Porgendo il foglio, che MANRICO legge.)

Manrico.

"In nostra possa è Castellor: ne dêi,
Tu, per cenno del prence,
Vigilar le difese. Ove ti è dato,
Affrettati a venir. Giunta la sera
Tratta in inganno di tua morte al grido,
Nel vicin claustro della croce il velo
Cingerà Leonora." Oh, giusto cielo!
(Con dolorosa esclamazione.)

Azucena
(scuotendosi).

(Che fia!)

Manrico
(al Messo).

Veloce scendi la balza,
E d'un cavallo a me provvedi—

Messo.

Corro—

Azucena (interposing).

Manrico!

Manrico.

The time flies swiftly.   Haste thee, and yonder

My coming awaits thee.

(The MESSENGER departs hastily.)

Azucena.

What hopest thou? what wouldst thou?

Manrico.

(Lose her thus! Oh, torment!

Thus lose that angel!)

Azucena.

(His brain is turned!)

Manrico.

Farewell now.

(Replacing his helmet upon his head, and wrapping his cloak around him.)

Azucena.

No! stay thee! hear me!

Manrico.

Release me!

But a moment lost may wither

All the hopes that now sustain me;

Earth and heaven, combined together,

Would be powerless to restrain me!

Azucena.

Insensate!

Manrico.

Ah, release me, O mother, I pray thee!

Woe betide if here I stay me!

Thou wilt see thy son, extended

At thy feet, with grief expire.

Azucena.

No, I'll ne'er permit thy going.

In thy veins my blood is flowing;

Every crimson drop thou losest

From thy mother's heart doth flow.

(MANRICO departs, AZUCENA striving in vain to detain him.)

SCENE II—Cloister of a Convent in the vicinity of Castellor.   Night.

(The COUNT, FERRANDO and followers advance cautiously, enveloped in their cloaks.)

Count.

All is deserted; through the air comes yet

No sound of th' accustomed chanting.

I come in time then.

Azucena (frapponendosi).

Manrico!—

Manrico.

Il tempo incalza—

Vola; m'aspetta dell cole a' piedi.

(Il Messo parte, affrettatamente.)

Azucena.

E speri, e vuoi?

Manrico.

(Perderla?—Oh, ambascia!—

Perder quell' angelo?—)

Azucena.

(E fuor di sè!)

Manrico.

Addio—

(Postosi l'elmo sul capo, ed afferrando il mantello.)

Azucena.

No—forma—odi—

Manrico.

Mi lascia—

Un momento può involarmi

Il mio ben, la mia speranza!

No, che basti ad arrestarmi

Terra e ciel non ha possanza.

Azucena.

Demente!

Manrico.

Ah! mi sgombra, o madre, i passi—

Guai per te, s'io qui restassi:

Tu vedresti a' piedi tuoi

Spento il figlio di dolor!

Azucena.

No soffrirlo non poss' io.

Il tuo sangue è sangue mio!

Ogni stilla che ne versi

Tu la spremi dal mio cor!

(Si allontana, indarno trattenuto da AZUCENA.)

SCENA II—Chiostro d'un cenobio, in vicinanza di Castellor.   E notte.

(Il CONTE, FERRANDO, ed alcuni sequaci, ed avviluppati nei loro mantelli, inoltrandesi cautamente.)

Conte.

Tutto è deserto; nè per l'aura ancora

Suona l'usato carme—

In tempo io giungo!

Ferrando.

A daring labor here, my lord,
Awaits thee.

Count.

'Tis daring; and such alone as burning passion
And wounded pride from me should demand.
My rival dead—each hindrance opposed to
my wishes
Seemed fallen and vanquished;
Till lately she discovered one still more potent,
The altar. Ah, no! For none else is
Leonora!
She is mine, mine only!

Ferrando.

Ardita opra, o signore,
Imprendi.

Conte.

Ardita, e quel furente amore
Ed irritato orgoglio
Chissero a me. Spento il rival, caduto
Ogni ostacol sembrava a' miei desiri;
Novello e più possente ella ne appresta—
L'altare!—Ah no, non fia
D'altri Leonora!—Leonora è mia!

IL BALEN DEL SUO — *OF HER SMILE THE RADIANT*   Air (Count)

Il ba - len del suo sor - ri - so d'u - na stel - la, vin - ce il
Of her smile, the ra-diant gleam-ing Pales the star-light's bright-est re-

rag - gio; il ful - gor del suo bel vi - so no - vò in -
flec -tion; While her face with beau - ty beam - ing, Brings me fresh

fon - de no - vo in - fon - de a me co - rag - gio. Ah! l'a - mor, l'a - mo - re on -
ar - dor, ar - dor lends to my af - fec - tion. Ah! this love, this love with - in me

d'ar - do le fa - vel - li in mi - o - fa - vor. Sper - da il so - le d'un suo
burn-ing, More than words shall plead on my part. Her bright glan - ces on me

sguar - do la tem - pes - ta, la tem - pes - ta del mio cor. Ah! l'a - mor, l'a - mor on -
turn-ing, Calm the tem - pest, Calm the tem - pest in my heart. Ah! this love with - in me

d'ar-de le fa-vel-li in mio fa-vo-re, sper-da il so-le d'un suo
burn-ing, More than words shall win me fa-vor, Her bright glan-ces on me

sguar-do la tem-pe-sta del mio cor. Ah! l'a-mor, l'a-mor on-
turn-ing calm the tem-pest in my heart. Ah! this love with-in me

d'ar-do le fa-vel-li in mio fa-vore, sper-da il so-le d'un suo sguar-do la tem-pe-sta,
burn-ing More than words shall win me fa-vor, Her bright glan-ces on me turn-ing, Calm the tem-pest,

Ah! _____ si. la tem-pes-ta del mio cor.
Ah! _____ calm the tem-pest in my heart.

(A sound of bells is heard.)	(Odesi il rintocco de' sacri bronzi.)
What soundeth? Oh, heaven!	Qual suono!—oh, ciel!—
Ferrando.	*Ferrando.*
The bell	La squilla
That proclaims the rite's commencing.	Vicino il rito annunzia!—
Count.	*Conte.*
Ere at the altar she kneels	Ah! pria che giunga.
I must seize her.	All' altar, si rapisca!
Ferrando.	*Ferrando.*
Ah! heed thee!	Oh, bada!
Count.	*Conte.*
Silence!	Taci!
Didst hear not? Depart then! 'Mid the trees' dark shadows	Non odo—andate—Di quei faggi all' ombra
Conceal yourselves.	Celatevi—Ah! fra poco.
(FERRANDO and followers retire.)	(FERRANDO e gli altri seguaci si allontanano.)
Ah! how quickly mine she will be!	Mia diverrà!—Tutto m' investe un foco!
Fires in my heart are burning!	
(Watching anxiously in the direction from which LEONORA is expected.)	(Ansioso, guardingo osserva dalla porte onde deve giungere LEONORA.)
Ferrando and Followers.	*Ferrando e Seguaci.*
How bold! Let's go—conceal ourselves	Ardire!—Andiam—celiamoci
Amid the shades in haste.	Tra l'ombre—nel mister!—
How bold! Come on—and silence keep,	Ardire!—Andiam—silenzio!—
The prize he soon will hold.	Si comia il suo voler!

PER ME ORA FATALE — OH, FATAL HOUR   Air (Count)

Alla marcia

Per me o-ra fa-ta-le, i tuoi mo-men-ti af-fret-ta, af-fret-ta. La
Oh, fa-tal hour im-pend-ing, Thy mo-ments urge with speed e-lat-ing, The

gio-ja che m'a-spet-ta, gio-ja mor-tal non è,___ gio-ja mor-
joy my heart's a-wait-ing Is not of mor-tal birth,___ of mor-tal

tal, no, no, no, non è.   In va-no un Dio, ri-va-le S'op-
birth, no, it can-not be. In vain doth Heav'n, con-tend-ing With

po-ne all' a-mor mi-o,___ non può nem-men un Di-o, don-na, ra-
ri-val claims, op-pose me,___ If once these arms en-close thee, No pow'r in

pir-ti a me,___ non può, ra-pir-ti a me.
heav'n or earth,___ no pow'r shall tear thee from me.

Chorus of Nuns (within).	Coro de Religioso (interno).
Error thy soul encumbers,	Ah! se l' error t'ingombra,
Daughter of Eve, but know thee,	O figlia d'Eva, i rai,
Death's swift approach will show thee	Presso a morir, vedrai
Life's but a fleeting dream.	Che un' ombra, un sogno tù,
Phantoms in restless slumbers	Anzi del sogno un' ombra
All earthly hopes will seem!	La speme di quaggiù!
Come, let this veil concealing,	Vieni, e t'asconda il veio
Hide thee from human vision,	Ad ogni sguardo umano.
Nor worldly thought, nor feeling	Aura, o pensier mondano
Can here admitted be.	Qui vivo più non è.
To heaven, for grace appealing,	Al ciel ti volgi, e il cielo
Opening it waits for thee.	Si schiuderà per te.
(Enter LEONORA with INEZ and female followers.)	(Entra LEONORA con INES, e seguiti.)
Leonora.	*Leonora.*
Why art thou weeping?	Perchè piangete?

Inez.

Ah! truly
Thou wilt leave us forever!

Leonora.

Oh, dear companions,
No fond smile, no hope to cheer me,
No flower remaining on earth for me!
Now must I turn unto Him, the whole
support
Of those in affliction, and after days of
prayer and penitence,
I may haply rejoin my lost beloved one
With the blest in heaven. Restrain thy
weeping;
To the altar now lead me.
(About to proceed.)
(Enter the Count, suddenly.)

Count.

No, withhold!

Ladies.

The Count here!

Leonora.

Gracious heaven!

Count.

For thee no altar now waits
But one hymenial.

Ladies.

Such daring boldness!

Leonora.

Why comest thou here, insensate?

Count.

To make thee mine now!
(On saying so, he approaches, and seizes Leonora—but
Manrico appears, like a phantom, and places himself between
them—general consternation.)

Leonora.

And can I still my eyes believe
That see thee here before me!
Or is it but a dream of bliss,
A charm that hovers o'er me!
Unused to such excessive joy
My heart with doubts contended!
Art thou from heaven descended,
Or am I there with thee?

Count.

Do souls departed thus return
From death's domains eternal?

Ines.

Ah!—dunque
Tu per sempre ne lasci!

Leonora.

O dolci amici
Un riso, una speranza, un fior la terra
Non ha per me! Degg' io
Volgermi a quei che degli afflitti è solo
Conforto, e dopo i penitenti giorni,
Púò fra gli eletti al mio perduto bene
Ricongiungermi un di. Tergete i rai,
E guidatemi all' ara.
(Incamminandosi.)

(Entra il Conte, irrompendo ad un tratte.)

Conte.

No, giammai!—

Donne.

Il conte!

Leonora.

Giusto ciel!

Conte.

Per te non havvi
Che l' ara d' imeneo—

Donne.

Cotanto ardia!—

Leonora.

Insano! e qui venisti?

Conte.

A farti mia.
(E si dicendo, scagliasci verso de Leonora onde impadro
nirsi di lei; ma fra esso e la preda trovasi, qual fantasm
surle di sotterra, Manrico. Un grido universal irrompe.)

Leonora.

E deggio?—e posso crederlo?—
Ti veggo a me d'accanto!
E questo un sogno, un' estasi,
Un sovrumano incanto!
Non regge a tanto giubilo
Rapito il cor, sorpreso!—
Sei tu dal ciel disceso,
O in ciel son io con te?

Conte.

Dunque gli estinti lasciano
Di morte il regno eterno!

Thus to condemn me, doth hell indeed
Renounce its prey infernal!
But if as yet thy fatal thread
Of time remains unmeasured,
If life by thee is treasured,
Then fly from her and me.

Manrico.

Heaven's blest abode, nor regions infernal
Have yet possessed me.
True, base assassins mortal blows may deal,
Thy deeds impressed me.
O'erwhelming power that naught can stay
Have ocean's waves unbounded!
He, who thy guilt confounded!
His arm has aided me.

Ladies.

In heaven thy faith reposing,
(To LEONORA.)
Thence comes this aid to thee.

Ferrando and Followers.

'Tis fate thou'rt now opposing,
From harm it holds him free.
(Enter RUIZ and Soldiers.)

Ruiz and Followers.

Long live Urgal!

Manrico.

My brave-hearted soldiers!

Ruiz.

Come then.

Manrico
(To LEONORA).
Lady, I wait thee.

Count.

Wouldst thou rob me of her?
(Opposing him.)

Leonora.

Oh!

Manrico
(to the COUNT).
Withhold there!

Count.

Wouldst thou deprive me of her?
No!
(Drawing his sword.)

Ruiz and Soldiers.

He raveth!
(Surrounding the COUNT.)

A danno mio rinunzia
Le prede sue l' inferno!—
Ma se non mai si fransero
De' giorni tuoi gli stami,
Se vivi e viver brami,
Fuggi da lei, da me.

Manrico.

Nè m' ebbe il ciel, nè l' orrido
Varco infernal sentiero—
Infami sgherri vibrano
Colpi mortali, è vero!
Potenza irresistibile
Hanno de fiumi l' onde!—
Ma gli empj un Dio confonde!—
Quel Dio soccorse a me!

Donne.

Il cielo in cui fidasti,
(A LEONORA.)
Pietade avea di te.

Ferrando e Seguaci.

Tu col destin contrasti;
(Al CONTE.)
Suo difensore egli è.
(Entra RUIZ, seguito da lunga tratta d' armati.)

Ruiz.

Urgel viva!

Manrico.

Miei prodi guerrieri!—

Ruiz.

Vieni.

Manrico
(A LEONORA.)
Donna, mi segui.

Conte.

E tu speri?
(Opponendosi.)

Leonora.

Oh!

Manrico
(Al CONTE.)
T'arretra.

Conte.

Involarmi costei!
No!
(Sguainando la spada.)

Ruiz e Armati.

Vaneggi!
(Accerchiando il CONTE.)

Ferrando and Followers.

What wouldst thou, my lord?

(The COUNT is disarmed by the soldiers of RUIZ.)

Count.

All my reason in fury is lost!

(with gestures and accents of fury.)

Leonora.

(He affrights me!)

Count.

Furies dwell in my heart!

Ruiz and Soldiers.

Come then, a future of smiles waits for thee.

(To MANRICO.)

Ferrando and Followers.

Yield thee, since yielding no baseness implies.

(Exit MANRICO, leading LEONORA—the COUNT is driven back, the ladies retreat to the Convent, as the curtain falls.)

END OF THE SECOND ACT.

Ferrando e Seguaci.

Che tenti, signor!

(Il CONTE è disarmato aa quei di RUIZ.,

Conte.

Di ragione ogni lumi perdei!

(Con gesti ed accenti di maniaco furore.)

Leonora.

(M'atterrisce.)

Conte.

Ho lo furie nel cor!

Ruiz e Armati.

Vieni; è lieta la sorte per te.

(A MANRICO.)

Ferrando e Seguaci.

Cedi; or ceder viltade non è!

(MANRICO tragge seco LEONORA—il CONTE è respinto, le donne rifuggono al cenobio—scende subito la tela.)

FINE DELL' ATTO SECONDO.

ACT III.

THE GIPSY'S SON.

SCENE I—A camp. On the right, the tent of the COUNT DI LUNA, on which is displayed a banner, indicative of his supremacy. The fortress of Castellor seen in the distance. The scene full of Soldiers, some playing, some polishing their accoutrements, some walking in apparent conversation, while others are on duty as Sentinels.

(Enter FERRANDO, from the tent of the COUNT.)

Some of the Soldiers.

Now with dice, may fortune speed us;
Other games will shortly need us!
From our swords this blood we burnish,
Coming deeds fresh stains will furnish.

(Sounds of warlike instruments are heard; all start and turn towards the sounds.)

Some Soldiers.

Lo! they come for succor praying!

(A strong band of soldiers crosses the camp.)

Other Soldiers.

Still, they make a brave display!

All.

Let us, without more delaying
Castellor attack to-day.

Ferrando.

Yes, brave companions; at dawn, to-morrow,

ATTO III.

IL FIGLIO DELLA ZINGARA.

SCENA I—Accampamento—A destra, il padiglione del CONTE DI LUNA, su cui sventola la bandiera in segno di supremo comando—da lungi Torreggia Castellor.—Scolte di uomini d'arme da per tutto; altri giocano, altri forbiscono le armi, altri passeggiano.

(Entra FERRANDO, dal padiglione del CONTE.)

Alcuni Uomini d'Arme.

Or co' dadi, ma fra poco
Giocherem ben altro gioco!
Questo acciar, dal sangue or terso,
Fia di sangue in breve asperso!

(Odonsi strumenti guerrieri; tutti si volgono là dove si avanza il suono.)

Alcuni.

Il soccorso dimandato!

(Un grosso drappello di balestrieri, in completa armatura, traversa il campo.)

Altri.

Han l'aspetto del valor!

Tutti.

Più l'assalto ritardato
Or non fia di Castellor.

Ferrando.

Sì prodi amici; al dì novello, è mente

Our leader has now resolved
On storming the fortress on all sides.
Within its walls a booty immense
We're sure to find; 'tis more than hopeful;
If conquered 'tis ours then.

Some of the Soldiers.

Pleasure there invites us.

Ferrando and Chorus.

Now let the trumpet in war tones resound-
ing,
Call to arms; with courage bold, we'll march
undaunted.
Haply, to-morrow, our proud foes confound-
ing,
On those walls shall our banners be planted.
Ne'er more brilliant were prospects victor-
ious
Than the hopes which our hearts now elate.
Thence, we'll gather renown, bright and
glorious;
Pleasure, honor and profit there await us,
Honor and booty for us there await.

(Enter the COUNT, from the tent; turns with lowering
gaze towards Castellor.)

Count.

Within my rival's arms! How this reflec-
tion,
Like a taunting demon, follows me
Wherever I wander. Within my rival's
arms! To-morrow
Ere the day dawns, I'll hasten to sunder
them forever!
Oh! Leonora!

(A tumult is heard.)
(Enter FERRANDO.)

Count.

What now?

Ferrando.

Around the camp
Was seen a gipsy-woman, loitering:
Surprised by the sentinels on duty
To escape she attempted. With reason
They suspected her of spying out our move-
ments,
And pursued.

Count.

Was she taken?

Del capitan la rôcca
Investir da ogni parte.
Colà pingue bottino
Certezza è rinvenir, più che speranza.
Si vinca, è nostro.

Uomini d'Arme.

Tu c'inviti a danza!

Ferrando con Coro.

Squilli, echeggi la tromba guerriera
Chiami all' armi, alla pugna, all' assalto:
Fia domani la nostra bandiera
Di quei merli piantata sull' alto.
No, giammai non sorrise vittoria
Di più liete speranze finor!
Ivi l'util ci aspetta e la gloria;
Ivi opimi la preda e l'onore!
Ivi opimi la preda e l'onor!

(Entra il CONTE, uscito dalla tenda, volge uno sguardo
bieco a CASTELLOR.)

Conte.

In braccio al mio rival!—Questo pensiero
Come persecutor demone ovunque
M'insegue! In braccio al mio rival!—Ma
corro
Surta appena l'aurora,
Io corro a separavi—Oh, Leonora!

(Odesi tumulti.)

(Entra FERRANDO.)

Conte.

Che fu?

Ferrando.

D'appresso il campo
S'aggirava una zingara; sorpresa
Da' nostri esploratori,
Si volse in fuga; essi, a ragion temendo
Una spia nella trista,
L'inseguir—

Conte.

Fu raggiunta?

Ferrando.

They seized her.

Count.

Hast seen her yet?

Ferrando.

No; the conductor
Of the escort hath so
Informed me.

Count.

Here she comes.

(AZUCENA, with her hands bound together, is dragged in by the Sentinels.)

Soldiers.

Come on, thou sorceress, come forward!

Azucena.

Oh, help me! Pray release me! Ah, maddened wretches,
Of what accuse me?

Count.

Come hither.

(AZUCENA is led before the COUNT.)

To me reply now, and tremble if thou liest.

Azucena.

Ask, then.

Count.

Whither bound?

Azucena.

I know not.

Count.

How?

Azucena.

'Tis a custom of the gipsies
Without purpose to wander
Wherever fancy leads them,
Their only shelter heaven,
The wide world their country.

Count.

Whence comest thou?

Azucena.

From Biscalia, where, till of late,
Was my sole abode, amid its wild, barren
mountains.

Count.

(From Biscalia!)

Ferrando.

E presa.

Conte.

Vista l' hai tu?

Ferrando.

No; della scorta
Il condottier m'apprese
L'evento.

(Tumulto più vicino.)

Conte.

Eccola.

(Entra AZUCENA, con le mani avvinte, è trascinata dagli Esploratori—un codazzo d'altri soldati.)

Esploratori.

Innanzi, o strega, innanzi.

Azucena.

Aìta!—Mi lasciate—Oh! furibondi,
Che mal fec' io?

Conte.

S'appressi.

(AZUCENA è tratta innanzi il CONTE.)

A me rispondi.
E trema dal mentir!

Azucena.

Chiedi.

Conte.

Ove vai?

Azucena.

Nol so.

Conte.

Che?

Azucena.

D'una zingara è costume
Muover senza disegno
Il passo vagabondo,
Ed è suo tetto il ciel, sua patria il mondo.

Conte.

E vieni?

Azucena.

Da Biscaglia, ove finora
La sterili montagne ebbi ricetto.

Conte.

(Da Biscaglia!)

Ferrando.

(What heard I? oh, dark suspicion.)

Ferrando.

(Che intesi!—Oh, qual sospetto!)

GIORNI POVERI— *I WAS POOR, YET UNCOMPLAINING* (Azucena)

Con espressione

Gior- ni po- ve- ri vi- ve- a, pur con - ten- ta del mio
I was poor, yet un-com - plain-ing, Lived con - tent- ed, grate-ful

sta- to; so- la spe-me un fi-glio a- ve- a, Mi la- sciò! m'ob-
heart- ed, With one son, sole hope re - main- ing, But, a - las! from

bli- a l'in- gra- to. Io de - ser- ta, va- do er- ran- do di quel
me he hath part- ed. Now I wan - der sad and lone - ly Through the

fi - glio ri- cer- can- do, di quel fi - glio che al mio co -
world, seek- ing him on - ly; All my heart's trou- bled e - mo -

re pe- ne or- ri- bi- li- co- stò!— Qual per es - so pro-vo a- mo- re,
tion For his loss, no words can show!— Ah! for him my warm de - vo- tion,

qual per es - so pro-vo a- mo- re ma- dre in ter- ra non- pro- vò.
Ah! for him, my warm de - vo - tion, No earth-ly moth- er else— can know.

Ferrando.

Ah! those features!

Count.

Say, long time
Didst thou abide among those mountains?

Azucena.

Long time, yes.

Ferrando.

(Il suo volto.)

Conte.

Di' traesti
Lunga etade fra quei monti?

Azucena.

Lunga, sì.

Count.

> Dost thou remember
> A child, son of a noble,
> Who was stolen from his castle
> Many years since and carried thither?

Azucena.

> And thou, tell me—art?

Count.

> A brother
> Of the lost one.

Azucena.

> Ah!

Ferrando.

> Yes!
>> (Noting the ill-concealed terror of AZUCENA.)

Count.

> Hast heard what there befell him?

Azucena.

> I?—No!—Oh! grant
> That I may now my search continue.

Ferrando.

> Stay, impostor!

Azucena.

> (Alas!)

Ferrando.

> Thou seest here
> The guilty wretch who that dark crime
> Committed!

Count.

> Continue!

Ferrando.

> Behold her.

Azucena.

> Silence!
>> (Softly to FERRANDO.)

Ferrando.

> 'Tis she, who stole the child, and burned
>   him!

Count.

> Ah! guilty one!

Chorus.

> 'Tis the same one!

Azucena.

> He speaks falsehood.

Conte.

> Rammenteresti
> Un fanciul, prole di conti,
> Involato al suo castello,
> Son tre lustri, e tratto quivi?

Azucena.

> E tu, parla—sei?

Conte.

> Fratello
> Del rapito.

Azucena.

> (Ah!)

Ferrando.

> (Sì!)
>> (Notando il mal nascoto terrore di AZUCENA.)

Conte.

> Ne udivi
> Mai novella?

Azucena.

> Io?—No!—Concedi
> Che del figlio l'orme io scopra.

Ferrando.

> Resta, iniqua—

Azucena.

> (Ohimè!)

Ferrando.

> Tu vedi
> Chi l'infame, orribil opra
> Commettea!

Conte.

> Finisci.

Ferrando.

> E dessa!

Azucena.

> (Taci.)
>> (Piano a FERRANDO.)

Ferrando.

> E dessa, che il bambino arse!

Conte.

> Ah, perfida!

Coro.

> Ella stessa!

Azucena.

> Ei mentisce

Count.

    Thou canst not fly
    Thy fate impending.

Azucena.

    Ah!

Count.

    Those bonds
    Draw still more closely.
           (The soldiers obey.)

Azucena.

    Oh! heaven! Oh! heaven!

Chorus.

    Vent thy rage!

Azucena.

    And comest thou not,
    My son, Manrico, to release me?
    Thy unhappy mother now
    To aid and succor?

Count.

    Thou the mother of Manrico?

Ferrando.

    Tremble!

Count.

    Oh! fate! thus in my power!

Azucena.

    Ah! loose awhile, ye monsters vile,
    These bonds that now confine me.
    Such fierce and cruel torments
    To lingering death consign me!
    Descendant of a wicked sire,
    Than he more guilty, tremble!
    For God protects the weak,
    And he will punish thee!

Count.

    Thy son, oh, wretched Zingara,
    Is he that base betrayer?
    And can I, thee condemning,
    Strike, too, the traitor's heart?
    The joy my soul o'erflowing,
    Words lack the power of showing!
    To my arm, for vengeance, a brother's ashes
        call!
    Avenged in full shall they be!

Ferrando and Chorus.

    Base wretch, the fatal pile prepared,

Conte.

    Al tuo destino.
    Or non fuggì.

Azucena.

    Deh!

Conte.

    Quei nodi
    Più stringete
           (I soldati esequiscono.)

Azucena.

    Oh, Dio! Oh, Dio!

Coro.

    Uria pure.

Azucena.

    E tu non m'odi,
    Oh, Manrico,—oh, figlio mio?
    Non soccorri all' infelice
    Madre tua!

Conte.

    Di Manrico genitrice!

Ferrando.

    Trema!

Conte.

    Oh, sorte! in mio poter!

Azucena.

    Deh, ralentate, o barbari,
    Le acerbe mie ritorte—
    Questo crudel supplizio
    E prolungata morte!
    D' iniquo genitore
    Empio figliuol peggiore,
    Trema—V' è Dio pe' miseri,
    E Dio ti punirà!

Conte.

    Tua prole, o turpe zingara,
    Colui, quel seduttore!
    Portò col tuo supplizio
    Ferirlo in mezzo al core!
    Gioja m'inonda il petto,
    Ciu non esprimo il detto!
    Meco il fraterno cenore
    Piena vendetta avrà!

Ferrando e Coro.

    Infame, pira sorgere;

Ah! yes, thou soon shalt see
Bright flames the heavens illuming!
Not this alone awaits thee,
These earthly fires consuming!
Condemned to flames infernal
There shall thy wicked spirit dwell!

*(Azucena is dragged away by the soldiers, by command
of the Count. He enters the tent, followed by Ferrando.)*

SCENE II—Hall adjoining the Chapel of Castellor; a
balcony in the background.

(Manrico, Leonora, Ruiz.)

Leonora.

Ah! what clamor of arms
Is that which reached me?

Manrico.

Great is the danger;
Vain are all my attempts to hide it!
At early dawn to-morrow
The foe will assail us.

Leonora.

Alas! what sayst thou?

Manrico.

Be assured that our swords will be victori-
ous!
We can equal them
In arms, boldness, and courage.
Depart.
                    (To Ruiz.)
The preparations for the strife
In my absence, thou wilt accomplish.
Let nought be wanting.
                    (Exit Ruiz.)

Leonora.

What a sombre splendor
Is o'er our bridal shining!

Manrico.

All this mournful foreboding
Pray banish, dearest!

Leonora.

And can I?

Manrico.

'Tis love, sublime emotion, at such a mo-
ment
Bids thy heart still be hopeful.
Ah! love; how blest our life will be

Empia, vedrai tra poco—
Nè solo tuo supplizio
Sarà l'orrendo foco!
Le vampe dell' inferno
A te fian rogo eterno;
Ivi penare ed ardere
L'anima tua dovrà!

*(Al cenno del Conte, i soldati traggono seco loco Azucena.
Egli entra nella sua tenda, seguito da Ferrando.)*

SCENA II—Sala adjacente alla Cappella in Castellor, co
verone in fondo.

(Manrico, Leonora, e Ruiz.)

Leonora.

Quale d'armi fragore
Foc' anzi intesi?

Manrico.

Alto è il periglio!—Vano
Dissimularlo fora!
Alla novella aurora
Assaliti saremo!

Leonora.

Ahimè!—che dici!

Manrico.

Ma de' nostri nemici
Avrem vittoria.—Pari
Abbiamo al loro ardir, brando e coraggio.
Tu va.
                    (a Ruiz).
Le belliche opre,
Nell' assenza mia breve, a te commetto.
Che nulla manchi!
                    (Ruiz parte.)

Leonora.

Di qual tetra luce
Il nostro imen risplende!

Manrico.

Il presagio funesto,
Deh, sperdi, o cara!

Leonora.

E il posso?

Manrico.

Amor—sublime amore,
In tal istante ti favella al core.
Ah! sì, ben mio, coll' essere
Io tuo, tu mia consorte,

Our fond desires attaining,
My soul shall win fresh ardor,
My arm new courage gaining.
But, if, upon the fatal page
Of destiny impending,
I'm doomed among the slain to fall,
'Gainst hostile arms contending,
In life's last hour, with fainting breath,
My thoughts will turn to thee.
Preceding thee to heaven, will death
Alone appear to me.

(Tones of organ heard from the neighboring chapel.)

Leonora.

The mystic tide of harmony
Within our hearts doth flow!
The church unfolds the raptures
From holy love that grow!

(While they are about to enter the chapel, RUIZ enters hurriedly.)

Ruiz.

Manrico!

Manrico.

How?

Ruiz.

The Zingara,
Yonder, in chains, behold her!

Manrico.

Oh, heaven!

Ruiz.

Led on by cruel men,
They near the stake already.

Manrico.

Oh, heavens! my limbs are failing me;
Shadows my eyes are veiling!
(Approaching the balcony.)

Leonora.

Thou tremblest!

Manrico.

With reason. Know the cause:
I am—

Leonora.

Thou'rt what?

Manrico.

Her offspring.
Ah! monsters! this dark revolting scene
Almost of my breath deprives me!

Avrò più l' alma intrepida,
Il braccio avrò più forte.
Ma pur, se nella pagina
De' miei destini è scritto,
Ch' io resti fra le vittime,
Dal ferro ostil trafitto,
Fra quegli estremi aneliti,
A te il pensier verrà, verrà,
E solo in ciel precederti
La morte a me parrà!

(Odesi il suono dell' organo dalla vicina cappella.)

Leonora.

L'onda de suoni mistici
Pura discende al cor!
Vieni; ci schiude il tempio
Gioje di casto amor!

(Mentre s' avviano giubilanti al tempio, RUIZ soppragiunge frettoloso.)

Ruiz.

Manrico!

Manrico.

Che?

Ruiz.

La zingara,
Vieni, tra ceppi mira!

Manrico.

Oh, Dio!

Ruiz.

Per man de' barbari
Accesa è girà la pira.

Manrico.

Oh, ciel! mie membra oscillano—
Nube me copre il ciglio!
(Accostandosi al verone.)

Leonora.

Tu fremi.

Manrico.

E il deggio! Sappilo,
Io son—

Leonora.

Che mai?

Manrico.

Suo figlio!
Ah, vili! Il rio spettacolo
Quasi il respir m'invola!

Collect our forces without the least delay.	Raduna i nostri—affrettati.
Ruiz—go—speed thee, quickly!	Ruiz—va—torna—vola!
(RUIZ departs hastily.)	(RUIZ parte.)

DI QUELLA PIRA — *OF THAT DARK SCAFFOLD*   Air. (Manrico)

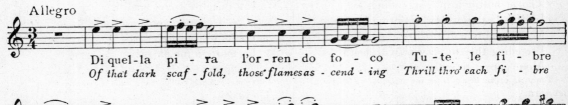

Di quel-la pi - ra l'or - ren-do fo - co Tu - te le fi - bre
Of that dark scaf - fold, those flames as - cend - ing Thrill thro' each fi - bre

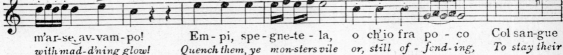

m'ar-se av-vam-po! Em - pi, spe-gne-te - la, o ch'io fra po - co Col san-gue
with mad-d'ning glow! Quench them, ye mon-sters vile or, still of - fend-ing, To stay their

vos - tro la spe-gne - rò. E - ra già fi - glio pri - ma d'a -
fu - ry, your blood shall flow! I was her off - spring, ere love I

mar - ti, Non puo fre - nar - mi il tuo mar - tir!__ Ma-dre in-fe-
gave__ thee, In vain to hold__ me, thy griefs would try.__ Moth- er un-

li - ce, cor-ro a sal - var - ti, O te-co al-me - no cor-ro a mo-rir!
hap - py! I fly to save thee, Or, all else fail - ing, with thee to die.

Leonora.	*Leonora.*
Such heavy sorrows my heart o'erpowering.	Non reggo a colpi tanto funesti.
Oh! better far would it be to die!	Oh, quanto meglio saria morir!
(Re-enter RUIZ, with Soldiers.)	(Entra RUIZ, torna armati.)
Ruiz.	*Ruiz.*
Arouse ye to arms now!	All' armi, all' armi! eccone presti
The foe we will defy!	A pugnar teco, teco a morir.
(MANRICO rushes out, followed by RUIZ and Soldiers. From within a noise of arms and warlike instruments is heard.)	(MANRICO parte frettoloso seguito da RUIZ, e dagli armati, mentre odesi dall' interno fragor d'armi e di bellici strumenti.)

END OF THE THIRD ACT.	**FINE DELL' ATTO TERZO.**

ACT IV.

THE PUNISHMENT.

SCENE I—A wing of the palace of Aliaferia; in the angle, a tower with window secured by iron bars. Night; dark and clouded.

(Enter LEONORA and RUIZ, enveloped in cloaks.)

Ruiz   (in an undertone).

Here stay we;
Yonder's the tower where are confined the
     prisoners for state offences;
Hither they brought him whom we are seek-
     ing.

Leonora.

Go thou:
Leave me here; be not anxious for my safety;
Perchance I yet may save him.
                    (RUIZ retires.)
Afraid for me? Secure
And ready are my defences!

(She gazes upon a jewel which she wears on her right hand.)

In this dark hour of midnight
I hover round thee near approaching.
Unknown to thee, love! Ye moaning breezes
     around me playing.
In pity aid me, my sighs to him conveying!

ATTO IV.

IL SUPPLIZIO.

SCENA I—Un' ala del palazzo dell' Aliaferia—all' angolo una torre, con finestre assicurate da spranghe di ferro. Notte oscurissima.

(Si avanzano due personne ammentellate; sono RUIZ e LEONORA.)

Ruiz   (sommessamente).

Siam giunti:
Ecco la torre, ove di stato
Gemono i prigionieri.—Ah! l'infelice
Ivi fu tratto!

Leonora.

Vanne.
Lasciami, nè timor di me te prenda—
Salvarlo io potrò, forse.
                    (RUIZ si allontana.)
Timor di me?—Sicura,
Presta è la mia difesa!

(I suoi occhi figgonsi ad una gemma che le fregia la man destra.)

In questa oscura
Notte ravvolta, presso a te son io,
E tu nol sai! Gemente
Aura, che intorno spiri,
Deh, pietosa gli arreca i miei sospiri.

D'AMOR SULL' ALI ROSEE — *ON ROSY WINGS OF LOVE* Air. (Leonora)

D'a-mor sull'a - li ro-se - e Van-ne, so-spir do-len - te,
On ro-sy wings of love de - part, Bear-ing my heart's sad wail - ing,

Del pri-gio-nie-ro mi - se-ro Con - for-ta l'e - gra-men - te.— Com'
Vis - it the pris'ner's lone - ly cell, Con - sole his spir-it fail-ing.— Let

au - ra di spe - ran - za A - leg-gia in quel - la stan - za. Lo
hope's soft whis-pers— wreath - ing A - round him, com - fort breath-ing, Re-

de-sta al-le me - mo - rie, Ai so-gni, ai so-gni dell' a - - mor,
call to his fond re - mem - brance Sweet vi-sions, sweet vi-sions of our____ love;

dolce

Ma, deh! non dir-gli im-prov-vi-do le pe - ne, le pe-ne, le pe-ne del mio cor.
But, let no ac - cent re - veal to him The sor - rows, the sor-rows, the griefs my heart doth prove.

con forza *dolce*

Deh! non dir - gli im-prov-vi-do le pe - - ne del mio cor, le pe-
Let no ac - cent re - veal to him the tri - - als I now prove, the sor -

ne, le pe - - - - - - - ne del cor.
rows, the sor - - - - - - - rows I prove.

Chorus (The passing bell.) (within).	Voci (Suona la campana dei morti.) (interne).
Have compassion upon a soul departing	Miserere d'un' alma già vicina
For that abode, from whence there's no re-turning;	Alla partenza che non ha ritorno;
Thy forgiveness, oh! power divine, impart-ing,	Miserere di lei, bontà divina,
Let him not be a prey to endless burning.	Preda non sia dell' infernal soggiorno.
Leonora.	*Leonora.*
That solemn petition, so sadly ascending,	Quel suon, quelle preci solemni, funeste,
With terror and mystery the air seems to fill!	Empiron quest' aere di cupo terrore!
'Gainst fatal foreboding my heart is con-tending,	Contende l'ambascia, che tutta m'investe
My breath is suspended, my pulses are still.	Al labbro il respiro, i palpiti al core!

AH, CHE LA MORTE — *AH, HOW DEATH* Air (Manrico)

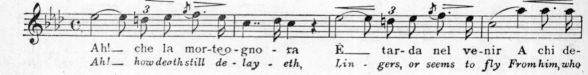

Ah!__ che la mor-te o-gno - ra È__ tar-da nel ve-nir A chi de-
Ah!__ how death still de - lay - eth, Lin - gers, or seems to fly From him, who

si - a, a chi de-si - a mo-rir! Ad-dì - o, ad-dio, Leo-no-ra ad-di - o!
long-eth, from him who long-eth to die! Fare-well,— love, fare-well, Leo-no-ra, fare-well)

Leonora.	**Leonora.**
Oh, heaven! faintness o'erpowers me!	Oh, ciel!—sento mancarmi!
Chorus	**Voci**
(within).	(internè).
Have compassion upon a soul departing	Miserere d'un' alma già vicina
For that abode, from whence there's no re-turning;	Alla partenza che non ha ritorno!
Thy forgiveness, oh! power divine, impart-ing,	Miserere di lei, bontà divina,
Let him not fall a prey to endless burning.	Preda non sia dell' infernal soggiorno!
Leonora.	**Leonora.**
O'er yonder dark tower, ah, death waits the morrow	Sull' orrida torre, ah! par che la morte
With wings pale and shadowy his watch seems to hold.	Con ali di tenebre librando si và!
Ah! ne'er will they open those portals of sor-row	Ahi! forse dischiuse gli fian queste porte
'Till after the victim is lifeless and cold.	Sol quando cadavere già freddo ei sarà!
	(Rimane assorta, dopo qualche momento scuotesi, ed è in procinto di partire, allorchè vienne dalla torre un gemito, e quindi un mesto suono; elle si ferma.)
Manrico	**Manrico.**
(in the tower).	(Dalla torre.)
Now with my life fulfilling	Sconto col sangue mio
Love's fervent vows to thee!	L'amor che posi in te!
Do not forget; let me remembered be.	Non ti scordar di me!
Farewell, my love, farewell, Leonora!	Leonora, Addio!
Leonora.	**Leonora.**
And can I ever forget thee!	Di te, di te scordar me!
Thou shalt see that more enduring	(S'apre una porta.)
Love, than mine, ne'er had existence,	Tu vedrai che amore in terra
Triumph over fate securing,	Mai del mio non fù più forte:
Death shall yield to its resistance.	Vinse il fato in aspra guerra,
At the price of mine, now blighted,	Vincerà la stessa morte.
Thy dear life will I defend,	O col prezzo di mia vita
Or again with thee united,	La tua vita salverò,
To the tomb will I descend!	O con te per sempre unita
	Nella tomba scenderò.
(Enter the COUNT and his followers. LEONORA stands aside.)	(Entra il CONTE, ed alcuni seguaci. LEONORA si pone in disparte.)
Count.	**Conte.**
You hear me? Give the son to the axe	Udiste? Come albeggi,
At daybreak; lead to the stake the mother.	La scure al figlio, ed alla madre il rogo.
(The followers enter the tower.)	(Entrano i seguaci per un piccolo uscio nella torre.)
Perhaps, thus acting, I abuse the power	Abuso io forse quel poter che pieno

The prince to me confided.
To such excesses that woman's love constrains me!
But where to find her? Since Castellor is ours
Of her no tidings have reached me;
All my researches on every side are fruitless!
Ah! cruel love, where art thou?

Leonora (advancing).

Standing before thee!

Count.

Those accents! Lady! thus near me?

Leonora.

Thou see'st me.

Count.

What brought thee hither?

Leonora.

Already his last hour approaches
And thou dost ask me?

Count.

Thou still wouldst dare me?

Leonora.

Ah, yes! for him
I would ask of thee compassion.

Count.

How? art thou raving?
Mercy to him, my rival, show?

Leonora.

May heaven with mercy inspire thee!

Count.

My whole desire is for vengeance. Go!

(LEONORA throws herself despairingly at his feet.)

In me trasmise li prence! A tal mi trag
Donna per me funesta!—Ov' ella è mai?
Ripresso Castellor, di lei contezza
Non ebbi, e furo indarno
Tante ricerche e tante!
Oh!—dove sei crudele?

Leonora (avanzandosi).

A te dinante.

Conte.

Qual voce!—Come!—tu, donna?

Leonora.

Il vedi.

Conte.

A che venisti?

Leonora.

Egli è gia presso
All' ora estrema, e tu lo chiedi?

Conte.

Osar potresti?

Leonora.

Ah, si, per esso
Pietà domando—

Conte.

Che! tu deliri!
Io del rivale sentir pietà?

Leonora.

Clemente il Nume a te l'inspiri—

Conte.

E sol vendetta mio nume. Va!

(LEONORA si getta disperata ai suoi piedi.)

MIRA DI ACERBE — *WITNESS THE TEARS OF AGONY* Air (Leonora)

Andante mosso

Mi - ra, dia-cer-be la-gri-me
Wit-ness the tears of ag-o-ny
Spar - go al tuo pie-de un ri - o.
Here, at thy feet, now rain-ing

Non bas-ta il pian-to? sve-na-mi,
If these suf-fice not, tor-ture me,
Ti be - vi il san-gue mi - o!
My life's crim-son cur-rent drain-ing!

Sve - na - mi, sve - na - mi; Ti be - vi il san - gue mi - o
Tor - ture me, tor - ture me, My life's crim - son cur - rent drain - ing!

Cal - pe - sta il mio ca - da - ve - re, Ma sal - va il Tro - va - tor.
Breath-less, thy feet may tram-ple me, But spare thou the Trou - ba - dour!

Count. 　　Ah! rather would I speedily 　　Add to his fate impending 　　Thousands of bitter cruelties, 　　Torments and death unending; 　　The more thy love to his replies 　　My rage inflames the more. 　　　　　　(About to go.) **Leonora.** 　　Hear me! 　　　　　(Clinging to him.) **Count.** 　　What more now? **Leonora.** 　　Mercy! **Count.** 　　Price is there none, which offered, 　　Could obtain it. Leave me now! **Leonora.** 　　One yet there is, one only, 　　And that price I offer. **Count.** 　　Offer, what? 　　Explain then! speak! **Leonora.** 　　Myself, then! (Extending her right hand to the COUNT, with anguish.) **Count.** 　　Heaven! what dost tell me? **Leonora.** 　　That I will perform 　　What here I promise. **Count.** 　　Am I not dreaming?	**Conte.** 　　Ah! dell' indegno rendere 　　Vorrei peggior la sorte— 　　Fra mille atroci spasimi 　　Centuplicar sua morte— 　　Più l'ami, e più terribile 　　Divampa il mio furor! 　　　　　　(Vuol partire.) **Leonora.** 　　Conte! 　　　　Si aviticchia ed esso.) **Conte.** 　　Nè cessi. **Leonora.** 　　Grazia! **Conte.** 　　Prezzo non avvi alcuno 　　Ad ottenerla—scostati! **Leonora.** 　　Uno ve n' ha—sol uno, 　　Ed io ta l'offro. **Conte.** 　　Spiegati, 　　Qual prezzo, di'? **Leonora.** 　　Me stessa! 　　(Stendendogli la sua destra con dolore.) **Conte.** 　　Ciel! tu dicesti? **Leonora.** 　　E compiere 　　Saprò la mia promessa. **Conte.** 　　E sogno il mio?

Leonora.

Unclose for me
The gates of yonder prison;
Escaping, let the prisoner but hear me—
Then I'll be thine.

Count.

Wilt swear it?

Leonora.

I swear to him, whom my innermost spirit
Beholdeth!

Count.

What ho!

(A jailer appears, in whose ear the COUNT whispers.
While the COUNT is speaking to him, LEONORA sucks the
poison concealed in the ring.)

Leonora.

(A cold and lifeless bride
Thou wilt have in me!)

Count

(turning to LEONORA).

My foe shall live!

Leonora

(aside, her eyes filled with tears of joy).

Shall live! Oh heaven! this boundless joy
Too great is for words' expression;
But from my throbbing, panting heart
Flow thanks in grateful confession!
Unmoved, my fate I now await;
Rapture, thus life completing,
With dying breath repeating
Thou'rt saved from death through me!

Count.

What words are those? oh! turn once more
To me thy thoughts confiding.
Ah! like a rapturous vision
Seemeth thy kind decision.
Thou wilt be mine! again declare,
My heart of doubts relieving,
Scarce in its bliss believing,
Though promised still by thee!

Leonora.

Now come—

Count.

Remember! Thou hast sworn!

Leonora.

My oath is sacred still.

(They enter the tower.)

Leonora.

Dischiudimi
La via tra quelle mura;
Ch' ei m' oda—che la vittima
Fugga, e son tua.

Conte.

Lo giura?

Leonora.

Lo giuro a Dio, che l'anima
Tutta mi vede!

Conte.

Ola!

(Correndo al uscio della torre. Si presenta un custode-
mentre il CONTE gli parla all' orecchio, LEONORA sugge il
veleno chiuso nell' anello.)

Leonora.

(M'avrai, ma fredda, esanime
Spoglia.)

Conte

(a LEONORA tornado).

Colui vivrà.

Leonora

(Da sè, alzando gli occhi, cui fan velo lagrime di letizia.)

(Vivra! Contende il giubilo
I detti a me, Signore!)
Ma coi frequenti palpiti
Mercè ti rende il core!
Ora il mio fine impavida,
Piene di gioja attendo—
Dirgli potrò, morendo;
Salvo tu sei per me!

Conte.

Fra te che parli?—Ah! volgimi.
Volgimi il detto ancora,
O mi parrà delirio
Quan ascoltai finora—
Tu mia! tu mia! ripetilo,
Il dubbio cor serena—
Ah! ch'io lo credo appena
Udendolo da te!

Leonora.

Andiam.

Conte.

Giurasti—pensaci!

Leonora.

E sacra la mia fè!

(Entrano nella torre.)

SCENE II—A gloomy dungeon.

(AZUCENA lying upon an old mattress, MANRICO seated near her.)

Manrico.

Mother, thou sleepest not?

Azucena.

I have sought for slumber,
But, ah! it flies from my weary eyelids!—
    I'll pray.

Manrico.

'Tis the air, cold and damp,
Perchance, with chills disturbs thee?

Azucena.

No; but from this tomb
Of the living would I escape forever,
Where confinement o'erpowers and suffo-
    cates me.

Manrico.

Escape!   (Wringing his hands.)

Azucena.

Do not distress thee;
            (Rising.)
These cruel tyrants cannot long oppress me.

Manrico.

Ah, wherefore?

Azucena.

Look ye! and behold already upon my brow
The finger of death has left its impress!

Manrico.

Ah!

Azucena.

They will find here
But a lifeless form, silent, cold and dead!
Merely a skeleton!

Manrico.

Cease ye!

Azucena.

Dost hear not?—coming footsteps—
Ah! the jailors approach, who to the stake
    will drag me!
Defend, and save thy mother!

Manrico.

There's no one,
Resume thy courage.   There's no one here
    approaching.

SCENA II—Orrido carcere.

(AZUCENA giacente sopra una specie di rozza coltre, MAN-RICO seduto a lei d'appresso.)

Manrico.

Madre, non dormi!

Azucena.

L'invocai più volte,
Ma fugge il sonno a queste luci, prego.

Manrico.

L'aura fredda è molesta
Alle tue membre forse?

Azucena.

No; da questa
Tomba di vivi sol fuggir vorrei,
Perchè sento il respiro soffocarmi!

Manrico.

Fuggir!   (Torcendosi le mani.)

Azucena.

Non attristarti;
            (Sorgendo.)
Far di me strazio non potranno i crudi!

Manrico.

Ah! come?

Azucena.

Vedi? le sue forsche, impronte
M' ha già stampate in fronte
Il dito della morte!

Manrico.

Ahi!

Azucena.

Troveranno
Un cadavere muto, gelido!—anzi
Uno scheletro!

Manrico.

Cessa!

Azucena.

Non odi?—gente appressa!
I carnefici son—vogliono al rogo
Trarmi!—Difendi la tua madre!

Manrico.

Alcuno,
Ti rassicura, quì non volge.

Azucena.

    The scaffold!

    That word of terror!

Manrico.

    Oh! mother! oh! mother!

Azucena.

    One morning

    Fierce crowds assembled, seized my mother and led her

    To torture! Mark how the abhorrent flames curl!

    Round her they madly cling! her hair consuming

    Now streams upward to heaven!

    Observe the glaring eyeballs

    From their orbits protruding! Ah! who has brought me

    To behold this dread vision?

      (Falls convulsed in the arms of MANRICO.)

Manrico.

    If filial love and words of affection

    Have power to move thy feelings maternal,

    Strive to banish these terrors,

    And seek in slumbers forgetful, both rest and composure.

      (Conducts her to the mattress.)

Azucena.

    Il rogo!

    Parola orrenda!

Manrico.

    Oh, madre!—oh, madre!

Azucena.

    Turba feroce l'ava tua condusse

    Al rogo—mira la terribil vampa!

    Ella n' è tocca già!—già l'arso crine

    Al ciel manda faville!—

    Osserva le pupille

    Fuor dell' orbita lor!—Ahi!—chi mi toglie

    A spettacol sì stroce!

      (Cadendo tutta convulsa tra le braccia di MANRICO.)

Manrico.

    Se m'ami ancor, se voce

    Di figlio ha possa di una madre in core,

    Ai terrori dell' alma

    Obli cerca nel sonno, e posa e calma.

      (La conduce presso la coltre.)

SI, LA STANCHEZZA — *YES, HEAVY WOES* Duet. (Manrico and Azucena)

AZUCENA

Andantino.   *Tutto a mezza voce*

Si; la stan-chez-za m'op-pri-me o fi - glio, Al - la qui- e - te io
Yes; heav - y woes, and fa - tigue op - press me, Clos - ing my eyes, I to

chiu-do il ci - glio. Ma, se del ro - go ar - der si ve - da L'or - ri - da
sleep ad - dress me. But, should that dark pile rise up be - fore thee, With flames as-

MANRICO

fiam-ma, de - sta-mi al-ler. Ri - po-sa, o ma - dre; Id - di - o con - ce - da
fiam - ing, wake me a - gain. Re - pose, O mo - ther: may Heav'n watching o'er thee

AZU.

Men tri-sti im - ma - gi - ni al tuo cor.
Send thee bright vi - sions, sooth-ing thy pain!

Ai no-stri mon - ti

ri - tor - ne - re - mo, L'an - ti - ca pa - ce i vi go - dre - mo! Tu can - te -
our steps re - tra-cing, There, peace and qui - et once more em - bra - cing, Songs thou wilt

ra - i, sul tuo li - u - to, In son - no pla - ci - do io dor - mi - rò.
sing me with lute at tend-ing, Sweet dreams shall vis - it our sleep as of yore.

MAN.

Ri - po - sa o ma - dre; io pro - no e mu - to La mente al cie - lo ri - vol - ge -
Re-pose, O moth - er; si - lent-ly bend-ing O'er thee, my spir - it heav'n-ward shall

AZU.

Tu can - te - ra - i sul tu - o li - u - to In son - no
Loved songs thou'lt sing me thy soft lute aid lend-ing, Sweet dreams shall

MAN.

rò.
soar.

La men - te al
My soul, with de -

pla - ci - do io dor - mi - rò, tu can - te - ra - i, sul tu - o li -
vis - it our sleep as of yore. Loved songs thou'lt sing me, thy soft lute aid

cie - lo ri - vol - ge - rò,
vo - tion heav'n-ward shall soar.

u - to, In son - no pla - ci - do io dor - mi - rò, Io
lend - ing, Sweet dreams shall vis - it our sleep as of yore, Sweet

La men - te al cie - lo___ ri - vol - ge - rò.
My soul, with de - vo - tion,___ heav'n-ward shall soar.

dor - mi - rò, Io dor - mi - rò, Io dor - mi - rò,
dreams of yore, Sweet dreams of yore, Sweet dreams of yore,

Ri - po - sa, o ma - dre, ri - po - sa, o
Re - pose thee, O moth - er, re - pose___ thee, O

Io dor - mi - ro, Io dor - mi - ro, Io dor - mi - ro.___
Sweet dreams of yore, Sweet dreams of yore, Sweet dreams of yore.___

ma - dre la men - te al ciel ri - vol - ge - rò.___
moth - er, my wear - y soul heav'n-ward shall soar.___

(AZUCENA yields herself to sleep; MANRICO remains kneeling beside her.)

SCENE III—The door opens; enter LEONORA.

Manrico.

　　How! In this darkness do I deceive me?

Leonora.

　　'Tis I, Manrico!

Manrico.

　　Oh! my Lenora!

　　Oh, heaven, dost grant me in thy compassion

　　Rapture so boundless ere to death they lead me?

(AZUCENA si addormenta; MANRICO resta genuflesso accant a lei.)

SCENA III—Si apre la porta, entra LEONORA.

Manrico.

　　Che!—non m'inganno! quel fioco lume!

Leonora.

　　Son io, Manrico—

Manrico.

　　Oh, mia Leonora!

　　Ah, mi concedi, pietoso Nume,

　　Gioja si grande, anzi ch'io morra?

Leonora.

Thou shalt not die, love! I come to save
thee.

Manrico.

Truly! to save me? What meanest thou?

Leonora.

Farewell, love!
Let nought delay thee, depart now, quickly!

Manrico.

Thou comest not with me?

Leonora.

I must remain here!

Manrico.

Remain!

Leonora.

Ah, fly thee!

Manrico.

No.

Leonora.

Woe awaits thee!
(Endeavoring to force him towards the door.)

Manrico.

No!

Leonora.

Life's before thee!

Manrico.

Ah! no, I scorn it!
But, lady, bend thy gaze upon me!
Whence comes this power? what price has
bought it?
Thou wilt not speak? oh, dark suspicion!
'Twas from my rival thou purchased thy
mission!
Ah! thou hast sold him thy heart's affection!
Bartered a love, once devoted to me!

Leonora.

Oh, how thine anger doth blind thy vis-
ion!
Oh, how unjust is thy cruel suspicion!
Obey, and fly thee, not heaven's protection,
If thou dost linger, can succor thee!

Azucena
(sleeping).

Back to our mountains, our steps retracing.
There peace and quiet once more embracing.

Leonora.

Tu non morrai—vengo a salvarti.

Manrico.

Come!—a salvarmi?—Fia vero!

Leonora.

Addio!
Tronca ogni indulgio!—t'affretta!—parti!
(Accennandogli la porta.)

Manrico.

E tu non vieni?

Leonora.

Restar degg' io!

Manrico.

Restar!

Leonora.

Deh! fuggi!

Manrico.

No.

Leonora.

Guai se tardi!
(Cercando di trarlo verso l'uscio.)

Manrico.

No!

Leonora.

La tua vita!

Manrico.

Io la dispresso—
Pur—figgi, o donna, in me gli sguardi!—
Da chi l'avesti?—ed a qual prezzo?—
Parlar non vuoi?—Balen tremendo!—
Dal mio rivale!—intendo—intendo!—
Ha quest' infame l'amor venduto—
Venduto un core che mio giurò!

Leonora.

Ahi, come l'ira ti rende cieco!—
Ahi, quanto ingiusto, crudel sei meco!—
T' arrendi—fuggi, o sei perduto!—
O, il ciel nemmen salvar ti può!

Azucena
(Dormendo.)

Ai nostri monti ritorneremo—
L'antica pace—ivi godremo!

Songs thou wilt sing me with lute attending,
Sweet dreams shall visit our sleep as of yore.

Manrico.

Begone now!

Leonora
(casting herself down at the feet of MANRICO).

Oh! repulse me not!
See'st thou? I languish,
Oppressed and fainting.

Manrico.

Go! I hate thee now;
May curses blight thee!

Leonora.

Ah! cease reviling;
Curse me no more, but raise thy thoughts
To heaven in prayers for me
At this dark moment!

Manrico.

A chill through my bosom is swiftly cours-
ing.

Leonora.

Manrico!
(Falls on her face.)

Manrico
(hastening to lift her up).

Lady! what mean you?
Tell me!

Leonora.

Death's cold hand is on me!

Manrico.

What, dying?

Leonora.

Ah! far more rapidly
The poison sped its mission
Than I intended!

Manrico.

Oh! mortal blow!

Leonora.

Feel now, my hand is freezing—
But here, within me, dread fires are burn-
ing!
(Placing her hand on her breast.)

Manrico.

Oh, heaven, what didst thou?

Leonora.

Sooner than live, another's bride,
Near thee, I preferred to die!

Tu canterai—sul tuo lïuto—
In sonno placido—io dormirò—

Manrico.

Ti scosta.

Leonora
(è caduta ai piedi di MANRICO).

Non respingermi—
Vedi?—Languente, oppressa,
Io manco—

Manrico.

Va—ti abbomino—
Ti maledico—

Leonora.

Ah, cessa!—
Non d'imprecar, di volgere
Per me la prece a Dio
E questa l'ora!

Manrico.

Un brivido corse nel petto mio!

Leonora.

Manrico!—
(Cade boccone.)

Manrico
(accorrendo a sollevarla).

Donna, svelami—
Narra—

Leonora.

Ho la morte in seno.

Manrico.

La morte!—

Leonora.

Ah, fu più rapida
La forza del veleno
Ch'io non pensava!—

Manrico.

Oh, fulmine!

Leonora.

Senti!—la mano è gelo—
Ma quì foco orribile
Arde—
(Toccandosi il vetto.)

Manrico.

Che festi—oh, cielo!

Leonora.

Prima che d'altri vivere,—
Io volli tua morir!—

Manrico.

Insensate! and I this angel's love
With curses dared repay!

Leonora.

I strive no longer!

Manrico.

Ah! hapless one!
(The COUNT enters, but stops on the threshold.)

Leonora.

Behold the moment! I'm dying, Manrico!
Now, heavenly Father, pardon me, I implore
    Thee!

Count.

(Ah! she deceived me purposely,
That for him she might die!)
The block awaits him!
(To the soldiers, pointing out MANRICO.)

Manrico.

Mother! farewell forever!
(Goes out with the soldiers.)

Azucena
        (awakening).

Manrico! my son, where art thou?

Count.

To death delivered!

Azucena.

Ah, stay thee! hear me—
(The COUNT drags AZUCENA to the window.)

Count.

Look ye!

Azucena.

Heaven!

Count.

'Tis over!

Azucena.

The victim was thy brother!

Count.

He! horrid fate!

Azucena.

Thou art avenged, O mother!
(Falls near the window.)

Count
        (with horror).

And I still live!

Manrico.

Insano!—Ed io quest' **angelo**
Osava malodir!

Leonora.

Più non—resisto!—

Manrico.

Ahi, misera!—
(Entra il CONTE, arrestandosi sulla **seglia.**)

Leonora.

Ecco l'instante—io moro—
Manrico!—Or la tua grazia,
Padre del cielo, imploro!

Conte.

(Ah! volle me deludere
E per costui morir!)
Sia tratto al ceppo!
(Indicando agli armati MANRICO.)

Manrico.

Madre!—Oh, madre, addio!
(Parte, tra gli armati.)

Azucena
        (Destandosi.)

Manrico!—Ov' è mio figlio?

Conte.

A morte ei corre!—

Azucena.

Ah ferma!—m'odi—
(Franscinando AZUCENA presso la **finestra.**)

Conte

Vedi!

Azucena.

Cielo!

Conte.

E spento!

Azucena.

Egli era tuo fratello!—

Conte.

Ei!—quale orror!

Azucena.

Sei vendicata, O madre!
(Cade a piè della finestra.)

Conte.

E vivo ancor!
(Inorridito.)

END OF THE OPERA.

LA TRAVIATA

by

GIUSEPPE VERDI

LIBRETTO ADAPTED FROM "LA DAME AUX CAMELIAS" BY ALEXANDRE DUMAS FILS

THE STORY OF "LA TRAVIATA"

THE first act commences with a gay party in the house of Violetta (the heroine), a young and beautiful creature, thrown by circumstances, and the loss of her parents in childhood, into a course of voluptuous living. She is surrounded by a circle of gay and thoughtless beings like herself, who devote their lives to pleasure. Amongst the throng who crowd to her shrine is Alfred Germont, a young man, who becomes seriously enamored with Violetta. Touched by the sincerity of his passion, she yields to its influence, a new and pure love springs up in her heart, and for the first time she becomes conscious of the misery of her position, and the hollowness of the pleasures in which she has basked. In the second act, we discover her living in seclusion with her lover, in a country-house near Paris, three months after the events narrated in the preceding act. Alfred accidentally discovers that Violetta has been secretly selling her houses and property in Paris, in order to maintain this establishment; and, revolting at the idea of being a dependent on her bounty, he leaves hurriedly for Paris, to redeem his honor from this disgrace. During his absence, his father, who has discovered his retreat, arrives, and, representing to Violetta that his son's connection with her is not only lowering him in the opinion of the world, but will be ruinous to his family, inasmuch as his sister was betrothed to a wealthy noble, who had, however, declared his intention of renouncing her, unless Alfred would give up Violetta, the generous girl resolves to sacrifice her affections and happiness for her lover's sake, and returns alone to Paris, whither Alfred, overwhelmed with despair when he discovers her flight, follows her. We are then transported to a saloon in the hotel of Flora, one of Violetta's former friends, during a festival given by the fair mistress of the mansion. There Alfred again meets Violetta, now under the protection of the Baron Dauphol, and being unaware of the generous motive which made her desert him, he overwhelms her with reproaches, and flings a purse containing money at her feet, in the presence of the company. Degraded and heartbroken, the unfortunate Violetta returns home to die; and in the last act we find the sad romance of her life drawing to its close. Alfred, too late, learns the truth, and discovers the sacrifice she has made to secure his happiness. Penetrated with grief and shame, he hastens, with his father, to comfort and console her, and to offer her his hand and name in reparation of the wrong he has done her, — but too late. The fragile flower, broken on its stem, can never more raise its beauteous head. One gleam of happiness, the purest and brightest that she has known, arising from her lover's assurance of his truth, and his desire to restore her reputation, gilds the closing moments of her life, and in a transport of joy her soul suddenly quits its fragile tenement of clay,

LA TRAVIATA

ACT I.	ATTO I.
SCENE I—A salon in the house of VIOLETTA; in the back scene is a door, which opens into another salon; there are also side doors; on the left is a fireplace, over which is a mirror. In the centre of the apartment is a dining-table, elegantly laid.	SCENA I—Salotto in casa di VIOLETTA; nel fondo è la porta che mette ad altra sala; ve ne sono altre due laterali; a sinistra un caminetto con sopra uno specchio. Nel mezzo è una tavola riccamente imbandita.
(VIOLETTA, seated on a couch, is conversing with the DOCTOR and some friends, whilst others are receiving the guests who arrive, among whom are the BARON, and FLORA on the arm of the MARQUIS.)	(VIOLETTA seduta sur un divano sta discorrendo col DOTTORE, e con alcuni amici, mentre altri vanno ad incontrare quelli che sopraggiungono, tra' quali sono il BARONE e FLORA al braccio del MARCHESE.)

Chorus 1.	*Coro* 1.
Past already's the hour of appointment—	Dell' invito trascorsa è già l' ora—
You are tardy.	Voi tardaste.
Chorus 2.	*Coro* 2.
We played deep at Flora's,	Giocammo da Flora,
And while playing the hours flew away.	E giocando quell' ore volâr.
Violetta.	*Violetta.*
Flora, and kind friends, the night is before us.	Flora, amici, la notte che resta
Other pleasures we here will display.	D'altre gioie quì fate brilla—
(Goes to meet them.)	(Andando ore incontre.)
'Mid the wine-cups the hours pass more gaily.	Fra le tazze è più viva la festa.
Flora. *Marquis.* } Can you there find enjoyment?	*Flora.* *Marchese.* } E goder voi potrete?
Violetta.	*Violetta.*
I strive to;	Lo voglio;
Yes, to pleasure I yield, and endeavor	Alla danza m'affido, ed io soglio
With such remedies illness to stay.	Con tal farmaco i mali sopir
All.	*Tutti.*
Yes! enjoyment will lengthen our days.	Sì, la vita s'addoppia al gioir.

SCENE II—The same. GASTON and ALFRED enter. Servants are busy about the table.	SCENA II—Detti, il Visconte GASTONE DI LETORIERES, ALFREDO GERMONT; servi affaccendati interno all mensa.
Gaston.	*Gastone.*
In Alfred Germont, fairest lady,	In Alfredo Germont, o signora,
Another behold, who esteems you;	Ecco un altro che molto vi onora;
There are few friends like him; he's a treasure.	Pochi amici a lui simili sono.
Violetta.	*Violetta.*
Thanks, dear Viscount, for so great a pleasure.	Mio Visconte, mercè di tal dono.
(She gives her hand to ALFRED, who kisses it.)	(Dà la mano ad ALFREDO, che gliela bacia.)

Marquis.

Dear Alfred!

Alfred.

Kind Marquis!
　　　　　　(They shake hands.)

Gaston
　　　　　　(to ALFRED).

I told you

That combined here are friendship and pleasure.

(During this dialogue the servants have placed the viands
upon the table.)

Violetta.

All is ready?
　　　　　　(A servant bows assent.)

My dear friends, be seated;

'Tis at the banquet that each heart unfolds.

Chorus.

Thou hast wisely the maxim repeated,

Cure for trouble the wine-cup still holds.

(They seat themselves, VIOLETTA between ALFRED and GAS-
TON, and opposite to them FLORA, the MARQUIS, and the
BARON; the rest take their seats promiscuously; there is a
momentary silence, during which the dishes are passed round,
and VIOLETTA and GASTON converse in an undertone.)

Gaston
　　　　　　(to VIOLETTA).

Thou'rt the sole thought of Alfred.

Violetta.

Art jesting?

Gaston.

Thou wert ill, and each day in distress

He came to ask thy condition.

Violetta.

Be silent;

No, I am naught to him.

Gaston.

I deceive not.

Violetta
　　　　　　(to ALFRED).

Is it true then? Can it be? Ah, I know not.

Alfred
　　　　　　(sighing).

Yes, it is true.

Violetta
　　　　　　(to ALFRED).

Grateful thanks, then, I give you.
　　　　　　(To the BARON.)

You, dear Baron, were not so enamored.

Baron.

But 'tis only a year I have known you.

Marchese.

Caro Alfredo!

Alfredo.

Marchese!
　　　　　　(Si stringono la mano.)

Gastone
　　　　　　(ad ALFREDO).

T' ho detto

L' amistà quì s' intreccia al diletto.

(I servi frattanto avranno imbandite le vivande.)

Violetta.

Pronto è il tutto?
　　　　　　(Un servo accenna che sì.)

Miei cari, sedete;

E al convito che s' apre ogni cor.

Tutti.

Ben diceste—le cure segrete

Fuga sempre l'amico licor.

(Siedono in modo che VIOLETTA resti tra ALFREDO e GAS-
TONE; di fronte vi sarà FLORA, il MARCHESE ed il BARONE;
gli altri siedono a piacere. Vi ha un momento di silenzio;
frattanto passano i piatti, e VIOLETTA e GASTONE parlano
sotto voce tra loro.)

Gastone.

Sempre Alfredo a voi pensa.

Violetta.

Scherzate?

Gastone.

Egra foste, e ogni dì con affanno

Quì volò, di voi chiese.

Violetta.

Cessate.

Nulla son io per lui.

Gastone.

Non v' inganno.

Violetta
　　　　　　(ad ALFREDO).

Vero è dunque?—Onde ciò? Nol com
prendo.

Alfredo
　　　　　　(sospirande).

Sì, egli è ver.

Violetta.

Le mie grazie vi rendo.
　　　　　　(Al BARONE.)

Voi, barone, non feste altrettanto.

Barone.

Vi conosco da un anno soltanto.

Violetta.

And Alfred a few minutes only.

Flora

(softly to the BARON).

'Twould be better if you had not spoken.

Baron

(softly to FLORA).

For this youth I've no liking.

Flora.

But why?

As for me, now, he pleases me well.

Gaston

(to ALFRED).

Thou art silent; hast nothing to offer?

Marquis.

Madame alone has the power to arouse him.

Violetta

(fills the glass of ALFRED).

I will fill, then, like Hebe!

Alfred.

And, like her,

I proclaim thee immortal.

All.

We pledge thee!

Gaston

(to the BARON).

Can you not, in this moment of pleasure,

Give a toast, or a gay tuneful measure?

(The BARON declines.)

(To ALFRED.)

Then wilt thou—

All.

Yes, yes, a drinking song.

Alfred.

I've no inspiration.

Gaston.

Art thou not then a singer?

Alfred

(to VIOLETTA).

Will it please you?

Violetta.

Yes.

Alfred

(rising).

Yes? Then I yield.

Marquis.

Pay attention!

Violetta.

Ed ei solo da qualche minuto.

Flora

(piano al BARONE).

Meglio fora, se aveste taciuto.

Barone

(piano a FLORA).

M'è increscioso quel giovin.

Flora.

Perchè?

A me invece simpatico egli è.

Gastone

(ad ALFREDO).

E tu dunque non apri più bocca?

Marchese

(a VIOLETTA).

E a madama che scuoterlo tocca.

Violetta

(mesce ad ALFREDO).

Saro l'Ebe che versa.

Alfredo.

E ch' io bramo

Immortal come quella.

(Con galanteria.)

Tutti.

Beviamo.

Gastone.

O Barone, nè un verso, nè un viva

Troverete in quest' ora giuliva?

(BARONE accenna di nò.)

(Ad ALFREDO.)

Dunque a te.

Tutti.

Sì, sì, un brindisi.

Alfredo.

L'estro non m'arride.

Gastone.

E non se' tu maestro?

Alfredo

(a VIOLETTA).

Vi fia grato?

Violetta.

Sì.

Alfredo

(si alza).

Sì?—L'ho in cor.

Marchese.

Dunque attenti.

Yes, attention we'll pay!

Tutti.
Sì, attenti al cantor.

LIBIAMO NE' LIETI — *A BUMPER WE'LL DRAIN* (Alfred)

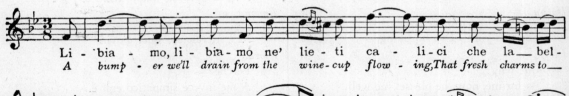

Li - bia - mo, li - bia-mo ne' lie - ti ca - li - ci che la __ bel-
A bump - er we'll drain from the wine-cup flow - ing, That fresh charms to __

lez - za in fio - ra, e la _____ fug-ge-vol, fug-gè - vol o -
beau - ty is lend - ing, O'er fleet - ing mo-ments, so quick-ly end -

-ra s'in - ne-brii a vo-lut - tà. Li - biam ne' dòl - ci __
ing, Gay pleas-ure a - lone should __ reign. We'll drink the thrill - ing __

fre - mi - ti che su - sci - ta l'a - mo - re, poi - chè quel l'oc-chio al
ec - sta - sies, That love ex - cites with - in us, When her bright eye doth __

co - re on - ni - po - ten - te __ và __ Li - bia - mo, a - mo-re a -
win us, And ev - 'ry heart re - tain __ A bump - er to love, mid the

mor fra i ca - li - cì più cal - di __ ba - ci a - vrà.
wine - cups flow - ing, Fresh warmth will our __ pleas - ures re - gain.

Ah! to love, 'mid wine-cups flowing	Libiamo; amor fra i calici
New delight our joys will gain.	Più caldi baci avrà.
Violetta.	*Violetta* (s' alza).
Surrounded by you, I shall learn to lighten	Tra voi, saprò dividere
The footsteps of time with gladness;	Il tempo mio giocondo;
All of this world is but folly and madness	Tutto è follia nel monde
That is not pleasure gay.	Ciò che non è piacer.
Enjoy the hour, for rapid	Godiam; fugace e rapido
The joys of life are flying--	E il gaudio dell' amore:

Like summer flow'rets dying—
Improve them while we may!
Enjoy! the present with fervor invites us,
Its flattering call obey.

All.

Enjoy then the wine-cup with songs of pleas-
ure
That make night so cheerful and smiling,
In this charming paradise, beguiling,
That scarcely we heed the day.

Violetta
   (to ALFRED).

The sum of life is pleasure.

Alfred
   (to VIOLETTA).

While still unloved, unloving?

Violetta
   (to ALFRED).

Experience ne'er has taught me.

Alfred
   (to VIOLETTA).

And thus my fate must be.
  (Music is heard in another room.)

All.

What's this?

Violetta.

Will you not join the gay group of dancers?

All.

Oh! a happy thought! We'll gladly join
them.

Violetta.

Then let us enter!
(Approaching the door, VIOLETTA, seized with a sudden
faintness, cries out:)

Alas!

All.

What ails thee?

Violetta.

Nothing, nothing.

All.

Why do you pause then?

Violetta.

Let's go now.
(Takes a few steps, but is obliged to re-seat herself.)

Oh, Heaven!

All.

Again still!

E un fior che nasce e muore
Nè più si può goder.
Godiam—c'invita un fervido
Accento lusinghier.

Tutti.

Godiam—la tazza e il cantico
Le notti abbella e il riso;
In questo paradiso,
Ne scuopra il nuovo dì.

Violetta
   (ad ALFREDO).

La vita è nel tripudio.

Alfredo
   (a VIOLETTA).

Quando non s'ami ancora.

Violetta
   (ad ALFREDO).

No! dite a chi l'ignora.

Alfredo
   (a VIOLETTA).

E il mio destin così.
  (S' ode musica dall' altra sala.)

Tutti.

Che è cio.

Violetta.

Non gradireste ora le danze?

Tutti.

Oh, il gentile pensier!—Tutti accetiamo.

Violetta.

Usciamo dunque?
(S' avviano alla porta di mezzo, ma VIOLETTA e colta di
subito pallore.)

Ohimè!

Tutti.

Che avete?

Violetta.

Nulla, nulla.

Tutti.

Che mai v'arresta?

Violetta.

Usciamo.
(Fà qualche passo, ma è obbligata a nuovamente fermar
e sedere.)

Oh Dio!

Tutti.

Ancora!

Alfred.

Ah! you suffer—

All.

Oh, Heaven! what means this?

Violetta.

A sudden tremor seized me. Now—there, pray enter.
(Pointing to the other room.)
I will rejoin you ere long.

All.

As you desire, then.
(All pass into the other room, except ALFRED.)

SCENE III—VIOLETTA, ALFRED, afterward GASTON.

Violetta
(rises and regards herself in a mirror).
Ah me! how pale!
(Turning, she perceives ALFRED.)
You here?

Alfred.

Are you relieved from recent distress?

Violetta.

I'm better!

Alfred.

Ah, these gay revels soon will destroy thee.
Great care is needful—on this depends your being.

Violetta.

Canst thou then aid me?

Alfred.

Oh! wert thou mine now, with vigilance untiring
I'd guard thee with tenderest care.

Violetta.

What say'st thou?
Some one, perchance, then, cares for me?

Alfred
(confusedly).
No one in all the world doth love you.

Violetta.

No one?

Alfred.

I, only, love you.

Violetta.

Ah! truly!
(Laughing.)
Your great devotion I had quite forgotten.

Alfredo.

Voi soffrite.

Tutti.

Oh ciel!—ch' è questo?

Violetta.

E un tremito che provo—or là passate,
(Indicando l' altra stanza.)
Tra poco anch' io sarò.

Tutti.

Come bramate.
(Tutti passano all' altra sala, meno ALFREDO, che resta indietro.)

SCENA III—VIOLETTA, ALFREDO, e GASTONE, a tempo.

Violetta
(si guarda nello specchio).
Oh, qual pallor!
Voi quì!
(Volgendosi s' accorge d' ALFREDO.)

Alfredo.

Cessata è l'ansia, che vi turbò?

Violetta.

Sto meglio.

Alfredo.

Ah, in cotal guisa v'ucciderete!
Aver v'è d'uopo cura dell' esser vostro.

Violetta.

E lo potrei?

Alfredo.

Se mia foste, custode io veglierei
Pe' vostri soavi dì.

Violetta.

Che dite?
Ha forse alcuno cura di me?

Alfredo.

Perchè nessuno al mondo v'ama.

Violetta.

Nessun?

Alfredo.

Tranne sol io.

Violetta.

Gli è vero!
(Ridende.)
Si grande amor dimenticato avea.

Alfred.
> Dost mock me? Have you a heart then?

Violetta.
> A heart? Yes—haply—but why do you thus question?

Alfred.
> Ah, if you had one you would not thus trifle with me.

Violetta.
> Are you then truthful?

Alfred.
> You, I deceive not.

Violetta.
> 'Tis long, that you have thus loved me?

Alfred.
> Ah, yes; a year now.

Alfredo.
> Ridete!—e in voi v' ha un core?

Violetta.
> Un cor? Sì, forse—e a che lo richiedete?

Alfredo.
> Oh, se ciò fosse, non potreste allora celiar.

Violetta.
> Dite davvero?

Alfredo.
> Io non v'inganno.

Violetta.
> Di molto è che mi amate?

Alfredo.
> Ah sì, da un anno.

UN DI FELICE——*ONE DAY, A RAPTURE* (Alfred)

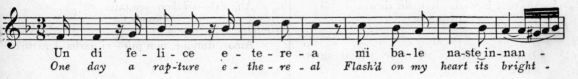

Un di fe-li-ce e-te-re-a mi ba-le na-ste in-nan-
One day a rap-ture e-the-re-al Flash'd on my heart its bright-

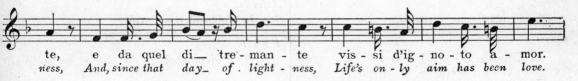

te, e da quel di__ tre-man-te vis-si d'ig-no-to a-mor.
ness, And, since that day__ of light-ness, Life's on-ly aim has been love.

Di quell' a-mor, quell' a-mor__ ch'e pal-pi-to dell' u-ni-
Ah, yes, of love, of the love__ that pal-pi-tates Thro' all the

ver-so, dell' u-ni-ver-so in-te-ro, mi-ste-ri-o-so, mi-ste-ri-o-so al-
world, thro' cre-a-tion wide, ex-tend-ed; Oh, pow'r mys-te-rious, pow'r yet un-com-pre-

te-ro, cro-ce, cro-ce e de-li-zia, cro-ce e de-li-zia, de-li-zia al cor.
hend-ed, Tor-ment, tor-ment and rap-ture, tor-ment and rap-ture, each do I prove.

Violetta.

    If this be true, ah! fly from me.
    Friendship alone I offer,
    I neither know nor suffer
    A feeling of such devotion.
    I am sincere and frank with thee;
    Look for one warmer, kinder;
    'Twill not be hard to find her,
    Then think no more of me.

Alfred.

    Oh love, sublime, yet mysterious,
    Power ne'er yet comprehended,
    Torments and raptures of love!

Gaston
                (appearing at the door).
    How now? What here employs you?

Violetta.

    Trifles and folly.

Gaston.

    Ah, that is well. Remain then.
             (Goes back.)

Violetta
             (to Alfred).
    Of love speak we no more. Is it agreed
    on?

Alfred.

    I will obey you—farewell.
             (About to depart.)

Violetta.

    Is such your pleasure?
       (Takes a flower from her bosom.)
    Then take with thee this flow'ret.

Alfred.

    And why?

Violetta.

    Soon to return it.

Alfred
              (returning).
    How soon?

Violetta.

    When its gay bloom is faded.

Alfred.

    Oh, joy! To-morrow!

Violetta.

    'Tis well—to-morrow!

Alfred.

    I am at last so happy!
       (Seizes the flower with transport.)

Violetta.

    Ah, se ciò è ver, fuggitemi—
    Pura amistade io v'offro;
    Amar non sò, nè soffro
    Di cosi eroico ardor.
    Io sono franca, ingenua;
    Altra cercar devoto—
    Non arduo troverete
    Dimentecarmi allor.

Alfredo.

    Oh amore misterioso,
    Misterioso altero,
    Croce e delizia al cor.

Gastone
          (presentandosi sulla porta di **mezzo**).
    Ebben?—che diavol fate?

Violetta.

    Si folleggiava.

Gastone.

    Ah, ah!—stà ben—restate.
             (Rientra.)

Violetta.

    Amor, dunque, non più—vi garba il patto?

Alfredo.

    Io v'obbedisco.—Partò.
          (Par andarsene.)

Violetta.

    A tal giungeste?
       (Si toglie un fiore dal **seno.**)
    Prendete questo fiore.

Alfredo.

    Perche?

Violetta.

    Per riportarlo.

Alfredo
              (tornando).
    Quando?

Violetta.

    Quando sarà appassito.

Alfredo.

    Allor domani?

Violetta.

    Ebbene domani.

Alfredo.

    Io son felice!
       (Prende con trasporto il fiore.)

Violetta.

You still declare you love me?

Alfred.

How much I love thee!

Violetta. (Going.)

You go then.

Alfred.

Yes, love! (Returns and kisses her hand.)

Violetta.

To-morrow—

Alfred.

More I will ask not.

(Exit.)

SCENE IV—Violetta, and all the others, returning from the dancing-room.

All.

In the east the dawn is breaking,
And perforce we must depart,
Gentle lady, leave now taking,
Thanks we give thee from each heart.
Full the city is of pleasure,
Brief the time for love and joy,
To repose give needful measure,
Lest enjoyment we destroy!

(Exeunt.)

SCENE V—Violetta, alone

How wondrous! how wondrous! those accents
Upon my heart are graven!
Will it misfortune bring me, a love in earnest?
What shall be thy resolve, my troubled spirit?
No living man hath yet enflamed thee!
Oh, rapture that I have known not, to be loved and loving.
Can my heart still disdain it
For follies dry and heartless, which now enchain me?

Violetta.

D' amarmi dite ancora?

Alfredo.

Oh, quanto v'amo!

Violetta. (Per partire.)

Partite?

Alfredo.

Parto. (Torna a lei, e le bacia la mano.)

Violetta.

Addio.

Alfredo.

Di più non bramo.

(Esce.)

SCENA IV—Violetta e tutti gli altri che tornano dalla sala della danza.

Tutti.

Si ridesta in ciel l' aurora,
E n' è forza ripartire;
Mercè a voi, gentil signora,
(a Violetta).
Di sì splendido gioir
La città di feste è piena,
Volge il tempo del piacer;
Nel riposo omai la lena
Si ritempri per goder.

(Partono dalla destra.)

SCENA V—Violetta sola.

E strano!—è strano!—In core
Scolpiti ho quegli accenti!
Saria per mia sventura un serio amore?
Che risolvi, o turbata anima mia?
Null' uomo ancora t' accendeva.—Oh, gioia,
Ch'io non conobbi, esser amata amando!
E sdegnarla poss' io
Per l' aride follie del viver mio?

AH, FORS' È LUI —— 'TWAS HE PERCHANCE (Violetta)

Ah, fors' è   lui che l'a-ni-ma   so-lin-ga ne' tu-mul-ti,
'Twas he, per-chance, my long-ing soul, Lone-ly, 'mid scenes of pleas-ure,

so - lin - ga ne' tu - mul - ti,   go - dea so - ven - te pin - ge - re
lone - ly, 'mid scenes of pleas - ure, Oft loved to paint in col - ors bright,

de' suoi co - lo - ri oc - cul - ti,   de' suoi co - lo - ri oc - cul - ti!   Lui che, mo - des - to e
In its own gold and   a - zure, In its own gold and a - zure.   He, who with mod - est

vi - gi - le,   all' e - gre sog - lia - sce - se,   e nuo - va feb - bre ac - ce - se
vi - gi - lance, To my sick room re - turn - ing, Kin - dled new flames, still burn - ing,

des - tan - do - mi all' a - mor!   A quell a - mor, quell' a - mor che è pal - pi - to dell' u - ni -
Des - tined my heart to love!   Yes! this is love, 'tis the love that pal - pi - tates Through all the

ver - so, dell' u - ni - ver - so in - te - ro,   mi - ste - ri - o - so, mi - ste - ri - o - so al -
world, through cre - a - tion wide - ly ex - tend - ed, Oh, pow'r mys - te - rious, Pow'r ne'er yet com - pre -

te - ro, cro - ce, cro - ce e de - li - zia, cro - ce e de - li - zia, de - li - zia al cor.
hend - ed, Tor - ment, tor - ment and rap - ture, tor - ment and rap - ture each do we prove.

To my young heart, all guileless then,	A me, fanciulla, un candido
Filled with intrepid yearning,	E trepido desire
This dream was imaged, fair, serene,	Quest' effigiò, dolcissimo
Bright o'er my pathway burning.	Signor dell' avvenire,
When like a star from heaven,	Quando ne' cieli il raggio
Radiant he stood before me,	Di sua beltà vedea,
Visions of hope came o'er me.	E tutta me pascea
Like the fond dreams I wove.	Di quel soave error
Then beat my heart with the love that pal-	Sentia che amore è palpito
pitates	Dell' universo intero,

Through all the world, thro' creation wide
  extended.

Oh! pow'r mysterious, pow'r ne'er yet comprehended.

Torment and rapture, each do we prove.

(Remains for an instant buried in thought, then says:)

What folly! All this is vain delirium!

Child of misfortune, lonely,

By all abandoned, in this gay crowded desert,

This vortex of pleasure they call Paris,

What hope remains? what must I do, then?

Surrender to pleasure's maddening whirl
  again?

Misterioso, altero,

Pena e delizia al cor.

(Resta concentrata un istante poi dice.)

Follie!—follie!—delirio vano è questo!

In quai sogni mi perdo!

Povera donna, sola,

Abbandonata in questo popoloso deserto,

Che appellano Parigi,

Che spero or più?—Che far degg' io?—
  gioire.

Di voluttà nei vortici finire.

SEMPRE LIBERA — *EVER FREE, SHALL I STILL WANDER* (Violetta)

Sem-pre li - be - ra__ degg' i - o fol - leg - gia - re di gio-ja in
Ev - er free, shall I__ still wan - der Mad - ly on from pleas-ure to

gio - ja, vo' che scor-ra il vi -- ver mi - o pei sen - tie - ri del pia -
pleas - ure? Life's short mo-ments shall__ I squan-der In pur - suit of fol - lies.

cer? Nas-ca il gior-no, o il gior-no muo - ja sem-pre lie - ta ne' ri -
gay? Days pass by me in rap-id meas-ure, Hap-piest where light hearts are.

tro - vi,_____ a di - let - ti sem - pre nuo - vi dee vo -
throng - ing,_____ For new pleas - ures ev - er long -- ing, Shall my

la - re il __ mio pen - sier, dee __ vo - lar, dee __ vo - lar, dee __ vo -
thoughts fly i - dly a - way, fly __ a - way, fly __ a - way, Shall __ my

la — re il mio pen - sier, dee___ vo - lar, dee___ vo
thoughts fly i - dly a - way, fly___ a - way, i - dly

lar !   il pen - sier.
fly, ___   fly a - way.

(Exit on the left.)	(Parte, a sinistra.)
END OF THE FIRST ACT.	**FINE DELL' ATTO PRIMO.**

ACT II.

SCENE I—A country house near Paris. A salon on the ground floor. At the back, facing the audience, a fireplace, over which is a looking-glass. A clock hangs between two glass doors, which are closed. There are also two side doors, seats, tables, and writing materials.

(ALFRED enters, in sporting costume.)

Alfred.

Out from her presence, for me there's no enjoyment.

(Puts down his gun.)

Three months have flown already
Since my beloved Violetta
So kindly left for me her riches, admirers,
And all the haunts of pleasure,
Where she had been accustomed
To homage from all hearts, for charms transcendent.
Yet now contented in this retreat, so quiet,
She forgets all for me. Here, near my loved one,
New life springs within me;
From the trials of love restored and strengthened,
Ah! in my present rapture past sorrows are forgotten.

ATTO II.

SCENA I—Casa di Campagna presso Parigi. Salotto terreno. Nel fondo, in faccia agli Spettatori, è un camino, sopra il quale uno specchio ed un orologio, fra due porte chiuse da cristalli, che mettono ad un giardino. Al primo panno due altre porte, una di fronte all' altra. Sedie, tavolini, qualche libro, l'occorrente per scrivere.

(ALFREDO entra, in costume da caccia.)

Alfredo.

Lunge da lei per me non v' ha dilette!

(Depone il fucile.)

Volaron già tre lune
Dacchè la mia Violetta
Agi per me lascio, dovizie, onori.
E le pompose feste,
Ove agli omaggi avvezza,
Vedea schiavo ciascun di sua bellezza—
E dal suffio d'amor rigenerato
Solo esiste per me—qui presso a lei
Io rinascer mi sento,
E dal suffio d' amor rigenerato
Scordo ne' gaudj suoi tutto il passato.

DI MIEI BOLLENTI SPIRITI—— *ALL MY IMPULSIVE ECSTASIES* (Alfred)

De miei bol-len-ti spi - ri - ti il gio-va-ni le ar-do - re, el - la tem-prò col
All my im-pul-sive ec - sta-sies, Sprung from a youth-ful ar - dor, She hath sub-dued with

pla - ci - do sor - ri - so dell' a - mor, dell' a - mor! Dal di che dis - se:
peace - ful smiles, The smiles of hap - py love, hap - py love! Thus, since she whis-per'd,

vi - ve - re io vo - glio, io vo-glio a te fe - del, dell' u - ni - ver - so im-
"Live for me, Still faith - ful, I will be true to thee." Of all the world for-

me - mo - re io vi - vo, io vi - vo qua - si, io vi - vo qua - si in
get - ful, free, The earth___ seems like heav'n to me, Yes, I seem in heav'n to

ciel. Dal di che dis - se: vi - ve - re io vo-glio a te fe - del, si si,
be. Thus, since she whis-per'd "Live for me, I will be true to thee;" Ah! yes,

dell' u - ni - ver - so im-me-mo - re io vi - vo,___ vi - vo qua - si, io vi - vo qua - si in
of all the world for - get - ful, free, The earth___ seems heav'n to me; now, I seem in heav'n to

ciel, io vi - vo in ciel, dell u - ni - ver-so im-me-mo - re io vi - vo qua - si in
be! 'tis heav'n to me, Of all___ the world for-get-ful, now I seem in heav'n to

ciel,___ ah si, io vi - vo qua-si in cie - lo, io vi - vo qua - si in ciel.
be,___ Ah, yes, in heav'n I seem to be, now in heav'n I seem to be.

SCENE II—The same, ANNINA, entering hastily, in a trav-
lling dress.

Alfred.

    Whence have you come, Annina?

Annina.

    From the city.

Alfred.

    By whom sent thither?

SCENA II—Detto, ed ANNINA in arnese da viaggio.

Alfredo.

    Annina! donde vieni?

Annina.

    Da Parigi.

Alfredo.

    Chi tel commise!

Annina.

    My kind mistress sent me.

Alfred.

    For what purpose?

Annina.

    To sell her jewels, horses, carriages, and all that's left to her.

Alfred.

    Heard I rightly?

Annina.

    Great are the expenses of living here secluded.

Alfred.

    You ne'er told me!

Annina.

    My silence was commanded.

Alfred.

    Commanded! Much still is needed?

Annina.

    One thousand louis'!

Alfred.

    Now leave me. I go to Paris.

    Mind that your mistress knows nothing of these questions.

    Ere long I shall be able to repair all. Go—go!   (ANNINA goes out.)

Annina.

    Fu la mia signora.

Alfredo.

    Perchè?

Annina.

    Per alienar cavalli, cocchi, e quanto ancor possiede.

Alfredo.

    Che mai sento!

Annina.

    Lo spendio è grande a viver quì solinghı.

Alfredo.

    E tacevi?

Annina.

    Mi fu il silenzio imposto.

Alfredo.

    Imposto!—e v'al bisogna?—

Annina.

    Mille luigi.

Alfredo.

    Or vanne—Andrò a Parigi—

    Questo colluquio ignori la signora—

    Il tutto valgo a riparere ancora.

     (ANNINA parte.)

SCENE III—ALFRED, alone.   SCENA III—ALFREDO, solo.

O MIO RIMORSO! — OH! DARK REMORSE! (Alfred)

O_ mio ri-mor-so! oh in-fa-mia! io ____ vis-si in ta-le er - - ro - re! ma il
Oh, dark re-morse! oh! in-fa-my! To ____ live in such blind ____ er-ror! From.

tur - pe son-no a fran-ge-re il ____ ver mi ba - le - no! Per
dreams so base, I wake at last To ____ truth, all now re - veal'd! One

po-coin se - no ac-que-ta-ti, o gri-do o gri-do dell' o'-no-re ____ m'a-
mo-ment more thy voice re-strain, Oh, cry, oh, cry of in-jured hon-or! ____ For

vrai se cu - ro - vin-de - ce, quest'___ on - ta la - ve - rò. oh, mio ros -
soon, ex-punged shall be the stain, Such___ shame-ful acts re - peal'd. Oh, blush of___

sor! oh in-fa - 'mia! ah si, quest' on - ta la - ve - rò si,___ la - ve -
shame! oh, base - ness! ah, yes such acts must be' re - peal'd, must be re -

- rò, oh mio ros - sor! oh in-fa - mia! ah! si, quest' on - ta, sì quest'
peal'd. Oh, blush of___ shame! oh,___ base - ness!. ah, yes, this base-ness, yes, this

on - ta la - ve - rò quest' on - ta, quest' on - ta la - ve - rò.
shame must be re - peal'd, This base - ness, this act must be re - peal'd.

(Departs.)	(Esce.)
SCENE IV—VIOLETTA enters with papers in her hand; ANNINA, JOSEPH.	SCENA IV—VIOLETTA, ch'entra con alcune carte, parlando, con ANNINA, poi GIUSEPPE a tempo.
Violetta	*Violetta.*
(to ANNINA). Alfred?	Alfredo!
Annina.	*Annina.*
He has gone to Paris, madame.	Per Parigi or or partiva.
Violetta.	*Violetta.*
When to return?	E tornerà?
Annina.	*Annina.*
Before the day is ended, He bade me tell you.	Pria che tramonti il giorno—dirvel m'impose.
Violetta.	*Violetta.*
'Tis strange, this!	E strano!
Joseph	*Giuseppe*
(presents a letter). For you.	(le presenta una lettera). Per voi.
Violetta.	*Violetta*
'Tis well. A business agent shortly will arrive here; At once admit him.	(la prende). Sta bene. In breve Giungerà un uom d' affari—entri all' istante.
(Exeunt ANNINA and JOSEPH.)	(ANNINA e GIUSEPPE escono.)

SCENE V—Violetta, afterwards Germont, introduced by Joseph, who places two chairs, and goes out.

Violetta
(reading the letter).
Ah! ah!
So Flora hath my home discovered,
And invites me to join a dance this evening!
She'll look for me in vain!
(Throws the letter on a table and seats herself.)

Joseph.
A man would see you.

Violetta.
'Tis the one I look'd for.
(Bids Joseph show him in.)

Germont.
Are you the lady of the house?

Violetta.
I am, sir.

Germont.
In me behold Alfred's father.

Violetta.
You?
(With surprise, invites him to be seated.)

Germont.
Yes, of the imprudent, who goes fast to ruin,
Led away by your follies.

Violetta
(rising, resentfully).
Stay, sir, I am a lady in my own dwelling,
And perforce I must leave you, for your
sake more than mine.
(About to retire.)

Germont.
(What manners!)   But then—

Violetta.
You have been led in error.
(Returns to her seat.)

Germont.
He will spend all his fortune upon you.

Violetta.
He has not yet offered.   I should refuse.

Germont.
How then such grandeur?
(Looking around.)

Violetta
(gives him a paper).
This deed is to all else a mystery—to you
'twill not be

SCENA V—Violetta, quindi il Sig. Germont, introdotto da Giuseppe, che, avanza due siede, e parte.

Violetta
(leggendo la lettera).
Ah, ah,
Scoopriva Flora il mio ritiro!—
E m'invita a danzar per questa sera!—
In van m'aspetterà.
(Getta il foglio sul tavolino e siede.)

Giuseppe.
Giunse un signore.

Violetta.
Ah! sarà lui che attendo.
(Accenna a Giuseppe d'introd.)

Germont.
Madamigella Valery?

Violetta.
Son io.

Germont.
D' Alfredo il padre in me vedete.

Violetta.
Voi!
(Sorpresa gli accenna di sedere.)

Germont.
Sì, dell' incanto, che a rovina corre,
Ammaliato da voi.
(Sedendo.)

Violetta
(alzandosi risentita).
Donna son io, signore, ed in mia casa
Ch'io vi lasci assentite,
Più per voi, che per me.
(Per uscire.)

Germont.
(Quai modi!)   Pure—

Violetta.
Tratto in error voi foste.
(Torna a sedere.)

Germont.
De' suoi beni donovuol farvi.

Violetta.
Non l' oso finora.—Rifiuterei.

Germont.
Pur tanto lusso—

Violetta
(gli dà le carte)
A tutti è mistero quest atto.—A voi no! si

Germont   (reads the paper).
  Heav'n, what a statement!
  Have you then determined all your wealth
    to dispose of?
  But, your past life, ah, why must that accuse
    you?

Violetta.
  It does so no longer; Alfred I love now, and
    Heav'n
  Has cancell'd all the past with my repent-
    ance.

Germont.
  Ah, you have noble feelings.

Violetta.
  Like sweet music my ear receives your ac-
    cents.

Germont   (rising).
  And of such feelings a sacrifice I ask now.

Violetta   (rising).
  Ah, no, pray do not!
  A dreadful thing thou wouldst require, I'm
    certain.
  I foresaw it, with terror; ah, I was far too
    happy!

Germont.
  A father's honor requires it,
  And the future of his two dear children
    claims it.

Violetta.
  Of two children?

Germont.
  Yes.

Germont   (dopo averle scorse coll' occhio).
  D'ogni avere pensate dispogliarvi!--
  Ah, il passato perchè, perchè v'accusa!

Violetta.
  Più non esiste—or amo Alfredo, e Dio
  Lo cancellò col pentimento mio.

Germont.
  Nobile sensi invero!

Violetta.
  Oh, come dolce mi suona il vostra accento!

Germont.
  Ed a tai sensi un sacrifizio chieggo.

Violetta   (alzandosi).
  Ah, no, tacete—
  Terribil cosa chiedereste certo—
  Il predevi, v'attesi, era felice troppo.

Germont.
  D'Alfredo il padre la sorte,
  L'avvenir domanda or qui de' suoi due figli.

Violetta.
  Di due figli?

Germont.
  Sì.

PURA SICCOME UN ANGELO — *PURE AS AN ANGEL* (Germont)

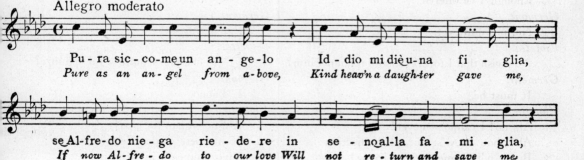

l'a - ma-to e a-man-te   gio - vi - ne,   cui spo-sa an-dar do -
He, the be - lov'd and   lov - ing youth,   Who soon should wed my

ve - a,   or si ri-cu-sa al vin - co - lo__ che,
daugh - - ter, Must then with-draw his plight-ed troth, With

lie - ti, lie-ti ne ren - de - va.   Deh non mu-ta-te in tri-bo-li
all the joy, the joy it brought her.   Then do not change love's ro - ses fair

le ro-se dell' a - mor, ah, non mu-ta-te in tri-bo-li le ro-se dell' a -
To thorns of grief and pain, Ah, do not change love's ro - ses fair To thorns of grief and

mor a' prie-ghi miei re-sis-te-re no, no, non vo-glia il vos-tro cor, no, no.
pain, Your gen-'rous heart, to my fond pray'r, no, no, Will not op-posed re-main, no, no.

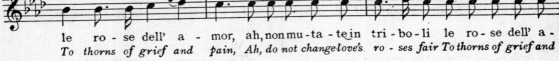

Violetta.
Ah! I see now, that I must for a season
Be from Alfred parted. 'Twill be painful,
Dreary for me, yet—

Germont.
That will not suffice me!

Violetta.
Heav'ns! What more dost seek for?
Enough I've offered!

Germont.
No, not quite yet.

Violetta.
You wish that I forever should renounce him?

Germont.
It must be.

Violetta.
Ah, no! I cannot—never!
Ah! thou know'st not what affection
Burns within me, ardent, living!

Violetta.
Ah, comprendo—dovrò per alcun tempo
Da Alfredo allontanarmi—doloroso
Fora per me—pur—

Germont.
Non è ciò che chiedo.

Violetta.
Cielo!—che più cercate?—offersi assai!

Germont.
Pur non basta.

Violetta.
Volete che per sempre a lui renunzi?

Germont.
E d'uopo.

Violetta.
Ah, no—giam no, mai!
Non sapete quale affetto
Vivo, immensò in' arda il petto?

Not one kind friend or connexion
Can I number, still surviving?
But Alfred has declared it,
All in him my heart should find!
Ah! thou know'st not what dark sorrow
Mocked my being with its shadow?
All is over—how sad the morrow,
Parted thus from dear Alfred!
Ah! the trial is too cruel;
It were better far to die.

Germont.

The sacrifice is heavy;
But hear me with tranquillity.
Lovely thou art still, and youthful, too.
Hereafter—

Violetta.

No more persuade me. I know all,
But it cannot be. Him only I love and
live for!

Germont.

So be it. But the men are oft unfaithful
still—

Violetta (astounded).
Great Heaven!

Germont.

Some day, when love hath colder grown,
And time's broad gulf yawns wider;
When all the joys of life have flown,
What then will be? Consider!
No healing balm shall soothe your rest,
No warm and deep affection,
Since Heav'n your ties will ne'er have blest
With holy benediction.

Violetta.

'Tis all true!

Germont.

Then haste to dissipate the spell
Of this bright dream, controlling;
Be to my home and loved ones
Our angel, good, consoling.
Violetta, oh, consider well
While yet there may be time.
'Tis Heav'n itself that bids me speak,
'Tis Heav'n inspiring
These words in faith sublime.

Che nè amici, nè parenti
Io non conto tra' viventi?
E che Alfredo m' ha giurato
Che in lui tutto io troverò?
Non sapete che colpita
D'atro murbo è la mia vita?
Che già presso il fin ne vedo?
Ch'io mi separi da Alfredo!
Ah, il supplizio è si spietato,
Che morir preferiro.

Germont.

E grave il sacrifizio,
Ma pur, tranquilla udite.
Bella voi siete e giovane—
Col tempo—

Violetta.

Ah, più non dite—v'intendo—
M' è impossibile—Lui solo amar vogl'io.

Germont.

Sia pure—ma volubile sovente è l'uom.

Violetta (colpita).
Gran Dio!

Germont.

Un di, quando le veneri
Il tempo avrà fugate,
Fia presto il tedio a sorgere—
Che sarà allor!—pensate—
Per voi non avran balsamo
I più soavi affetti!
Da un genitor non furono
Tai nodi benedetti.

Violetta.

E vero!

Germont.

Ah, dunque, sperdasi
Tal sogno seduttore—
Siate di mia famiglia
L'angiol consolatore—
Violetta, deh pensateci,
Ne siete in tempo ancor.
E Dio che inspira, o giovane,
Tai detti a un genitor.

Violetta.

Thus, to the wretched, who falls, frail and
erring,

When once again she would rise, hope is
silent.

Though Heaven's indulgent, its pardon con-
ferring,

Man unforgiving to her will be.

Say to this child of thine, young, pure and
lovely,

Thou hast a victim found, whose life of
sadness

Had but one single ray of rapture and gladness

Which she will yield to her, then gladly die.

Germont.

Weep on, thou hapless one,

Weep on; I witness thy trial

In what I ask of thy selfdenial.

Bear up, thou noble heart, triumph is nigh.

Violetta.

Now command me.

Germont.

Tell him that thou lovest him **not**.

Violetta.

He'll not believe.

Germont.

Then leave him.

Violetta.

He'll follow.

Germont.

Well, then—

Violetta.

Embrace me as thy daughter, then will my
heart be strong.
(They embrace.)

Ere long, restored you'll find him; but sad
beyond all telling.

Then, to console him, from the arbor approach him.
(Points to the garden and sits down to write.)

Germont.

What art thinking?

Violetta.

Cosi alla misera, ch' è un di caduta,

Di più risorgere speranza è muta!

Se pur benefico le ìndulga Iddio

L'uomo implacabile per lei sarà.

Dite alla giovine si bella e pura.

Ch'avvi una vittima, della sventure

Cui resta un unico raggio di bene

Che a lei il sagrifica e che morrà.

Germont.

Piangi, piangi, o misera,

Supremo il veggo è il sagrifizio

Ch'orati chieggo.

Sento nell' anima già le tue pene

Coraggio, è il nobile cor vincerà.

Violetta.

Imponete.

Germont.

Non amarlo ditegli.

Violetta.

Nol crederà.

Germont.

Partite.

Violetta.

Seguirammi.

Germont.

Allor.

Violetta.

Qual figlia m'abbraciate—forte così sarò.
(S'abbracciano.)

Tra breve ei vi fia reso, ma afflitto oltal
ogni dire;

A suo conforto di colà volerete.
(Indicandogli il giardino, va ver iscrivere.)

Germont.

O che pensate!

Violetta.

If you my thoughts could know, you would
then oppose me.

Germont.

Generous-hearted! How can I e'er repay
thee?

Violetta.

I shall die! let not my memory
By him be execrated,
But let my woes and trials dark
To him be all related.
This sacrifice o'erwhelming
I make of love to duty,
Will be the end of all my woe,
The last sigh of my heart.

Germont.

No, noble heart, thou still shalt live!
A bright fate shall redress thee;
These tears announce the happy day
That Heav'n will send to bless thee.
This sacrifice unbounded
You make of love to duty,
So noble is, 'twill soon a glow
Of pride to you impart.

Violetta.

Some one comes, retire now.

Germont.

Oh, how my heart is grateful!

Violetta.

We meet no more forever!
(They embrace.)

Both.

May you be happy—Heav'n bless thee!
(GERMONT goes out by the garden door.)

SCENE VI—VIOLETTA, then ANNINA, then ALFRED.

Violetta.

Oh, grant me strength, kind Heaven!
(Sits down, writes, and then rings the bell.)

Annina.

Do you require me?

Violetta.

Yes; take and deliver thou this letter.

Annina
(looks at the direction with surprise).

Oh!

Violetta.

Sapendo, v' opporreste al pensier mio.

Germont.

Generosa!—e per voi che far poss' io?

Violetta
(tornando a lui).

Morrò—la mia memoria;
Non fia ch' ei maledica,
Se le mie pene orribili
Vi sia chi almen gli dica.
Conosca il sacrifizio
Ch' io consumai d'amor.
Che sarà suo fin l'ultimo
Sospiro del mio cor.

Germont.

No, generosa, vivere,
E lieto voi dovrete,
Mercè di queste lagrime
Dal cielo un giorno avrete,
Premiato il sacrifizio
Sarà del vostro cor.
D'un' opra cosi nobile
Andrete fiera allor.

Violetta.

Quì giunge alcun; partite!

Germont.

Ah, grato v' è il cor mio!

Violetta.

Non ci vedrem più, forse.
(S'abbracciano.)

A due.

Felice siate—Addio!
(GERMONT esce la porta del giardino.)

SCENA VI—VIOLETTA, poi ANNINA, quindi ALFREDO.

Violetta.

Dammi tu forza, o cielo!
(Siede, scrive, poi suona il campanelle.)

Annina.

Mi chiedeste?

Violetta.

Sì, reca tu stessa questa foglio.

Annina
(ne guarda la direxione, a se na mestra sorpresa).

Oh!

Violetta.

Be silent; go directly.
                    (Exit Annina.)
I must write to him now. What shall I
    say?
Where shall I find the courage?
                    (Writes, then seals the letter.)

Alfred   (coming in).

What now?

Violetta   (conceals the letter).

Nothing.

Alfred.

Wert writing?

Violetta.

Yes—no—

Alfred.

What strange confusion! To whom wert
    writing?

Violetta.

To thee.

Alfred.

Give me the letter.

Violetta.

No—directly.

Alfred.

Forgive me; my thoughts are quite disturbed.

Violetta   (rising).

By what?

Alfred.

News from my father.

Violetta.

Hast seen him?

Alfred.

Ah no! but he hath sent a cruel letter!
I soon expect him. At a glance he will
    love thee.

Violetta   (with agitation).

Let him not here surprise me.
Allow me to retire now, thou wilt calm him;
Then at his feet—I'll humbly fall—
                    (Scarcely restraining her tears.)
He cannot will that we should part—we
    shall be happy—
Because thou lov'st me, Alfred—is it not
    so?

Violetta.

Silenzio—va all'istante.
                    (ANNINA parte.)
Ed or si scriva a lui—che gli dire?
Chi men darà il coraggio?
                    (Scrive e poi suggella.)

Alfredo.

Che fai?

Violetta   (nascendendo la lettera).

Nulla.

Alfredo.

Scrivevi? ·

Violetta.

No—sì—   (Confusa.)

Alfredo.

Qual turbamento?—a chi scrivevi?

Violetta.

A te.

Alfredo.

Dammi quel foglio.

Violetta.

No, per ora.

Alfredo.

Mi perdona—son io preoccupato.

Violetta   (alzandosi).

Che fu?

Alfredo.

Giunse mio padre.

Violetta.

Lo vedesti?

Alfredo.

Ah, no; un severo scritto mi lasciava—
Ma verrà—t'amerà solo in vederti.

Violetta   (molte agitata).

Ch'io quì non mi sorprenda—
Lascia che m'allontani—tu lo calma—
Ai piedi suoi mi getterò—divisi
                    (Mal frenande il piante.)
Ei più non è vorrà—sarem felici—
Perchè tu m'ami, Alfredo, non è vero?

Alfred.

>Oh, dearly! Why dost weep thus?

Violetta.

> My heart, o'ercharged, had need of weep-
> ing—I now am tranquil,
> Thou seest it?—Smiling on thee!
> > (With great effort.)
> I'll be there—'mid the flow'rs, ever near
> thee,—
> Love me, Alfred, love me as I now love
> thee.
> Farewell, love!
> > (Runs to the garden.)

SCENE VII—ALFRED, then JOSEPH, then a MESSENGER.

Alfred.

> Ah, that fond heart lives only in my de-
> votion!

(Sits down and opens a book, reads a little, then rises, and looks at the clock, which is upon the chimneypiece.)

> 'Tis late now! to-day it's doubtful
> If I shall see my father.

Joseph
> > (enters hurriedly).

> Sir, my lady has departed,
> In a carriage that awaited,
> And is already upon the road to Paris.
> Annina, too, disappeared some time before
> her.

Alfred.

> I know—be quiet.

Joseph.

> (What does this mean?)
> > (Retires.)

Alfred.

> She goes, perhaps, to hasten
> The sale of all her property.
> Annina will stay all that.

(His father is seen in the distance, crossing the garden.)

> Some one is in the garden!
> Who's there?
> > (Going out.)

Messenger
> > (at the door).

> You, sir, are Germont?

Alfred.

> I am, sir.

Alfredo.

> Oh, quanto!—perchè piangi?

Violetta.

> Di lagrime avea duopo—or son tranquilla—
> Lo vedi?—ti sorrido—
> > (Forzandosi.)
> Sarò là, tra quei fior, presso a te sempre—
> Amami, Alfredo, quant' io t'amo.—Addio.
> > (Corre in giardino.)

SCENA VII—ALFREDO, poi GIUSEPPE, indi un COMMISSIONARO, a tempo.

Alfredo.

> Ah, vive sol quel core all' amor mio!

(Siede, prende a caso un libro, legge alquanto, quand s'alza, guarda l'ora sull' orologio sovrappesto al camino.)

> E tardi; ed oggi forse.
> Più non verrà mio padre.

Giuseppe
> > (entrando frettoloso).

> La signora è partita—
> L' attendeva un calesse, e sulla via
> Già corre di Parigi.—Annina pure
> Prima di lei spariva.

Alfredo.

> Il sò, ti calma.

Giuseppe
> > (da se).

> Che vuol dir ciò!
> > (Esce.)

Alfredo.

> Va forse d' ogni avere
> Ad affrettar la perdita—
> Ma Annina la impedirà.

(Si vede il Padre attraversare in lontane il giardino.)

> Qualcuno è nel giardino!
> Chi è là?
> > (Per uscire.)

Commissionaro
> > (alla porta).

> Il Signor Germont?

Alfredo.

> Son io.

Messenger.

    Sir, a lady in a coach, gave me,

    Not far from this place, a note, to you directed.

    (Gives a letter to Alfred, is paid and departs.)

SCENE VIII—ALFRED, then GERMONT, from the garden.

Alfred.

    From Violetta! ah, why am I thus moved?

    To rejoin her, perhaps she now invites me.

      I tremble.

    Oh, Heav'n! send courage!

           (Opens and reads.)

    "Alfred, at the moment this note shall reach you"—

    Ah!

    (He utters a cry like one struck by a thunderbolt, and in turning finds himself in the presence of his father, into whose arms he throws himself, exclaiming:)

    Oh, my father!

Germont.

    My dear son!

    How thou dost suffer! restrain thy weeping,

    Return and be the glory, the pride of thy father.

    (ALFRED despairingly sits at a table, with his face concealed in his hands.)

Commissionaro.

    Una dama, da un cocchio, per voi,

    Di quà non lunge mi diede questo scritto.

    (Da una lettera ad ALFREDO, ne riceve qualche moneta, e parte.)

SCENA VIII—ALFREDO, poi GERMONT, ch'entra dal giardino.

Alfredo.

    Di Violetta!—Perchè son io commosso?—

    A raggiungerla forse ella m' invita—

    Io tremo!—Oh ciel!—Coraggio!

          (Apre e legge.)

    "Alfredo, al giungervi di questo foglio"—

        (Come fulminato, grida.)

    (Volgendosi, si trava a fronte del padre, nelle cui braccia si abbandona, esclamando:)

    Ah!—Padre mio!

Germont.

    Mio figlio!

    Oh, quanto soffri—tergi, ah, tergi il pianto—

    Ritorna di tuo padre orgoglio e vanto.

    (ALFREDO disperato siede presso il tavolino col volte tra le mani.)

DI PROVENZA IL MAR — *FROM FAIR PROVENCE'S SOIL AND SEA*   (Germont)

Di Pro - ven-za il mar il suol chi dal cor-ti can-cel-lò? chi dal
From fair Pro-vence soil and sea, Who hath won thy heart a - way, Who hath

cor-ti can-cel-lò? di Pro-ven-za il mar il suol? al na-tio ful-gen-te sol qual de-
won thy heart a-way, From fair Pro-vence soil and sea? From thy na-tive sunny clime, What strange

sti-no ti fu-rò? qual de-sti-no ti fu-rò? al na-tio ful-gen-te sol? Oh, ram-
fate caused thee to stray, What strange fate caused thee to stray From thy na-tive sun-ny clime? Oh, re-

men -ta' pur nel duol ch'i - vi gio-ja a te bril-lò, e che pa - ce co - la sol su te
mem-ber in thy woe All the joy that waits for thee, All the peace thy heart would know, On-ly

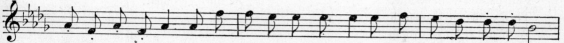

splen-de-re an-cor può, e che pa - ce co - la sol su te splen-de-re an-cor può.
there still found may be. All the peace thy heart would know, On-ly there, still found may be.

Dio mi gui - dò!——— Dio mi gui - dò! Dio mi gui - dò!
Heav'n guid - ed me!——— Heav'n guid - ed me! Heav'n guid - ed me!

Ah! thy father old and worn,
    What he felt, thou ne'er canst know.
In thine absence, so forlorn
    Seemed his home, with grief and woe.
But I find thee now again,
    If my hope doth not mislead,
If yet honor doth remain
    With its voice not mute or dead,
Heav'n sends me aid!
Wilt not answer a father's affection?
          (Embracing him.)

Alfred.

Countless furies within my heart are rag-
    ing!
Go and leave me—
        (Repulses his father.)

Germont.

How, leave thee?

Alfred.

(Oh, for vengeance!)

Germont.

Do not linger, let's go now, oh, haste thee!

Alfred.

(It was Dauphol!)

Germont.

Dost thou not hear?

Alfred.

No!

Oh! il tuo vecchio genitor
    Tu non sai quanto soffri—
Te lontano, di squallor
    Il suo tetto si copri—
Ma se alfin ti trovo ancor
    Se in me speme non falli.
Se la voce dell' onor
    In te appien non ammuti—
Dio m'esaudi!
Nè rispondi d'un padre all'affeto.
          (Abbracciando.)

Alfredo.

Mille furie divorammi il petto—
Mi lasciate—
        (Respingendolo.)

Germont.

Lasciarti!

Alfredo

(Oh, vendetta!)
        (risoluto).

Germont.

Non più indugi; partiamo—t'affretta.

Alfredo.

(Ah, fu Douphol!)

Germont.

M'ascolti tu?

Alfredo.

No!

Germont.

    All in vain then my search will have been?
    No, no, I will not chide thee now,
    But hide the past forever;
    The love that guides me ever
    Full pardon will bestow.
    Then come and drown thy cares in joy
    With me again returning;
    For thee loved ones are yearning;
    Such hopes thou'lt not destroy!
    Fond hearts at home are burning
    Their soothing care to show.

Alfred

(Arousing himself; sees upon the table the letter of FLORA, glances at its contents, and exclaims:)

    Ah! She's at the fête, then!
    Thither will I fly, and seek revenge.

Germont.

    What say'st thou? ah, stay thee!

(ALFRED departs precipitately, followed by his father.)

SCENE IX—A salon in FLORA's palace, richly furnished and lighted up. A door in the back scene, and two lateral ones. On the right, a little forward, a table, on which are cards and other implements of play. On the left a small table, with flowers and refreshments; chairs and a settee.

(FLORA, the MARQUIS, the DOCTOR, and other guests, enter from the left, and converse amongst themselves.)

Flora.

    There'll be fun here to-night with maskers
        merry;
    The Count will be their leader;
    Violetta and Alfred both will be here.

Marquis.

    Have you not heard the news then?
    Germont and Violetta are divided.

Flora.
Doctor. } Is that true?

Marquis.

    Yes, and she will come with the Baron.

Doctor.

    I saw them yesterday, appearing quite happy.
        (A noise is heard on the right.)

Flora.

    Be silent—you hear them?

All.

    Yes, our friends are coming.

Germont.

    Dunque invano trovoato t'avrò!
    No, non udrai rimproveri;
    Copriam d'oblio il passato;
    L'amor che m'ha guidato
    Sa tutto perdonar.
    Vieni, i tuoi cari in giubilo
    Con me rivedi ancora;
    A chi penò finora
    Tal gioja non niegar
    Un padre ed una suora
    T'affretta a consolar.

Alfredo

(Scuotendosi, getta a caso gli occhi sulla tavola i vede la lettera di FLORA, la scorre ed esclama:)

    Ah!—ell' è alla festa!—volisi
    L' offesa a vendicar.

Germont.

    Che dice? ah ferma!

(Fugge precipitoso seguito dal padre.)

SCENA IX—Galleria nel palazzo di FLORA, riccamente addobata ed illuminata. Una porta nel fondo e due laterali. A destra piu avanti un tavoliere con quanto occorre pei giuoco; a sinistra, ricco tavolino con fiori e rinfreschi, varie sedis e un divano.

(FLORA, il MARCHESE, il DOTTORE, ed altri invitati entrano dalla sinistra, discorrendo tra loro.)

Flora.

    Avrem lieta di maschere la notte;
    N' è duce il viscontino—
    Violetta ed Alfredo anco invitai.

Marchese.

    La novita ignorate?
    Violetta e Germont son disgiunti.

Dottore.
Flora. } Fia vero.

Marchese.

    Ella verrà qui col barone.

Dottore.

    Li vidi jeri ancor—parean felici.
        (S' ode rumore a destra.)

Flora.

    Silenzio—Udite?

Tutti

        (vanno verso la destra).
    Giungono gli amici.

SCENE X—The same, and a number of ladies masked as GIPSIES, some of whom hold a staff in the hand, some have tambourines, with which to beat time.

SCENA X—Detti, e molte Signore mascherate da ZINGARE, che entrano dalla destra.

NOI SIAMO ZINGARELLE — WE'RE GIPSIES GAY AND YOUTHFUL (Chorus)

Allegro moderato

Noi sia-mo zin-ga-rel-le ve-nu-te da lon-ta-no: d'o-
We're gip-sies gay and youth-ful, From dis-tant shores ar-riv-ing: With

gnu-no sul-la ma-no leg-gia-mo l'av-ve-nir, Se—
skil-ful art con-triv-ing The fu-ture to fore-tell, We—

con-sul-tiam le stel-le, con-sul-tiam le stel-le null' av-via noi d'os-cu-ro no, null'
read the plan-ets truth-ful, read the plan-ets truthful, Their se-crets dark un-fold-ing, all their

av-via noi d'os-cu-ro, e i ca-si del fu-tu-ro pos-sia-mo al-trui pre-
se-crets dark un-fold, The realms of fate be-hold-ing, We can your for-tunes

dir. Se—con-sul-tiam le stel-le null' av-via noi d'os-cur, e i ca-si del fu-
tell. We—read the plan-ets truth-ful, Their se-crets dark un-fold, The realms of fate be-

tu-ro pos-sia-mo al-trui pre-dir, e i ca-si del fu-tu-ro, e—i ca-si del fu-
hold-ing, We can your for-tunes tell, The realms of fate be-hold-ing, We can thus your fortunes

tur e i ca-si del fu-tu-ro pos-sia-mo al-trui, pos-sia-mo al-trui pre-
tell, All the realms of fate be-hold-ing, we thus can tell, For-tunes we thus can

dir e_ i ca - si del fu - tu ro, e_ i ca - si del fu - tur, e_ i ca - si del fu-
tell, All the realms of fate be-hold-ing, We can thus your for-tunes tell, All the realms of fate be-

tu - ro_ pos - sia - mo al - trui, pos-sia-mo al-trui pre - dir.
hold - ing, We thus can tell, for-tunes we thus can tell.

First Gipsy
   (examining the hand of FLORA).
Let's see now. You, fair lady,
Have rivals gay and sprightly.
	1. Zingara
	   (prendono la mano a FLORA, e la osservano).
	Vediamo?—Voi, signora,
	Rivali alquante avete.

Second Gipsy
   (examining the hand of the MARQUIS).
And you, if we read rightly,
Are not the type of truth.
	2. Zingara
	   (fanno lo stesso al MARCHESE).
	Marchese, voi non siete
	Model di fedeltà.

Flora (to the MARQUIS). You play me false already? I'll take good care to pay you.	*Flora* (al MARCHESE). Fate il galante ancora? Ben vo' me la paghiate.
Marquis (to FLORA). Ah, what the deuce thus say you? The charge is base untruth.	*Marchese* (a FLORA). Che diacin vi pensate? L' accusa è falsità.
Flora. The fox, howe'er disguising, Will yet be low and vicious; Gay Marquis, be judicious, Or else you may repent.	*Flora.* La volpe lascia il pelo, Non abbandona il vizio— Marchese mio, giudizio, O vi faro pentir.

All.
Let now a veil oblivious
Be o'er the past extended;
What's done may not be mended,
But future wrongs prevent.
   (FLORA and the MARQUIS shake hands.)
	Tutti.
	Su via, si stenda un velo
	Sui fatti del passato;
	Già quel ch' è stato è stato,
	Badiano al l'avvenir.
	   (FLORA ed il MARCHESE si stringono la mano.)

SCENE XI—The same; GASTON and others, masked as Spanish Mattadores, and others as Piccadores, who enter in a lively manner from the right.

Gaston and Tenors.

We are Mattadores from Madrid, so famous;
Bold and valiant in Bull-fights all name us;
Just arrived here, to join with discretion
In the fun of the "Fat ox" procession.
If a tale may command your attention,
You will find us gallants of pretention.

SCENA XI—Detti, GASTONE ed altri mascherati di Mattadori e Piccadori spagnuoli, ch'entrano vivacemente dalla destra.

Gastone e Mattadori.

Di Madride noi siam mattadori,
Siamo i prodi del circo de' tori;
Testè giunti a godere del chiasso
Che a Parigi si fa pel Bue grasso;
E una storia se udire vorrete,
Qualti amanti noi siamo, saprete.

All the Others.
   Yes, yes, bravi! go on now relating.
   With much pleasure we'll listen.

Gaston and Chorus.
   Hear then.

Gli Altri.
   Sì, sì, bravi; narrate, narrate;
   Con piacere l'udremo.

Gastone e Mattadori.
   Ascoltate.

E PIQUILLO UN BEL GAGLIARDO — *YOUNG PIQUILLO* (Gaston and Chorus)

E__ Pi-quil-lo un bel__ ga-gliar-do bi-sca-gli-no mat-ta-dor,
Young Pi-quil-lo, gay__ and dar-ing, Was__ a val-iant mat-ta-dor,

for-te il brac-cio, fie-ro il guar-do, del-le gio-stre e-gli è sig-nor.
Strong his arm was, proud his bear-ing, In__ all sports, the prize he bore.

D'An-da-lu-sia gio-vi-net-ta fol-le-men-te in-na-mo-rò;
One of Spain's fair maids en-chant-ing, With this youth fell mad-ly in love:

ma-la bel-la ri-tro-set-ta. co-sì al gio-va-ne__ par-lò:
But__ the maid, ere fa-vors grant-ing, Bade__ him thus his val-or prove—

Cin-que to-ri in un__ sol gior-no vo' ve-der-ti ad at-ter-rar,
"Five stout bulls, in one brief morn-ing I would see__ thee meet and slay;

e se vin-ci, al tuo__ ri-tor-no ma-no e cor-ti vo'__ do-nar.
If suc-cess-ful, here re-turn-ing, Hand and heart shall thee re-pay."

Sì__ gli dis-se il mat-ta-do-ro al-le gio-stre mos-se il piè;
Then the mat-ta-dor__ as-sent-ed, To__ the tri-al led__ the way;

cin - que to - ri vin - ci - to - re   sull' a - re - na e - gli sten - dè,
Five fierce bulls, in turn pre - sent - ed,   *His strong arm did van-quish that day,*

cin - que to - ri vin - ci - to - re   sull' a - re - na e - gli sten - dè.
Five fierce bulls, in turn pre - sent - ed,   *His strong arm did van-quish that day.*

Flora and Others.

Bravely he with courage daring
Did his gallantry display!
While his love, with strength unsparing,
He declared in such gallant way.

Gaston and Chorus.

Then, 'mid plaudits loud, returning
To the maid, with winning grace,
Took the prize with blushes burning,
Held her fast in love's embrace.

Others of the Chorus.

Proofs we Mattadores thus render,
How we can vanquish all the fair!

Gaston.

Here, the hearts are far more tender,
We content with trifling are.

All.

Yes, let's try now to discover
All the various moods of fate;
The arena we uncover,
And for all bold players wait!

(The men take off their masks—some walk about, while others commence playing.)

SCENE XII—The same, and ALFRED; then VIOLETTA with the BARON; afterwards, a servant.

All.

Alfred!—you!

Alfred.

Yes, my kind friends.

Flora.

Violetta?

Alfred.

I don't know.

All.

What cool indifference! Bravo! We'll now commence to play.

(GASTON shuffles the cards, ALFRED and others put up their stakes. VIOLETTA enters, leaning on the arm of the BARON.)

Gli Altri.

Bravo invero il mattadore
Ben gagliardo si mostrò,
Se alla giovine l' amore
In tal guisa egli provò.

Gastone e Mattadori.

Poi, tra plausi, ritornato
Alla bella del suo cor,
Colse il premio desïato
Dal a fede, dall' amor.

Gli Altri.

Con tai prove i Mattadori
San le amanti conquistar!

Gastone e Mattadori.

Ma diù sen più miti i cori;
A noi basta folleggiar.

Tutti.

Sì, sì allegri—Or pria tentiamo
Della sorte il vario umor.
La palestra dischiudiamo
Agli audaci giuocator.

(Gli uomini si tolgono la maschera, chi passeggia e chi s accinge a giuocare.)

SCENA XII—Detti, ed ALFREDO, quindi VIOLETTA coi BARONE; un Servo a tempo.

Tutti.

Alfredo!—Voi!

Alfredo.

Sì, amici.

Flora.

Violetta?

Alfredo.

Non ne so.

Tutti.

Ben disinvolto!—Bravo!—Or via, giuocar
Si può.

(GASTONE si pone a tagliare; ALFREDO ed altri puntano, VIOLETTA entra al braccia del BARONE.)

Flora
> (going to meet them).
>
> Here comes the guest most welcome.

Violetta.
> To your kind wish I yielded.

Flora.
> Thanks to you, also, Baron, for your polite acceptance.

Baron
> (softly to VIOLETTA).
>
> Germont is here! do you see him?

Violetta.
> (Heav'n! 'tis he, truly!)   I see him.

Baron.
> Let not one word escape you, addressed to this Alfred!

Violetta.
> (Why, ah, why came I hither?   In mercy, Heaven, thy pity send to me!)

Flora.
> Sit here beside me.   Tell me now, what new and strange is passing.

(To VIOLETTA, making her sit beside her on the settee. The DOCTOR approaches them while they are conversing in an undertone. The MARQUIS converses with the BARON. GASTON continues to play. ALFRED and others stake, and the rest walk about.)

Alfred.
> A four-spot!

Gaston.
> Ah! thou hast won it.

Alfred.
> Unfortunate in loving, makes fortunate in gaming—
> > (Stakes again and wins.)

All.
> Still he remains the victor.

Alfred.
> O I shall gain this evening, and with my golden winnings,
> To the green fields returning, I shall again be happy.

Flora.
> Singly?

Alfred.
> No, no. With some one like her who once was with me, but fled and left me!

Flora.
> (andandole incontro).
>
> Qui desïata giungi.

Violetta.
> Cessi al cortese invito.

Flora.
> Grata vi son, Barone, d' averlo pur gradito.

Barone
> (piano a VIOLETTA).
>
> Germont è qui! il vedete?

Violetta.
> Cielo!—egli è vero!
> > (Da sè.)
>
> Il vedo.

Barone.
> (piano a VIOLETTA).
>
> Da voi non un sol detto si volga a questo Alfredo.

Violetta
> (da sè).
>
> Ah, perchè venni incauta! Pieta di me, gran Dio!

Flora.
> Meco t' assidi; narrami—quai novità vegg' io?

(A VIOLETTA, facendola sedere presso dis è sul divano. Il DOTTORE si avvicina ad esse. che commessamente conversano. Il MARCHESE si trattiene a parte col BARONE; GASTONE taglia; ALFREDO ed altri puntano altri passegiano.)

Alfredo.
> Un quattro!

Gastone.
> Ancora hai vinto!

Alfredo.
> Sfortuna nell' amore vale fortuna al giuco.
> > (Punta e vince.)

Tutti.
> E sempre vincitore!

Alfredo.
> Oh, vincerò stàssera; e l' oro guadagnato
> Poscia a goder fra' campi ritornerò beato.

Flora.
> Solo?

Alfredo.
> No, no, con tale, che vi fu meco ancor,
> Poi mi sfuggia.

Violetta.

  (Oh, Heaven!)

Gaston
          (to ALFRED, pointing to VIOLETTA)
  Some pity show.

Baron
          (with ill-restrained anger).
  Beware!

Violetta
          (softly to the BARON).
  Be calm, or I must leave you.

Alfred
          (carelessly).
  Did you address me, Baron?

Baron
          (ironically).
  You are in such good fortune
  I fain would try against you.

Alfred.
  Yes? I accept your challenge.

Violetta.

  (Who'll aid me? Death seems approaching.
  O Heaven, look down and pity me!)

Baron
          (staking).
  Here at the right one hundred.

Alfred
          (staking).
  I, at the left one hundred.

Gaston
          (dealing off).
  An ace there, a knave, too; thou'st won it!
          To ALFRED.)

Baron.
  Wilt double?

Alfred.
  A double be it.

Gaston
          (dealing off).
  A four-spot—a seven.

Alfred.
  Then I'm again victorious.

All.
  Bravely indeed! good fortune seems partial to Alfred!

Violetta
          (da sè).
  Mio Dio!

Gastone
          (ad ALFREDO indic. VIOLETTA).
  Pietà di lei.

Barone
          (ad ALFREDO, con mal frenata ira).
  Signor!

Violetta
          (piano al BARONE).
  Frenatevi, o vi lascio.

Alfredo
          (disinvolto).
  Barone, m' appellaste?

Barone
          (ironico).
  Siete in si gran fortuna,
  Che al gioco mi tentaste.

Alfredo.
  Sì!—la disfida accetto.

Violetta
          (da sè).
  Che fia?—morir mi sento!
  Pietà, gran Dio, di me!

Barone
          (punta).
  Centro luigi a destra.

Alfredo
          (punta).
  Ed alla manca cento.

Gastone
          (ad ALFREDO).
  Un asso—un faute—hai vinto!

Barone.
  Il doppio?

Alfredo.
  Il doppio sia.

Gastone
          (tagliando).
  Un quattro, un sette—

Tutti.
  Ancora!

Alfredo.
  Pur la vittoria è mia!

Coro.
  Bravo davver!—la sorte è tutta per Alfredo.

Flora.

Ah! for the rustic dwelling the **Baron** pays expenses.

Alfred
(to the BARON).

Now we'll go on!

Servant
(entering).

The banquet is ready!

Flora.

Let's go then.

All
(starting).

Let's go, then.

Alfred
(to the BARON).

Shall we our game continue?

Baron.

At present, no, we cannot;
Ere long, my losses I'll regain.

Alfred.

At any game that suits you.

Baron.

Our friends we'll follow. After—

Alfred.

Whene'er you call, you'll find me.

(All retire through a door in the centre—the stage left empty for a moment.)

SCENE XIII—VIOLETTA returns, breathless, followed by ALFRED.

Violetta.

I have asked him to come hither.
Will he do so? And will he hear me?
Yes, he will, for bitter hate
Controls him more than my sad accents.

Alfred.

Didst thou call me? What dost wish for?

Violetta.

Quickly leave this place, I pray you;
Danger o'er you is suspended.

Alfred.

Ah! you're clearly comprehended.
E'en so base you then believe me?

Violetta.

Ah no, no, never!

Alfred.

But what then fear you?

Flora.

Del villeggia la spesa farà il Baron, già il vedo.

Alfredo
(al BARONE)

Seguite pur!

Serve.

La cena è pronta.

Flora.

Andiamo.

Coro
(avviandosi)

Andiamo.

Alfredo
(tra loro a parte)

Se continuar v' aggrada—

Barone.

Per ora nol possiamo.
Più tardi la rivincita.

Alfredo.

Al gioco che vorrete.

Barone.

Seguiam gli amici; poscia—

Alfredo.

Sarò qual mi vorrete.

(Tutti entrano nella porta di mezze: la scena rimane un istante vuota.)

SCENA XIII—VIOLETTA, che ritorna affannata. indi ALFREDO.

Violetta.

Invitato a qui seguirmi,
Verrà desso?—vorrà udirmi?
El verrà—chè l' odio atroce
Puote in lui più di mia voce.

Alfredo.

Mi chiamaste?—Che bramate?

Violetta.

Questi luoghi abbandonate—
Un periglio vi sovrasta.

Alfredo.

Ah, comprendo!—Basta, basta—
E si vile mi credete?

Violetta.

Ah, no, mai.

Alfredo.

Ma che temete?

Violetta.

Ah, I fear the Baron's fury.

Alfred.

An affair of death's between us;
Should this hand in death extend him,
One sole blow would then deprive thee
Both of lover and protector;
Would such losses sorrow give thee?

Violetta.

But if he should prove the victor!
There behold the sole misfortune,
That, I fear, would prove me fatal.

Alfred.

Pray, what care you for my safety?

Violetta.

Hence, depart now, this present instant!

Alfred.

I will go, but swear this moment,
Thou wilt follow now and ever,
Where I wander.

Violetta.

Ah, no; never.

Alfred.

No! and never!

Violetta.

Go, thou, unhappy! and forget me.
Thus degraded, go and leave me!
At this moment, to escape thee
I a sacred oath have taken!

Alfred.

To whom? tell me! who could claim it?

Violetta.

One who had the right to name it.

Alfred.

'Twas Dauphol?

Violetta

(with great effort).

Yes.

Alfred.

Then thou lov'st him?

Violetta.

Ah, well, I love him.

Alfred

(Runs furiously, throws open the doors and cries out:)

Come hither all!

Violetta.

Tremo sempre del Barone.

Alfredo.

E tra noi mortal quistione—
S' ei cadrà per mano mia
Un sol colpo vi torria
Coll' amante il protettore—
V'atterrisce tal sciagura?

Violetta.

Ma s' ei fosse l' uccisore!—
Ecco l' unica sventura—
Ch' io pavento a me fatale!

Alfredo.

La mia morte!—Che ven cale?

Violetta.

Deh, partite, e sull' istante.

Alfredo.

Partiro, ma giura innante
Che dovunque seguirai
I miei passi.

Violetta.

Ah no, giammai.

Alfredo.

No!—giammai!

Violetta.

Va, sciagurato,
Scorda un nome ch' è infamato—
Va—mi lascia sul momento—
Di fuggirti un giuramento
Sacro io feci.

Alfredo.

E chi potea?

Violetta.

Chi diritto pien ne avea.

Alfredo.

Fu Douphol?

Violetta

(con supremo sforzo).

Sì.

Alfredo.

Dunque l'ami?

Violetta.

Ebben—l'amo.

Alfredo

(corre furente sulla porta, e grida:)

Or tutti a me.

SCENE XIV—The same, and all the others, who enter in confusion.

All.

Did you call us? Now what would you?

Alfred

(pointing to Violetta, who leans fainting against the table).

Know ye all this woman present?

All.

Who? Violetta?

Alfred.

Know ye, too, her base misconduct?

Violetta.

Ah! spare me!

All.

No!

Alfred.

All she possessed, this woman here
Hath for my love expended.
I blindly, basely, wretchedly,
This to accept, condescended.
But there is time to purge me yet
From stains that shame, confound me.
Bear witness all around me
That here I pay the debt.

(In a violent rage he throws a purse at Violetta's feet—she faints in the arms of Flora and the Doctor. At this moment Alfred's father enters.)

SCENE XV—The same, and Germont, the elder, who has entered at the last words.

All.

Oh, to what baseness thy passions have
  moved thee.
To wound thus fatally one who has loved
  thee!
Shameless traducer of woman defenceless,
Depart hence, speedily, scorned and despised!

Germont.

Of scorn most worthy himself doth render
Who wounds in anger a woman tender!
My son, where is he? No more I see him;
In thee, Alfred, I seek him, but in vain.

Alfred

(aside).

Ah! yes, 'twas shameful! a deed, abhorrent,
A jealous fury—love's maddening torrent

SCENA XIV—Detti, e Tutti i precedenti, che confusamente ritornano.

Tutti.

Ne appellaste?—Che volete?

Alfredo

(additando Violetta che abbattuta, si appeggia al tavolino).

Questa donna conoscete?

Tutti.

Chi? Violetta?

Alfredo.

Che facesse
Non sepete?

Violetta.

Ah, taci.

Tutti.

No.

Alfredo.

Ogni suo aver tal femina
Per amor mio sperdea.
Io cicco, vile, misero,
Tutto accettar potea,
Ma, è tempo ancora! tergermi,
Da tanta macchia bramo
Qui testimon vi chiamo,
Che qui pagato io l'ho!

(Alfredo getta con furente sprezzo il ritratto di Violetta ai piedi di lei, ed essa sviene tra le braccia di Flora e del Dottore. In tal momento entra il Padre.)

SCENA XV—Detti, ed il Signor Germont, ch' entra all' ultime parole.

Tutti.

Oh, infamia orribile tu commettesti!—
Un cor sensibile cosi uccidesti!—
Di donne ignobile insultatore,
Di qua allontanati, ne desti orror.

Germont.

Di sprezzo degno sè stesso rende
Chi pur nell' ira la donna offende.
Dov' è mio figlio?— Più non lo vedo.
In te più Alfredo—trovar non so.

Alfredo

(da se).

Ah, sì!—che feci!—ne sento orrore!
Gelosa smania, deluso amore

Oppressed my senses, destroyed my reason;
From her, no pardon shall I obtain!
To fly and leave her, strength was denied me,
My angry passions did hither guide me.
But now that fury is all expended,
Remorse and horror to me remain.

Germont
(aside).

I 'mid them only know what bright virtues
Dwell in that sad heart so torn and bleed-
ing.
I know she loves him, all else unheeding;
Yet must, tho' cruel, silent remain.

Gaston. ⎱Oh! thou dost suffer! but cheer thy
Flora. ⎰ heart,
Here in thy trials we all take part.
Kind friends surround thee, care o'er thee
keeping,
Cease then thy weeping, thy tears restrain.

Baron.

This shameful insult against this lady
Offends all present; behold me ready
To punish outrage! Here now declaring
Such pride o'erbearing I will restrain.

Violetta
(reviving).

Ah, loved Alfred, this heart's devotion
Thou canst not fathom yet—its fond emo-
tion!
Thou'rt still unknowing that at the meas-
ure
Of this displeasure. 'tis proved again.
But when, hereafter, the truth comes o'er
thee,
And my affection shall rise before thee,
May Heav'n in pity then spare thee re-
morse.
Ah, tho' dead, still loving, ever will I re-
main!

(GERMONT takes his son with him; the BARON follows;
VIOLETTA is taken into an adjoining room by the DOCTOR
and FLORA, and the rest disperse.

END OF THE SECOND ACT.

Mi strazian l'alma—più non ragiono—
Da lei perdono—più non avro.
Volea fuggirla—non ho potuto!—
Dall' ira spinto, son qui venuto!—
Or che lo sdegno ho disfogato,
Me sciagurato!—rimorso io n' ho.

Germont
(da se).

Io sol fra tutti so qual virtude
Di quella misera il sen racchiude—
Io so che l'ama, che gli è fedele;
Eppur, crudele, tacer dovrò!

Gastone. ⎱Oh quanto peni! ma pur fi cor
Flora. ⎰Quì soffre ognuno del tuo dolor;
Fracari amici quì sei soltanto,
Rascinga il pianto che t' inondò.

Barone.

A questa donna l' atroce insulto
Qui tutti offese ma non inulto
Fia tanto oltraggio! Provar vi voglio
Che il vostro orgoglio fiaccar saprò!

Violetta
(riavendosi).

Alfredo, Alfredo, di questo core
Non puoi comprendere tutto l'amore;
Tu non conosci che fino a prezzo
Del tuo disprezzo—provato io l' ho!
Ma verrà giorno, in che il saprai—
Com' io t'amassi confesserai—
Dio dai rimorsi ti salvi allora
Io penta ancora—pur t'amero.

(GERMONT trae seco il figlio; il BARONE lo segue. VIOLETTA
è condotta in altra stanza dal DOTTORE e da FLORA; gli
altri si disperdano.)

FINE DELL' ATTO SECONDO.

ACT III.

SCENE 1—Violetta's bed-room. At the back a bed, with the curtains partly drawn. A window shut by inside shutters. Near the bed a table with a bottle of water, a crystal cup, and different kinds of medicine on it. In the middle of the room a toilet-table and settee; a little apart from which is another piece of furniture, upon which a night-lamp is burning. Chairs and other articles of furniture. On the left a fireplace with a fire in it.

(Violetta discovered sleeping on the bed—Annina, seated near the fireplace, has fallen asleep.)

Violetta   (awaking).

Annina!

Annina   (waking up, confusedly).

Did you call me?

Violetta.

Poor creature, were you sleeping?

Annina.

Yes, but forgive me.

Violetta.

Bring me here some water.
                    (Annina does so.)
Look out now—is it yet daylight?

Annina.

It is seven.

Violetta.

To a little light give access.
(Annina opens the blinds, and looks into the street.)

Annina.

Doctor Grenvil has come—

Violetta.

A friend most faithful!
I wish to rise, assist me!

(She rises, but falls again—then, supported by Annina, she walks slowly towards the settee, and the Doctor enters in time to assist her to sit upon it—Annina places cushions about her.

SCENE II—The same, and the Doctor

Violetta.

How kind in you thinking of me thus early.

Doctor   (feeling her pulse).

Yes, are you somewhat better?

Violetta.

With pain I suffer; but my mind is tranquil.
A priest came here last evening and brought me comfort.
Ah! religion is a solace to us in affliction.

Doctor.

Last night, how were you?

ATTO III.

SCENA I—Camera da letto di Violetta. Nel fondo e un letto con cortine mezzo tirate; una finestra chiusa da imposte interne; presso il letto uno sgabello su cui una bottiglia d'acqua, una tazza di cristallo, diverse medicine. A meta della scena una toilette, vicino un canapè; più distante un altro mobile, su cui arde un lume da notte, varie sedie ed altri mobili. La porta è a sinistra; di fronte v' è un caminnetto con fuoco acceso.

(Violetta dorme sul letto—Annina, seduta presso il caminetto, è pure addormita.)

Violetta   (destandosi).

Annina!

Annina   (svegliandosi confusa).

Comandate?

Violetta.

Dormivi, poveretta?

Annina.

Sì, perdonate.

Violetta.

Dammi d' acqua un sorso.
                    (Annina esequisce.)
Osserva, è pieno il giorno?

Annina.

Son sett' ore.

Violetta.

Dà accesso a un pò di luce.
                    (Apre le imposte, e guarda nella via.)

Annina.

Il Signor Grenvil!

Violetta.

Oh, il vero amico!—
Alzar mi vo'—m'aita.

(Si alza e ricade; poi sostenuta da Annina va lentamente verso il canapè, ed il Dottore entra in tempo per assisterla ad adagiarvisi—Annina vi aggiunge dei cuscini.)

SCENA II—Dette, ed il Dottore.

Violetta.

Quanta bontà!—Pensaste a me per tempo!

Dottore   (le tocca il polso).

Or come vi sentite?

Violetta.

Soffre il mio corpo, ma tranquilla ho l'alma.
Mi confertò ier sera un pio ministro.
Religione è sollievo a' sofferenti.

Dottore.

E questa notte?

Violetta.

Calmly I slept till morning.

Doctor.

Then keep your courage.

Convalescence, haply, is not far distant.

Violetta.

Oh! that's a kind deception

Allowed to all physicians.

Doctor
                    (pressing her hand).

Farewell now.   I'll return soon.

Violetta.

Be not forgetful.

Annina
        (in a low tone, whilst following the DOCTOR).

Is her case more hopeful?

Doctor.

But few brief hours of life are to her re-
    maining.

                    (Departs.)

SCENE III—VIOLETTA and ANNINA

Annina.

Now cheer thy heart.

Violetta.

Is this a festal morning?

Annina.

Paris gives up to folly—'tis carnival day.

Violetta.

Ah, 'mid this gay rejoicing, Heav'n alone
    doth know

How the poor are suffering!   What amount

Is there in that casket?

Annina
                    (opens and counts).

Just twenty louis'.

Violetta.

Take from it ten, and give them to the
    needy.

Annina.

Little you'll have remaining.

Violetta.

Oh, 'twill for me be plenty!
                    (Sighing.)

You can bring then my letters here.

Annina.

But you?

Violetta.

Ebbi tranquillo il sonno.

Dottore.

Coraggio adunque—la convalescenza

Non è lontana.

Violetta.

Oh, la bugia pietosa

A' medici è concessa.

Dottore
                    (stringendole la mano).

Addio—a più tardi.

Violetta.

Non mi scordate.

Annina
            (piano al DOTTORE, accompagnandolo).

Come va, Signore?

Dottore.

La tisi non le accorda che poch' ore.

            (Piano, e parte.)

SCENA III—VIOLETTA ed ANNINA.

Annina.

Or fate cor.

Violetta.

Giorno di festa è questo?

Annina.

Tutta Parigi impazza—è carnevale.

Violetta.

Oh, nel comun tripudio, sallo il cielo

Quanti infelici gemon!—Quale somma

V' ha in quello stipo?
                    (Indicandolo.)

Annina
                    (l'apre e conta).

Venti luigi.

Violetta.

Dieci ne reca ai poveri tu stessa.

Annina.

Poco rimanvi allora.

Violetta.

Oh, mi sarà bastante!—
                    (Sospirando.)

Cerca poscia mie lettere.

Annina.

Ma voi?

Violetta.

Naught will occur. You need not long be absent.

(Exit ANNINA.)

SCENE IV—VIOLETTA takes a letter from her bosom and reads:

"Thou hast kept thy promise. The duel took place. The Baron was wounded, but is improving. Alfred is in foreign countries. Your sacrifice has been revealed to him by me. He will return to you for pardon. I too will return. Haste to recover, thou deservest a bright future.

"GEORGIO GERMONT."

Violetta.

'Tis too late!

Still watching and waiting, but to me they come not!

(Looking in the mirror.)

Oh, how I'm changed and faded!

But the Doctor doth exhort me to be hopeful;

Ah! thus afflicted, all hope is dead within me!

Violetta.

Nulla occorrà, sollecita, se puoi.

(ANNINA esce.)

SCENA IV—VIOLETTA, che trae dal seno una lettera, e legge

"Teneste la promessa—La disfida ebbe luogo; il Barone fu ferito, però migliora Alfredo è in stranio suolo; il vostro sacrifizio io stesso gli ho svelato. Egli a voi tornerà pel suo perdono; io pur verrò—Curatevi—mertaste un avvenir migliore.

"GIORGIO GERMONT."

Violetta.

E tardi!—

(Desolata.)

Attendo, attendo—Nè a me giungon mai?

(Si guarda nello specchio.)

Oh, come son mutata!—

Ma il Dottore a sperar pure m' esorta!—

Ah, con tal morbo ogni speranza è morta.

ADDIO DEL PASSATO — *FAREWELL TO THE BRIGHT VISIONS* (Violetta)

Ad - di - o — del pas - sa - to — bei — sog - ni - ri - den - ti, le
Fare - well to — the bright vis - ions I — once fond - ly — cher - ish'd, Al -

ro - se - del — vol - to — gia — so - no — pal - len - ti l'a - mo - re d'Al -
read - y — the — ro - ses — that — deck'd me have — per - ish'd, The love of Al

fre - do — per - fi - no — mi nan - ca, con - for - to, so - ste - gno dell'
fre - do — is lost, past re - gain - ing, That cheer'd me when faint - ing, my

a - ni - ma stan-ca,   con - for-to,   so -
spir-it sus-tain-ing,   *sole com-fort,*   *sup -*

ste-gno ah! del-la tra - via-ta_ sor - ri-di al - de - si - o, a
port, ah! Pi - ty the_ stray one,_ and_ send her con-so - la - tion, Oh,

le - i deh per - do - na tu ac - co - gli-la, o Di-o!   ah!_ tut - to_
*par - don her trans-gress-ions, and grant her sal - va-tion.   Ah!_ thus all_*

_ tut-to fi - ni, or_ tut - to, tut - to fi - ni._
_ of life doth_ end, Ah!_ thus_ all of_ life doth_ end._

The sorrows and enjoyments of life will
soon be over,
The dark tomb in oblivion this mortal form
will cover!
No flowers for my grave, no kind friends
o'er me weeping.
No cross, with my name, mark the spot
where I'm sleeping.
Ah, pity the stray one, and send her con-
solation!
Oh, pardon her transgressions, and send her
salvation.
Thus all of life doth end.
(Sits down.)

BACCHANALIAN CHORUS (outside).
Room for the prize-ox, with honors appear-
ing!
Gay flowers and vine-leaves in garlands he's
wearing.
Room for the gentlest one of like creation,
Give him, with fife and horn, loud saluta-
tion.
Now, Parisians, make concession.
Clear the way for our procession.

Le gioie, i dolori fra poco avran fine;
La tomba al mortali di tutto è confine!—
Non lagrima o fiore avrà la mia fossa,
Non croce, col nome, che copra quest' ossa!—
Ah, della traviata sorridi al desio,
A lei, deh perdona, tu accoglila, o Dio!
Or tutto finì.

(Siede.)

CORO BACCANTE (esterno).
Largo al quadrupede sir della festa
Dio fiori e pampini cinto la testa—
Largo al più docile d' ogni cornuto.
Di corni e pifferi abbia il saluto.
Parigini, date passo al trionfo del Bue grasso
L' Asia, nè L' Africa vide il più bello,
Vanto ed orgoglio d' ogni macello—
Allegre maschere, pazzi garzoni,
Tutti plauditelo con canti e suoni!—
Parigini, etc.—

Asia or Afric ne'er saw one to beat him!

He is the proud boast of all those who meet
  him.

Maskers and merry boys with fun o'erflowing,

Songs in his honor raise, plaudits bestowing.

Now, Parisians, etc.

SCENE V—VIOLETTA, and ANNINA, returning hastily.

Annina   (hesitating).

  My lady—

Violetta.

  What has happened?

Annina.

  This morning—'tis true then? You are
    really better?

Violetta.

  Yes; but why?

Annina.

  Will you promise to be tranquil?

Violetta.

  Yes, what wouldst tell me?

Annina.

  I would now prepare you

  For a pleasure unexpected.

Violetta.

  For a pleasure, thou sayest?

Annina.

  Yes, gentle mistress.

Violetta.

  Alfred! Ah, thou hast seen him?

  He comes! oh, haste thee!

(ANNINA makes signs with her hand in the affirmative, and
goes to open the door.)

SCENE VI—VIOLETTA, ALFRED, and ANNINA.

Violetta.

  Alfred! (Going towards the door.)

Alfred.

(ALFRED enters, pale with emotion, and they throw themselves into each others' arms, exclaiming:)

Violetta.

  Beloved Alfred!

Alfred.

  My own Violetta!

  Ah! I am guilty! I know all, dearest.

Violetta.

  I only know, love, that thou art near me!

SCENA V—Detta, ed ANNINA, che torna frettolosa.

Annina   (esitando).

  Signora—

Violetta.

  Che t' accadde?

Annina.

  Quest oggi, è vero? vi sentite meglio?

Violetta.

  Sì; perchè?

Annina.

  D' esser calma promettete?

Violetta.

  Si; che vuoi dirmi?

Annina.

  Prevenir vi volli—

  Una gioia improvvisa.

Violetta.

  Una gioia!—dicesti?

Annina.

  Si, o Signora.

Violetta.

  Alfredo!—Ah, tu il vedesti!

  Ei vien! l' affretta.

(ANNINA afferma col capo, e va ad aprire la porta.)

SCENA VI—VIOLETTA, ALFREDO ed ANNINA.

Violetta.

  Alfredo?—(Andando verso l' uscio.)

Alfredo

(comparisce, pallido pella commozione, ed ambidue gettandosi le braccia al collo, esclamano:)

Violetta.

  Amato Alfredo!

Alfredo.

  Mia Violetta!—

  Colpevol sono—so tutto, o cara—

Violetta.

  Io so che alfine reso mi sei.

Alfred.

    This throbbing heart will show how I still love thee.

    I could no more exist, if from thee parted.

Violetta.

    If thou hast found me yet with the living,

    Believe that grief and woe no more can kill.

Alfred.

    Forget the sorrow in love forgiving,

    Both sire and son thou'lt pardon still.

Violetta.

    Ask me for pardon? 'Tis I am guilty,

    Thus rendered by my loving heart.

Both.

    No earthly power, nor friend, beloved,

    Shall tear us hence apart.

Alfredo.

    Da questo palpito, s' io t'ami, impara—

    Senza te esistere più non potrei.

Violetta.

    Ah, s'anco in vita m' hai ritrovata,

    Credi, che uccidere non può il dolor.

Alfredo.

    Scorda l'affanno, donna adorata.

    A me perdona e al genitor.

Violetta.

    Ch' io ti perdoni?—La rea son io;

    Ma solo amore tal mi rendè.

Alfredo e Violetta.

    Null' uomo o demone, angelo mio.

    Mai più staccarti portà da me.

PARIGI, O CARA — *GAY PARIS, DEAREST* (Duet, Alfred and Violetta)

de'_ cor si af - fan - ni com-pen-so a-vra - i la_ mia sa - lu - te
Joy_ shall re - pay_ thee for_ each dark sor - row, Thy_ cheek, so fad - ed,

ri - fio - ri - rà. So - spi-ro e lu - ce tu mi sa - ra - i, tut - to il fu -
shall bloom a - gain. Life, light and breath from me thou shalt bor - row, O'er com - ing

ALF.

tu - ro near - ri - de - Pa - ri - gi, o ca - ra, noi las - ce -
years, love, bright smiles shall Gay Par - is, dear - est, we'll leave with
reign.

VIOL.

re - mo. De cor-si af-fan - ni com-pen-so a-vra - i, tut-to il cre - a - to near-ri-de-
gladness, Joy shall re - pay us for each dark sor - row, O'er com - ing years, love, bright smiles shall

ALF.   VIOL.

La vi - tau - ni - ti tra - scor - re - re - mo, De' cor-si af-
reign. Our lives u - nit - ed, fly we from sad - ness, Joy shall re-

fan - ni com-pen-so a-vra - i; tut-to il fu - tu - re near ri - de -
pay_ thee for each dark sor - row, O'er com - ing years, love, bright smiles shall

VIOL.

rà, de' cor - si af - fan - ni com-pen - so a-
reign. For ev - 'ry dark sor - row some joy_ shall re-

ALF.

de' cor-si af- fan - ni com - pen-so a - vrai,
For all thy sor - rows thou'lt com-fort find.

vra - i, la mia sa - lu - te, la mia sa - lu - te ri-fio-ri - rà, ri-fio-ri,
pay thee, My cheek so fad - ed, My cheek so fad - ed, shall bloom a-gain, shall bloom a-

ah! si la tua sa - lu - te, la tua sa - lu - te ri-fio-ri - rà.
Ah! yes, thy cheek so fad - ed, thy cheek so fad - ed, shall bloom a - gain.

rà.
gain.

De' cor-si af-fan - ni com-pen-so a
Joy shall re - pay thee for ev-'ry

Pa-ri-gio ca - ra, noi la-sce-re-mo, si, noi
Gay Par-is, dear - est, we'll leave with glad-ness, Yes, we'll

vra - i, tut-toil cre - a - to ne ar-ri-de - rà.
sor - row, O'er com-ing years, love, bright smiles shall reign.

la - sce - re - mo, la vi-tau-ni - ti
leave with glad - ness, Our lives u - nit - ed,

De cor-si af-fan - ni com-pen-so a-vra - i tut-toil fu-
Joy shall re - pay thee for ev-'ry sor - row, O'er com-ing

tra-scor-re - re-mo, noi tra - scor - re -
fly we from sad - ness, we will fly from

tu - ro ne ar - ri - de - rà,
years, love, bright smiles shall reign.

de' cor - si af - fan - ni
For each hour of sor - row

re - mo,
sad - - ness,

de' cor - si af - fan - ni
each hour of sor - row

com - pen - so a -
joy shall re -

com - pen - so a - vra - i la mia sa - lu - te, la mia sa - lu - te ri - fio - ri -
some joy shall re - pay thee, my cheek so fad - ed, my cheek so fad - ed, shall bloom a -

vrai,
pay,

ah! sì, la tua sa - lu - te, la tua sa - lu - te ri - fio - ri -
Ah! yes, thy cheek so fad - ed, thy cheek so fad - ed, shall bloom a -

rà, ri - fio - ri - rà, ri - fio - ri - rà. De' _____ cor - si af - fan - ni,
gain, shall bloom a - gain, shall bloom a - gain. Joy _____ shall re - pay thee

rà, ri - fio - ri - rà, ri - fio - ri - rà. De' _____ cor - si af - fan - ni,
gain, shall bloom a - gain, shall bloom a - gain. Joy _____ shall re - pay thee

de' cor - si af - fan - ni com - pen - so a - vra - i, de' cor - si af - fan - ni com - pen -
for ev' - ry sor - row, shall joy re - pay thee, for ev' - ry sor - row, shall joy

de' cor - si af - fan - ni com - pen - so a - vra - i, de' cor - si af - fan - ni com - pen -
for ev' - ry sor - row, shall joy re - pay thee, for ev' - ry sor - row, shall joy

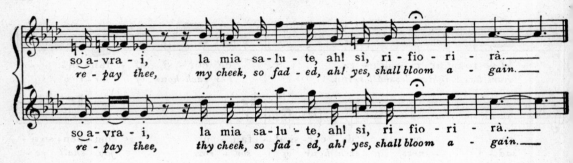

so a-vra-i,   la mia sa-lu-te, ah! sì, ri-fio-ri-rà.____
re-pay thee,   my cheek, so fad-ed, ah! yes, shall bloom a-gain.____

so a-vra-i,   la mia sa-lu-te, ah! sì, ri-fio-ri-rà.____
re-pay thee,   thy cheek, so fad-ed, ah! yes, shall bloom a-gain.____

Violetta.

Ah, no more! to church let us be going,

Our thanks to render with hearts o'erflowing.

(Staggers.)

Alfred.

'Thou'rt growing pale!

Violetta.

'Tis nothing, mark me; unlooked for pleasure can never enter

Without disturbing a heart o'erburdened.

(She sinks on a chair fainting, and her head falls backwards.)

Alfred.

Great Heaven!—Violetta!

(Alarmed, and supporting her.)

Violetta.

'Tis but the weakness

From recent illness. Now, love, I'm stronger—

See'st thou? and smiling—

(With effort.)

Alfred.

(Ah! cruel fortune!)

Violetta.

'Twas nothing! Annina, a shawl bring hither.

Alfred.

What now, love? but wait then—

Violetta.

No! I will go now.

(ANNINA presents the shawl, which she makes an effort to put on, but finds she is too weak, and exclaims:)

Great Heav'n, I cannot.

(She throws away the shawl vexedly, and sinks again on the chair.)

Alfred.

Heavens, what is it!

Go, call the Doctor.

(To ANNINA.)

Violetta.

Ah, non più—a un tempio—Alfredo, andiamo,

Del tuo ritorno grazie rendiamo.

(Vacilla.)

Alfredo.

Tu impallidisci!

Violetta.

E nulla, sai? Gioja improvvisa non entra mai,

Senza turbarlo, in mesto core.

(S' abbandona, come sfinita, sopra una sedia, col capo pendente all' indietro.)

Alfredo.

Gran Dio!—Violetta!

(Spaventato, sorreggendola.)

Violetta.

E il mio malore.

Fe debolezza—ora son forte—

Vedi?—sorrido.

(Sforzandosi.)

Alfredo.

(Ahi, cruda sorte!)

Violetta.

Fu nulla—Annina, dammi a vestire.

Alfredo.

Adesso!—Attendi.

Violetta.

No—voglio uscire.

(ANNINA le presenta una vesta ch'ella fa per indossare, impeditane dalla debolezza, exclama:)

Gran Dio!—non posso!

(Getta con dispetto la veste, e ricade sulla sedia.)

Alfredo.

Cielo, che vedo!

Va pel Dottore.

(Ad ANNINA.)

Violetta.

Ah, tell him—say that Alfred is now beside
   me.
Return'd and faithful to my affection—
Tell him I wish still to live.
      (ANNINA returns.)
      (To ALFRED.)
But though returned, love, thou hast not
   saved me,
No earthly power from the tomb can shield
   me.

SCENE VII—VIOLETTA and ALFRED.

Violetta.

Ah, cruel fate to die so young,
Tho' much I've borne of sorrow.
To die when hopes, to which I clung,
Reveal a brighter morrow!
Ah! then 'twas naught but madness.
The love to which I yielded!
In vain my heart was shielded,
Armed with faith, all, all in vain.

Alfred.

Oh, dearer far than breath or life,
Beloved one, fondly treasured!
My burning tears, in this dark hour,
With thine shall flow, unmeasured.
But, ah! far more than e'er before
I need thy fond devotion;
Yield not to sad emotion
While hope doth still remain!
   (VIOLETTA throws herself upon the lounge.)

SCENE THE LAST—The same, GERMONT, and the DOCTOR.

Germont
      (entering)

Ah! Violetta—

Violetta.

You, my friend?

Alfred.

My father—

Violetta.

Thou'st not forgot me?

Violetta.

Digli che Alfredo
E ritornato all' amor mio—
Digli che vivere ancor vogl' io.
      (ANNINA parte.)
      (Ad ALFREDO.)
Ma se tornando non m'hai salvato.
A niuno in terra salvarmi è dato.

SCENA VII—VIOLETTA ed ALFREDO.

Violetta.

Gran Dio! morir sì giovane,
Io, che penato ho tanto!
Morir si presso a tergere
Il mio si lungo pianto!
Ah, dunque fu delirio
La credula speranza;
Invano di costanza
Armato avrò il mio cor!
Alfredo—oh, il crudo termine
Serbato al nostro amor!

Alfredo.

Oh, mio sospiro,—oh, palpito
Diletto del cor mio!
Le mie colle tue lagrime
Confondere degg' io—
Or più che mai nostr' anime
Han duopo di costanza—
Ah, tutto alla speranza
Non chiudere il tuo cor!
Violetta mia, deh calmati,
M' uccide il tuo dolor.
   (VIOLETTA s'abbandona sul canapè.)

SCENA ULTIMA—Detti, GERMONT, ed il DOTTORE.

Germont
      (entrando).

Ah, Violetta!

Violetta.

Voi, signor!

Alfredo.

Mio padre!

Violetta.

Non mi scordaste?

Germont.

I redeem my promise—
And come, thou noble-hearted,
As my daughter to embrace thee.

Violetta.

Alas. too late thou comest!
Yet, in truth, I am grateful.
(They embrace.)
You see me, Grenvil? dying in the embrace
Of those I love most dearly!

Germont.

Ah, what say'st thou?
(Looking at her, aside.)
Oh, Heaven! 'tis true.

Alfred.

Oh, father, dost thou see her?

Germont.

Withhold! no more thus rend me;
For dark remorse devours my heart already!
Like the pealing of thunder each word confounds me—
Ah! incautious old father!
The wrong accomplished, now stands before me!

Violetta
(having opened a drawer over her toilet-table, she takes out a medallion, and says:)

Approach more nearly, beloved Alfred, and hear me;
Take this, a fair resemblance still
Of me in days of gladness;
A thought 'twill bring in sadness
Of her who loved thee well.

Alfred.

Oh, say not so, thou wilt not die,
But live, with love to bless me!
With such a dread bereavement
Kind Heav'n will not distress me.

Germont.

Oh, noble victim! noble sacrifice
To generous devotion!
Forgive me all the anguish
Thy heart has borne through me.

Violetta.

Should some young maiden, pure and fair,
Fresh as a flower, just blowing,

Germont.

La promessa adempio—
A stringervi qual figlia vengo al seno,
O generosa.

Violetta.

Ohimé! tardi giungeste!
Pure, grata ven sono—
(La abbraccia.)
Grenvil, vedete?—Tra le braccia io spiro
Di quanti ho cari al mondo.

Germont.

Che mai dite!
(Da se.)
Oh cielo!—è ver!
(La osserva.)

Alfredo.

La vedi, padre mio?

Germont.

Di più, non lacerarmi—
Troppo rimorso l'alma mi divora—
Quasi fulmin mi atterra ogni suo detto—
Oh, malcauto vegliardo!
Ah, tutto il mal che feci ora sol vedo!

Violetta
(frattanto avrà aperto a stento un ripostiglio della toilette e toltone un medaglione, dice:)

Prendi, quest è l'immagine
De' miei passati giorni.
A rammentar ti torni
Colei che sì t'amo.

Alfredo.

No, non morrai, non dirmelo.
Dêi vivere, amor mio—
A strazio così orribile
Qui non mi trasse Iddio.

Germont.

Cara, sublime vittima
D'un generoso amore
Perdonami lo strazio.
Recato al tuo bel core.

Violetta.

Se una pudica vergine
Degli anni suoi nel fiore

Love thee with heart o'erflowing,
Make her, I wish it, thy bride;
Show her this pictured likeness,
Say, 'tis a gift from me,
Who, now in heav'n, 'mid angels bright,
Prayeth for her, for thee.

Germont. ⎱ While yet these eyes have tears to
Doctor. ⎰ flow,
Annina. ⎰ I shall still weep, still weep for
         thee.

Go, join the blessed spirits now:
God calls thee heavenward, his own to be.

Violetta   (reviving).
'Tis wondrous!

All.
What?

Violetta   (speaking).
They all have ceased.
The paroxysms that distressed me.
Fresh life awakens within me, giving me
A vigor new and rare!
I am to life restored now!
Oh, rapture!
                (She falls upon the sofa.)

All.
Oh, heaven! Dead!

Alfred.
Violetta!

All.
May Heav'n her soul receive!

Doctor   (examining the pulse).
'Tis over!

All.
Oh, grief and woe!

A te donasse il core—
Sposa ti sia—lo vo'
Le porgi questa effigie,
Dille che dono all' è
Di chi, nel ciel tra gli angeli
Prega per lei, per te.

Germont. ⎱ Finchè avrà il ciglio lagrime
Dottore. ⎰ Io piangerò per te.
Annina. ⎰ Vola a' beati spiriti;
         Iddio ti chiama a sè.

Violetta   (alzandosi riammata).
E strano!

Tutti.
Che!

Violetta.
Cessarono
Gli spasmi del dolore.
In me rinasce, m'anima
Insolito vigore!
Ah!—io ritorno a vivere!
                (Trasalendo.)
Oh, gio—ia!
                (Ricade sul canapè.)

Tutti.
Oh, cielo!—muori!

Alfredo.
Violetta!

Tutti.
Oh, Dio!—soccorrasi.

Dottore   (dapo averle toccato il polso).
E spenta!

Alfredo e Tutti.
Oh, ⎰ rio ⎱ dolor!
    ⎱ mio ⎰

LA FORZA DEL DESTINO
(The Force of Destiny)

by

GIUSEPPE VERDI

ARGUMENT.

DONNA LEONORA has a lover, in the person of *Don Alvaro*, with whom she is on the point of eloping from the house of her father, the *Marquis of Calatrava*, when the latter enters; a scene ensues, and the *Marquis* is slain by the accidental discharge of *Don Alvaro's* pistol.

Leonora, after the death of her father, believing that *Alvaro* has deserted her, flies, and, disguised in male attire, becomes a recluse, living in a cavern, the privacy of which is secured to her by *Father Guardiano*, the superior of a religious community. Her brother, *Don Carlos di Vargas*, becomes imbued with the belief that it is his paramount duty to hunt the world through until he finds *Leonora* and her lover, and by their deaths to avenge his father's and the dishonor brought on the name he bears.

Don Carlos and *Don Alvaro*, under assumed names, and unknown to each other, being in the camp of the Italian and Spanish armies, *Alvaro* is the means of saving the life of *Don Carlos* from assassins, and they vow lasting friendship. Soon after this *Alvaro* is wounded in battle, it is supposed mortally. *Don Carlos* finds in the wounded man's possession a portrait of *Leonora*, which confirms him in his suspicion that his new friend is none other than *Alvaro*.

Alvaro, under the name of Father Raffaello, becomes a friar in a religious establishment situated in the immediate vicinity of the cavern in which *Leonora* is secluded. *Don Carlos* agains finds and compels him to fight; *Carlos* falls—this time mortally wounded. *Leonora* enters from her cavern, and the three recognize each other. *Don Carlos* calls upon his sister to embrace him ere he dies, seizes the opportunity to stab her, and then expires. *Leonora* implores the forgiveness of Heaven for *Alvaro*, who, humbled in heart by her earnest accents, throws himself penitent at her feet, and the curtain falls at the death of *Leonora*.

CHARACTERS.

IL MARCHESE DI CALATRAVA.

DONNA LEONORA,
DON CARLO DI VARGAS, } *his Children.*

DON ALVARO, *Donna Leonora's Lover.*

PREZIOSILLA, *a Young Gipsy.*

PADRE GUARDIANO,
FRA MELITONE, } *Franciscan Friars.*

CURRA, *Waiting-Woman to Leonora.*

MASTRO TRABUCO, *A Muleteer, afterwards a Pedlar.*

Alcade, a Magistrate.

A Spanish Military Surgeon.

Muleteers, Spanish and Italian Peasants, Spanish and Italian Soldiers, Franciscan Friars, Beggars, Vivandiers, Tumblers, Host, Hostess, Servants, Pedlars, Trumpeters, etc.

Scene, — SPAIN and ITALY. Time — End of the 18th Century.

LA FORZA DEL DESTINO

[THE FORCE OF DESTINY]

ATTO I	ACT I

SCENA I—Siviglia.—Una sala, tappezzata di damasco, con ritratti di famiglia, ed arme gentilizie, addobbata nello stile del secolo 18.0 pero in cattivo stato. Di fronte due finestre; quella a sinistra chiusa, l'altra a destra aperta e praticable, dalla quale si vede un cielo purissimo, illuminato dalla Luna, e cime d'alberi. Fra le finestre e un grande armadio chiuso, contenente vesti, biancherie, ecc. Ognuna delle pareti laterali ha due porte. La prima a destra della spettatore e la comune; la seconda mette alla stanza di CURRA. A sinistra in fondo e l' appartamento del MARCHESE; piu presso al proscenio quello di LEONORA. A mezza scena, alquanto a sinistra, e un tavolino coperto da tappeto di damasco, e sopra il medesimo una chitarra. vasi di fiori, due candel-abri d' argento accesi con paralumi, sola luce che schiarira la sala. Un seggiolone presso il tavolino; un mobile con sopra un oriuolo fra le due porte a destra; altro mobile sopra il quale e il ritratto, tutta figura, del MARCHESE, appoggiato alla parete sinistra. La sala sara parapettata.

Il MARCHESE DI CALATRAVA, con lume in mano, sta congedandosi da DONNA LEONORA preoccupata. CURRA viene dalla sinistra.

Marchese.

(Abbracciandola con affetto.)

Buona notte, mia figlia ! Addio, diletta !
Aperto ancora è quel verone !

(Va a chiuderlo.)

Leonora.

(Oh angoscia !)

Marchese.

Nulla dice il tuo amor ? Perchè si trista ?

(Tornando a lei.)

Leonora.

Padre—Signor—

Marchese.

La pura aura de' campi
Calma al tuo cor donova ;
Fuggisti lo straniero di te indegno
A me lascia la cura
Dell' avvenir. Nel padre tuo confida,
Che t' ama tanto.

Leonora.

Ah, padre !

SCENE I.—Seville.—A room, hung with damask, family portraits, and arms of nobility, furnished in the style of the 18th century, all, however, in a shabby condition. Two windows face the audience; that on the left is closed, that on the right open and practicable, from which is seen a clear sky, and the tops of trees, with a bright moonlight? Between the windows a large wardrobe, containing clothes, etc. Each side has two doors. The first to the right of the spectator is the common door; the second leads to CURRA's room. On the left side farthest off, is the apartment of the MARQUIS; that nearest the proscenium leads to LEONORA's room. Halfway, a little to the left, is a table with a damask cover, and on it a guitar, vases of flowers, and two lighted silver candlesticks with shades, the only light in the room. A large chair near the table; a piece of furniture with a clock on it between the two doors on the right; other furniture on the left, above which, hung against the wall, is the full-length portrait of the MARQUIS. The room is entirely enclosed.

MARQUIS OF CALATRAVA, with a light in his hand is taking leave of DONNA LEONORA, who is thoughtful. CURRA comes from the left.

Marchese

(Embracing her affectionately.)

Good night, my child ! Adieu, my dear one!
That balcony-window still open ?

(Goes and shuts it.)

Leonora.

(Oh, anguish !)

Marchese.

Not a word of love ? Why so sad ?

(Turning to her.)

Leonora.

Father—sir—

Marchese.

The pure air of the fields
Has brought peace to thy heart,
Thou hast left a stranger unworthy of thee,
And to me leave the care
Of thy future. In thy father confide,
Who so dearly loves thee.

Leonora.

Ah, my father !

Marchese.

Ebben, che t' ange ?
Non pianger, io t'adoro !

Leonora.

(Oh, mio rimorso !)

Marchese.

Ti lascio.

Leonora

(Gettandosi con effusione tra le braccia del padre.)

Ah, padre mio !

Marchese.

Ti benedica il cielo ! Addio !

Leonora.

Addio !

(Il MARCHESE bacia, riprende il lume, e va nelle sue stanze.)

SCENA II.—CURRA segue il MARCHESE, chiude la porta ond' e
uscito, e riviene a LEONORA abbandonatasi sul seggiolone piangente)

Curra.

Temea restasse qui fino a domani !
Si riapra il veron.
                    (Eseguisce.)
Tutto s'appronti. E andiamo.

Toglie dall' armadio un sacco da notte in cui ripone biancherie
e vesti.)

Leonora.

E si amoroso padre avverso
Fia tanto a' voti miei ?
No, no, decidermi non so.

Curra
              (Affaccendata.)

Che dite ?

Leonora.

Quegli accenti nel cor come pugnalia
Scendevanmi. Se ancor restava, appreso
Il ver gli avrei.

Curra
              (Smette il lavoro.)

Domani allor nel sangue
Suo saria don Alvaro,
Od a Siviglia prigioniero, e forse
Al patibol poi—

Leonora.

Taci !

Marchese.

What disturbs thee ?
Do not weep—I love thee dearly.

Leonora.

(Oh, what remorse !)

Marchese.

I leave thee.

Leonora

(Throwing herself with transport into his arms.)

Ah, dearest father !

Marchese.

Heaven bless thee ! Adieu !

Leonora.

Adieu !

(The MARQUIS kisses her, takes up a light, and goes to his room.)

SCENE II.—CURRA follows the MARQUIS, closes the door, at
which he went out, and returns to LEONORA, who has thrown herself in the chair.

Curra.

I thought he would stay till daylight !
Let us re-open the balcony.
                    (Opens it.)
Prepare everything and let us go.

(Takes travelling bag from the wardrobe, and fills it with linen
and clothes.)

Leonora.

Can so fond a father
Oppose my dearest wishes ?
No, no, I cannot leave.

Curra
              (Very busy.)

What do you say ?

Leonora.

His loving tones struck like a dagger
To my soul. Had he remained,
The truth I should have spoken.

Curra
              (Leaving off work.)

Then to-morrow
Don Alvaro would lie weltering in his
    blood,
Or be a prisoner in Seville,
And perhaps on the scaffold—

Leonora.

Be silent !

Curra.

   E tutto puesto
   Perch' egli volle amar chi non l' amava.

Leonora.

   Io non amarlo! Tu ben sai s'io l'ami!
   Patria, famiglia, padre,
   Per lui non abbandono!
   Ahi troppo!—troppo sventurata sono!
   Me pellegrina ed orfana
   Lungi dal natio nido,
   Un fato inesorabile
   Trascina a stranio lido,
   Colmo di triste immagini,
   Da' suoi rimorsi affranto
   E il cor di questa misera
   Dannato a eterno pianto.
   Ti lascio, ahimè, con lacrime,
   Dolce mia terra!—Addio!
   Ahimè, non avrà termine
   Si gran dolore!—Addio!

Curra.

   M' aiuti, signorina—
   Più presto andrem.

Leonora.

   S' ei non giungesse?
         (Guarda l' orologio.)
   E tardi.
   Mezzanotte è suonata!
         (Contenta.)
   Ah no, più non verrà!

Curra.

   Quale romore!
   Calpestio di cavelli!

Leonora

         (Corre al verone.)
   E desso!

Curra.

   Era impossibil
   Ch' ei non venisse!

Leonora.

   Ciel!

Curra.

   Bando al timore.

Curra.

   And all because he loves one
   Who does not return his love.

Leonora.

   Does not return it?
   Well thou knowest I love him!
   Country, family, father, for him do I not
     leave?
   Ah me!—I am indeed unhappy!
   A friendless wanderer,
   Far from my native land!
   An inexorable fate
   Drags me to a foreign country,
   Overwhelmed in dire woe,
   Crushed with deep remorse,
   My miserable spirit
   Is condemned to constant grief.
   With tears, alas! I leave thee,
   My own sweet native land.—Adieu!
   Never, never will end
   This bitter woe!—Adieu!

Curra.

   Help me, signora—   15:00
   We shall the sooner be ready.

Leonora.

   If he should not come?
         (Looks at the clock.)
   It is late—
   Midnight has struck!
         (Contentedly.)
   Ah no, he will not come.

Curra.

   What noise is that?
   It is the tread of horses!

Leonora

         (Running to balcony.)
   It is he!

Curra.

   It was impossible
   That he should fail to come.

Leonora.

   Heavens!

Curra.

   Away with fear.

SCENA III. Detti.—DON ALVARO senza mantello, con giusta-cuore a maniche larghe, e sopra una giubbetta da Majo, rete sul capo, stivali, speroni, entra dal verone e si getta tra le braccia di LEONORA.

SCENE III.—The same,—DON ALVARO, without a cloak, wearing a tight vest, with large sleeves and a slashed doublet, a net on his head, boots and spurs, he enters throught the balcony, and throws himself into LEONORA'S arms.

Alvaro.

Ah, per sempre, o mio bell' angelo,
Ne congiunse il cielo adesso
L'universo in questo amplesso
Con me veggo giubilar.

Leonora.

Don Alvaro !

Alvaro.

Ciel, che t' agita ?

Leonora.

Presso è il giorno.

Alvaro.

Da lung' ora
Mille inciampi tua dimora
M'han vietato penetrar;
Ma d' amor si puro e santo
Nulla opporsi può all' incanto,
E Dio stesso il nostro palpito
In letizia tramutò.

(A CURRA.)

Quelle vesti dal verone
Getta.

Leonora

(A CURRA.)

Arresta.

Alvaro

(A CURRA.)

No, no !

(A LEONORA.)

Seguimi;
Lascia omai la tua prigiane.

Leonora.

Ciel ! risolvermi non so !

Alvaro.

Pronti destrieri di già ne attendono;
Un sacerdote ne aspetta all' ara !
Vieni, d'amore in sen ripara
Che Dio dal cielo benedirà!
E quando il sole, nume dell' India,
Di mia regale stirpe signore,
Il mondo innondi del suo splendore,
Sposi, oh diletta, ne troverà.

Alvaro.

Ah, for ever, my lovely angel,
Heaven now unites us !
All the universe is glad
With me, in this embrace.

Leonora.

Don Alvaro !

Alvaro.

Oh Heaven, why thus agitated ?

Leonora.

The dawn is nigh.

Alvaro.

For a long time
Many obstacles kept me
From reaching thy dwelling;
But nought can stay the power
Of a love so pure and holy,
And Heaven itself our fears
Changes to contentment.

(To CURRA.)

Those vestments
Throw from the balcony.

Leonora

(To CURRA.)

Stay.

Alvaro

(To CURRA.)

No, no !

(To LEONORA.)

Follow me.
Leave thy prison now for ever.

Leonora.

Oh Heaven ! I cannot decide !

Alvaro.

Swift steeds are waiting,
A priest at the altar attends !
Come, shelter find in the love
Which Heaven will richly bless.
And when the sun, the god of India,
Sire of my royal race
Shall flood the earth with splendor,
Oh, beloved ! it will find us united.

Leonora.

E tarda l' ora.

Alvaro

(A CURRA.)

Su via t' affretta !

Leonora.

Ancor sospendi !

Alvaro.

Eleonora !

Leonora.

Diman.

Alvaro.

Che parli ?

Leonora.

Ten prego aspetta !

Alvaro

(Assai turbato.)

Diman.

Leonora.

Domani si partirà.
Anco una volta il padre, veder desio;
E tu contento, gli è ver, ne sei?

Sì perchè m'ami—

(Si confonde.)

Nè opporti dèi—
Oh anch' io, tu il sai— t' amo io tanto !
Ne son felice ! oh cielo, quanto !
Gonfio di gioia ho il cor ! Restiamo !

Sì, Don Alvaro, io t'amo, io t' amo !

(Piange.)

Alvaro.

Gonfio hai di gioia il core—e lagrimi!

Come un sepolcro tua mano è gelida !
Tutto comprendo—tutto, signora.

Leonora.

Alvaro !—Alvaro !

Alvaro

Eleonora !

(Lunga pausa.)

Saprò soffrire io solo. Tolga Iddio
Che i passi miei per debolezza segua—

Leonora.

The hour is late.

Alvaro

(To CURRA.)

Away--make haste !

Leonora

(To CURRA.)

Wait awhile !

Alvaro.

Eleonora !

Leonora.

To-morrow.

Alvaro.

What sayest thou ?

Leonora.

I pray thee, wait !

Alvaro

(Much disturbed.)

To-morrow.

Leonora.

To-morrow we will go .
Once more my father
I desire to see !
Thou art willing—is it not so ?
Yes, for thou lovest me, and wilt not
refuse.
I too, thou knowest, love thee !

(Confusedly.)

Am I not happy ? O heaven !
How my heart swells with joy !—Let us
wait !
Yes, Alvaro, I love thee ! I love thee !

(Weeps.)

Alvaro.

Thy heart swells with joy—then why
these tears ?
Thy hand is cold as death !
I understand all, signora—all !

Leonora.

Alvaro !—Alvaro !

Alvaro.

Eleonora !

(A long pause.)

I can suffer alone. Heaven forbid
That weakly thou shouldst follow me—

Sciolgo i tuoi giuri. Le nuziali tede Sarebbero per noi segnal di morte, Se tu, com' io non m' ami—se pentita—	I absolve thy vows. The nuptial tie Would be for us the stroke of death, If thou lovest not as I do—if, repenting—
Leonora.	*Leonora.*
Son tua, son tua col core e colla vita !	I am thine ! thine with heart and soul !

AH! SEGUIRTI FINO — *AH! I'LL FOLLOW* Air (Leonora)

Ah! se - guir - ti fi - no a - gl'ul - ti - mi Con - fi - ni del - la
Ah! I'll fol - low ev - er in thy path To earth's far con - fines

ter - ra; Con te sfi - dar - im - pa - vi - da Di rio des - tin la
wing - ing, And bold - ly with thee I de - fy The ter - rors war is

guer - ra; Mi fia pe - ren - ne gau - di - o D'e - te - rea vo - lut - ta. Ti
bring - ing, I'll share all dan - gers by thy side, With love and joy e - late, I'll

se - guo, an - diam di - vi - der - ci, Il fa - to, no,— no, non po - tra.
fol - low thee what - e'er— may be - tide, We win— a hap - py fate.

Alvaro.	*Alvaro.*
Sospiro, luce ed anima Di questo cor che t' ama ; Finchè mi batta un palpito, Far paga ogni tua brama Il solo ed immutabile Desio per me sarà. Mi segui ! Andiam, dividerci Il mondo non potrà.	Hope, light and life Of the heart that adores thee ! Till my pulses beat no more My sole desire will be To meet thy every wish, To cherish thee for aye. Follow me—let us go ! The world has no power to part us.
(S' avvicinano al verone, quando ad un tratto si sente a sinistra un aprire e chiudere di porte.)	(They approach the balcony when of a sudden is heard the opening and shutting of a door.)
Leonora.	*Leonora.*
Quale rumor !	What is that noise ?
Curra	*Curra*
(Ascoltando.)	(Listening.)
Ascendono le scale !	Some one is coming up stairs !

Alvaro.

Presto, partiamo !

Leonora.

E tardi.

Alvaro.

Allor di calma
E duopo.

Curra.

Vergin santa !

Leonora

(A ALVARO.)

Colà t' ascondi !

Alvaro.

No. Degg' io difenderti.

(Traendo una pistola.)

Leonora.

Ripon quell' arma—contro ai genitore
Vorresti ?

Alvaro.

No, contro me stesso.

(Ripone la pistola.)

Leonora.

Orrore !

SCENA IV.—Dopo vari colpi apresi con istrepito la porta del
fondo a sinistra, ed il MARCHESE DI CALATRAVA *entra infuriato
brandendo una spada e seguito da due servi con lume.*

Marchese.

Vil seduttor !—infame figlia !

Leonora

(Correndo a' suoi piedi.)

No, padre mio !

Marchese.

Più non lo sono.

(La respinge.)

Alvaro

(Al MARCHESE.)

Il solo colpevole son io
Ferite ' vendicatevi !

(Presentandogli il petto.)

Marchese

(Al ALVARO)

No la condotta vostra
Da troppo abbietta origine uscito vi dim-
　　ostra.

Alvaro.

Quick !　Let us go !

Leonora.

Too late !

Alvaro.

Well, then,
We must be calm and **firm**.

Curra.

Holy Virgin !

Leonora

(To ALVARO.)

Conceal thyself there !

Alvaro.

No. I must defend thee.

(Drawing out a pistol.)

Leonora.

Put back that weapon—
Wouldst use it 'gainst my father ?

Alvaro.

No, against myself.

(Replaces the pistol.)

Leonora.

Horrible !

SCENE IV.—After repeated blows the door at the back, on the
left, is burst open, and the MARQUIS OF CALATRAVA enters, enraged,
sword in hand, and followed by two servants with lights.

Marchese.

Vile seducer !—shameless daughter !

Leonora

(Rushing to his feet.)

No, father, no.

Marchese.

I am no longer thy father.

(Repulsing her.)

Alvaro

(To the MARQUIS.)

I alone am guilty.
Strike !—avenge thyself !

(Presenting himself.)

Marchese

(To ALVARO.)

No, thy conduct
Shows thee of origin too low.

Alvaro.

    Signor Marchese !
          (Risentito.)

Marchese
          (A LEONORA.)

    Scostati—
          (Ai Servia.)

    S' arresti l' empio !

Alvaro
          (Cavando nuovamente la pistola)

    Guai
    Se alcun di voi si move.
          (Ai Servi, che retrocedono.)

Leonora
          (Currendo a lut.)

    Alvaro, oh ciel, che fai !

Alvaro
          (Al MARCHESE.)

    Cedo a voi sol—ferite !

Marchese.

    Morir per mano mia !
    Per mano del cranefice tal vita estinta fia.

Alvaro.

    Signor di Calatrava,
    Pura siccome gli angeli è vostra figlia—
    Il giuro—reo son io solo. Il dubbio
    Che l' ardir mio qui desta, si tolga colla
      vita.
    Eccomi inerme.

(Getta la pistola, che percuote al suolo, scarica il colpo, e ferisce mortalmente il MARCHESE.)

Marchese.

    Io muoio !

Alvaro
          (Disperato.)

    Arma funesta !

Leonora
          (Correndo a' piedi del padre.)

    Aita !

Marchese
          (A LEONORA)

    Lungi da me—
    Contamina tua vista la mia morte !

Leonora.

    Padre !

Alvaro.

    Marquis !
          (Excitedly.)

Marchese
          (To LEONORA.)

    Stand aside—
          (To the Servants.)

    Seize the wretch !

Alvaro
          (Again taking out his pistol.)

    Approach me, if you dare !
          (To the Servants, who retire.)

Leonora
          (Running to him.)

    Alvaro, what madness is this ?

Alvaro
          (To the MARQUIS.)

    To thee alone I yield—strike !

Marchese.

    Not by my hand you die ;
    So base a life belongs only to the execu-
      tioner.

Alvaro.

    Signor de Calatrava, your child
    Is innocent as an angel ;
    I alone am guilty.
    Let the doubt which my rashness has raised
    Be dispelled with my life. Behold me
      unarmed.

(Throws away the pistol, which in falling, goes off, and kills the MARQUIS.)

Marchese.

    I am dying !

Alvaro
          (In despair.)

    Ill-fated weapon !

Leonora
          (Rushing to her father.)

    Help !

Marchese
          (To LEONORA.)

    Begone—
    Thy presence disgraces me in death!

Leonora.

    Father !

Marchese.

    Ti maledico !

           (Cade tra le braccia dei Servi.)

Leonora.

    Cielo pietade !

Alvaro.

    Oh sorte !

    (I Servi portano il MARCHESE alle sue stanze, mentre DON ALVARO trae seco verso il verone la sventurata LEONORA. Cade la tela.)

            FINE DELL' ATTO PRIMO:

Marchese.

    My curse upon thee !

           (Falls into the Servants' arms.)

Leonora.

    Have mercy, kind Heaven !

Alvaro.

    O cruel fate !

    (The Servants bear the MARQUIS to his apartments, whilst DON ALVARO drags the unhappy LEONORA towards the balcony. The Curtain falls.)

            END OF THE FIRST ACT

ATTO II.

SCENA I. Villaggio d' Hornachuelos e vicinanze.—Grande cucina d'una Osteria a pian terreno. A sinistra, e la porta d' ingresso che da sulla via; di fronte una finestra ed un credenzone con piatti, ecc. A destra, in fonda un gran focolare ardente con varie pentole;.piu vicino alle bocca-scena breve scaletta che mette ad una stanza, la cui porta e praticabile. Da un lato gran tavola apparecchiata con sopra una lucerna accesa. L' Oste e l' Ostessa che non parlano, sono affaccendati ad ammanir la cena. L' ALCADE e seduto presso al foco; uno STUDENTE presso la tavola. Alquanti MULATTIERI, fra quali MASTRO TRABUCO, ch' e al dinanzi sopra un suo basto. Due CONTADINI. due CONTADINE, la SERVA, ed un MULATTIERE. ballano la SEGUIDILLA. Sopra altra tavola, vino, bicchieri fiaschi, una bottiglia d'acquavite.

L'ALCADE, uno STUDENTE, MASTRO TRABUCO, MULATTIERI, PAESANI FAMIGLI, PAESANE ecc. A tempo LEONORA in vesti virile.

Coro.

　Hola, hola, hola !
　Ben giungi, o mulattier,
　La notte a riposar.
　Hola, hola, hola !
　　Qui devi col bicchier
　　Le forze ritemprar !

(L' Ostessa mette sulla tavola una grande zuppiera.)

Alcade.

　La cena è pronta.
　　　　　　(Sedendosi alla mensa.)

Tutti
　　　　(Prenendo posto presso la tavolo.)

　A cena, a cena !

Studente
　　　　　(Frattanto sul d' avanti dice.)

　(Ricerco invan la suora e il eduttore.)
　　Perfidi !

Coro
　　　　　　(All' ALCADE.)

　Voi la mensa benedite ?

Alcade.

　Può farlo il Licenziato.

Studente.

　Di buon grado. Benedetto
　E il pane che il Padre del ciel ci manda.

Tutti
　　　　　　(Sedendo.)

　Cosi sia.

ACT II.

SCENE I. The Village of Hornachuelos and neighborhood. A large kitchen on the ground-floor of an Inn. On the left, the entrance-door leading to the road, facing the audience; a window, and a large dresser, with plates, etc. On the right, at the back, a large fireplace, with cauldrons, etc., nearer the proscenium, a short staircase, leading to a room which has a practicable door. On one side a large table, laid out, and on it a lighted lamp. The Host and Hostess, who do not speak, are busy preparing the supper. The ALCADE is seated near the fire; a STUDENT s seated near the table. Some MULETEERS, amongst others MASTER TRABUCO, who is in front, leaning on his pack saddle. Two male and two female PEASANTS, the female SERVANT and a MULETEER dance the Seguidilla. Upon another table, wine, glasses, flasks, and a bottle of brandy.

The ALCADE, a STUDENT, MASTER TRABUCO, MULETEERS, PEASANTS ATTENDANTS, FEMALE PEASANTS, etc. Later LEONORA, in male attire.

Chorus.

　Hurrah, hurrah, hurrah !
　Now welcome, O muleteer,
　Who comes to pass the night ;
　Hurrah, hurrah, hurrah !
　Here is the brimming cup,
　Thy strength thou canst restore.

(The Hostess places a large soup-tureen on the table.)

Alcade.

　The supper is ready.
　　　　　　(Seating himself at table.)

All
　　　　　　(Taking their places at table.)

　To supper, to supper !

Student
　　　　　　(In the foreground.)

　In vain my sister and her betrayer I seek !
　The ingrates !

Chorus
　　　　　　(To the ALCADE.)

　Will you not ask a blessing ?

Alcade.

　The Licentiate can do it.

Student.

　With all my heart. Blessed be
　The bread that Heaven sends us from
　　　above.

All
　　　　　　(Seated.)

　Amen.

Leonora

Presentandosi alla potra della stanza a destra, che terra socchiusa

(Che vedo !—mio fratello !)

(Si ritira.)

(L' Ostessa avra gia distribuito il riso e siede cogli altri. In-eguito e servito altro piatto. TRABUCO e in disparte, sempre appog-iato al suo basto.

Alcade

(Assaggiando.)

Buono.

Studente

(Mangiando.)

Eccellente !

Mulattieri.

Par che dica mangiami.

Studente

(All' Ostessa.)

Tu das epulis accumbere divum.

Alcade.

Non sa Latino ma cucina bene.

Studente.

Viva l'Otessa !

Tutti.

Evviva !

Studente.

Non vien Mastro
Trabuco ?

Trabuco.

E Venerdi.

Studente.

Digiuna ?

Trabuco.

Appunto.

Studente.

E quella personcina con lei guinta?

SCENA II. Detti, e PREZIOSILLA, ch' entra saltellando.

Preziosilla.

Viva la guerra !

Leonora

(Appearing at the door of the room on the right, which she keeps half closed.)

What do I see !—my brother !

(She retires.)

(The Hostess has already distributed the rice, and sits down with the others. Other dishes are served up. TRABUCO on one side leans on his pack-saddle.)

Alcade

(Tasting.)

Capital !

Student

(Eating.)

Excellent !

Muleteer.

It seems to say, 'Come, eat me.'

Student

(To the Hostess.)

Tu das epulis accumbere divum.

Alcade.

She does not know Latin, but she cooks
well.

Student.

Long live the Hostess !

All.

Hurrah !

Student.

Does not Master Trabuco
Come to supper ?

Trabuco.

It is Friday.

Student.

Oh, you are fasting ?

Trabuco.

Just so.

Student.

And the little person who came with you '

SCENE II. The same, enter PREZIOSILLA, dancing.

Preziosilla.

Success to war !

Tutti.
    Preziosilla !—Brava !
    Brava !

Studente.
    Qui, presso a me.

Tutti.
    Tu la ventura.
    Dirne potrai.

Preziosilla.
    Chi brama far fortuna ?

Tutti.
    Tutti il vogliam.

Preziosilla.
    Correte allor soldati.
    In Italia, dov' è rotta la guerra
    Contro al Tedesco.

Tutti.
    Morte
    Ai Tedeschi !

Preziosilla.
    Flagel d' Italia eterno
    E de' figliuoli suoi.

Tutti.
    Tutti v' andremo.

Preziosilla.
    Ed io sarò con voi.

All.
    Preziosilla !—Bravo !
    Bravo !

Student.
    Here, sit by me.

All.
    You will be able
    To tell us our fortunes.

Preziosilla.
    Who wishes to make his fortune ?

All.
    Everyone wishes it.

Preziosilla.
    Haste, then, to Italy, as soldiers,
    Where war has broken out
    Against the Germans.

All.
    Death
    To the Germans !

Preziosilla.
    Of Italy and her sons
    They are the eternal scourge.

All.
    We will all go.

Preziosilla.
    And I shall be with you.

AL SUON DEL TAMBURO —*THE DRUM GAILY BEATING* (Preziosilla and Chorus)

Al suon del tam - bu - ro, Al brio del cor - sie - ro, Al nu - go - lo az-
The drum gai - ly beat - ing The hors - es swift fleet - ing, And vol - leys re -

zur - ro, Del bron - zo guer - rier! Dei cam - pi al su - sur - ro S'e-
peat - ing Give glo - ry to war! The bu - sy sounds a - bout the camp Drive

sal - ta il pen - sier! E bel - la la guer - ra, E bel - la la
anx - ious thought a - far! In bat - tle is glo - ry, In bat - tle is

guer - ra! Ev - vi - va la guer - ra, ev - vi va!
glo - ry! Hur - rah,— then, hur - rah, hur - rah, hur - rah!

E so-lo ob-bli-a-to Da vi-le chi muo-re; Al bra-vo sol-
No cow-ard can ev-er Make no-ble en-deav-er, But he-roes in

da-to Al ve-'ro va-lor E pre-mio ser-ba-to Di glo-ria d'o-
sto-ry Re-mem-ber'd will be: To them be the glo-ry By for-tune's de-

D.C. ℀ al Fine (Turning from one to the other)

nor! Se vie-ni, fra-tel-lo, Sa-rai ca-po-ra-le, E
cree! Good luck shall o'er-take you, A cor-po-ral make you, A

tu col-lon-nel-lo, E tu ge-ne-ra-le Il di-o fur-fan-tel-lo dall'
co-lonel's place take you, A gen-'ral you'll be; Be brave in the bat-tles When

D.C. ℀ al Fine

ar-co im-mor-ta-'le Fa-ro—di cap-pel-lo Al bra-vo uf-fi-zial.
mus-ket-ry rat-tles, And forth in dis-or-der The foe-men will flee.

Studente.	Student.
E che riserbasi Allo studente ?	And for the student What is reserved ?
(Le presenta la mano.)	(Holding out his hand.)
Preziosilla	*Preziosilla*
(Osservando.)	(Observing him)
O tu miserrime Vicende avrai.	Miserable man, Sorrow shortly will find thee.
Studente.	*Student.*
Che di'?	What do you say ?
Preziosilla	*Preziosilla*
(Fissandolo.)	(Earnestly)

Non mente
Il labbro mai—
Ma a te—carissimo,
Non presto fè
                    (Poi sotto voce.)
Non sei studenti ;
Non dirò niente,
Ma, gnaffe, a me,
Non se la fa,—
No per mia fè.
Tral la la là !

SCENA III.   Detti, e PELLEGRINI, che passao da furoi.

Voci Ie.
                    (Lontane.)
    Ah, pietade o Signor !

Voci 2e.
    Pieta di noi.

Voci Ie.
    Sii clemente, o Signor !

Voci 2e.
    Pietà di noi.

Voci Ie.
                    (Piu vicine.)
    Te lodiamo, o Signor !

Voci 2e.
    Pietà di noi.

Voci Ie.
    Deh, pietade, o Signorà!

Voci 2e.
    Pietà di noi.

Tutti.
    Chi sono ?
                    (Alzandosi e scoprendosi.)
Alcade.
    Pellegrini,
    Che vanno al giubileo.

Leonora.
    (Ricomparendo agitatissima sulla stessa porta.)
    Fuggir potessi.

Coro.
    Che passino attendiamo.

Alcade.
    Ebben, preghiam noi pure.

My lips
Ne'er utter falsehoods,
But on thee, dear sir,
I don't much rely.
                    (In an undertone.)
No student art thou.
I'll say nothing,
But with me, forsooth,
The ruse has failed,
By my faith !
Tra la la la !

SCENE III.   The same, and PILGRIMS, passing outside

1st Voice
                    (In the distance.)
    Pardon, gracious Heaven.

2nd Voice.
    Have pity on us.

1st Voice.
    Grant us grace !

2nd Voice.
    Have pity on us.

1st Voice
                    (Nearer.)
    We praise thee, O Heaven !

2nd Voice.
    Have pity on us.

1st Voice.
    We thank thee, O Heaven !

2nd Voice.
    Have pity on us.

All.
    Who are these ?
                    (Rising and showing themselves.)
Alcade.
    They are Pilgrims,
    Who are going to the jubilee.

Leonora
    (Appearing, in great agitation, at the same door.)
    If I could only escape !

Chorus.
    Let us wait till they pass.

Alcade.
    And let us also pray.

Coro.

Si preghiamo.

Tutti

(*Lasciando la mensa s' inginocchiano.*)

Suo noi concordi e supplici,
Stendi la man, Signore ;
Dall' infernal malore
Ne salvi tua pietà.

Leonora.

(Ah, da un fratello salvami
Che anela il sangue mio ;
Se tu nol vuoi, gran Dio,
Nessun mi salverà !)

(*Rientra nella stanza chiudendone la porta. Tutti riprendono
i loro posti. Si passano un fiasco.*)

Studente.

Viva la buona compagnia !

Tutti.

Viva !

Studente.

Salute qui, l' eterna gloria poi !

(*Alzando il bicchiere*)

Tutti.

Cosi sia.

(*Fanno altrettanto.*)

Studente.

Già cogli angioli, Trabuco ?

Trabuco.

E che ?—con questo inferno ?

Studente.

E quella personcina con lei giunta,
Venne pel giubileo ?

Trabuco.

Nol so.

Studente.

Per altro.
E gallo, oppur gallina ?

Trabuco.

De' forastier non bado che al danaro.

Studente.

Molto prudente !

(*Poi all' ALCADE.*)

Chorus.

Yes, let us pray.

All

(*Leaving the table and kneeling down.*)

O'er us, imploring Thee,
Extend Thy hand, O Lord,
From the power of ill
Let Thy mercy save us.
And mercy protect us.

Leonora.

Ah, from a brother save me,
Who thirsts for my blood ;
Thy hand alone, O Lord,
Can save me from his wrath.

(*Re-enters the room and shuts the door. All reseat themselves
and pass the bottle.*)

Student.

Long live this goodly company.

All.

Hurrah !

Student.

Health here, and happiness hereafter !

(*Raises the goblet.*)

All.

So be it.

(*They do the same.*)

Student.

Already dreaming, Trabuco ?

Trabuco.

What ? in this uproar ?

Student.

And the little person who came with you
Does she go to the Jubilee ?

Trabuco.

I do not know.

Student.

By the by,
Is it man or woman ?

Trabuco.

With strangers, I only think of the money

Student.

Most prudent !

(*To the ALCADE.*)

Ed ella
Che giungere la vide— perchè a cena.
Non vien ?

Alcade.
L'ignoro.

Studente.
Dissero chiedesse
Acqua ed aceto.—Ah ah !—per rinfrescarsi.

Alcade.
Sara.

Studente.
E ver ch' è gentile, e senza barba ?

Alcade.
Non so nulla.

Studente.
(Parlar non vuol !) Ancora
                    (To TRABUCO.)
A lei.
Stava sul mulo,
Seduta o a cavalcioni ?

Trabuco
                    (Impazientato.)
Che noia !

Studente.
Onde veniva ?

Trabuco.
So che andrè, presto o tardi, in Paradiso.

Studente.
Perchè ?

Trabuco
                    (Alzandosi.)
Ella il purgatorio.
Mi fa soffrir.

Studente.
Or dove va ?

Trabuco.
In istalla,
Dormir colle mie mule,
Che non san di Latino,
Nè sono Baccellieri.
                    (Prende il suo basto e parte.)

And you,
Who saw her arrive, say
Why she comes not to supper ?

Alcade.
I cannot tell.

Student.
They say she asked—ha ha !—
For vinegar and water, as refreshment.

Alcade.
May be.

Student.
Is it true that she is pretty, and has no
    beard ?

Alcade.
I really do not know.

Student.
(He will not speak.)
                    (To TRABUCO.)
Once more,
Was she seated on the mule,
Or rode astride ?

Trabuco
                    (Impatiently.)
What vexation !

Student.
Whence came she ?

Trabuco.
I know I shall go, sooner or later, to
    Paradise.

Student.
Why ?

Trabuco
                    (Rising.)
Because you make me
Suffer purgatory here.

Student.
Where are you going now ?

Trabuco.
To the stable,
To sleep with my mules,
Who don't know Latin,
And are not Bachelors of Arts.
                    (Takes his pack-saddle and goes.)

SCENA IV. I Suddettie meno MASTRO TRABUCO.

SCENE IV. The same. except TRABUCO.

Tutti.
　Ah ah ! è fuggito !

All.
　Ha ha ! he is off !

Studente.
　Poich' è imberbe l'incognito facciamgli
　Col nero du baffetti,
　Doman ne rideremo.

Student.
　As the unknown is a stripling,
　Let us paint on him a pair of moustaches,—
　That will make us all laugh to-morrow.

Alcuni.
　Bravo ! bravo !

Some of them.
　Bravo ! Bravo !

Alcade.
　Protegger debbo il viaggiator; m' oppongo.
　Meglio farebbe dirne

　D' onde venga, ove vade, e chi ella sia ?

Alcade.
　I am bound to protect travellers,
　And therefore object.—You had better tell us

　Whence you come, where going, and who you are.

Studente.
　Lo vuol saper ?—Ecco l'istoria mia.

Student.
　You wish to know ?—This is my tale.

SON PEREDA — *I'M PEREDA* Air (Student)

Son Pe - re - da, son ric-co do-no - re, Bac-cel - lie - re mi fe—Sa-la-
I'm Pè - re - da, from Sal-a - man-ca, Soon a—Doc-tor will be—my—

man-ca; Sa-ro presto in u-tro-que Dot-to - re, Che di— stu-dio an-cor
ti - tle; As a stu-dent I am a— rank-er, In— my— stu - dies I

po - co mi man-ca. Di la— Var-gas mi tol - se da un an - no E a Si -
ne'er was i dle. With one— Var-gas, I wentnow a year,— And to Se-

cresc.
vi - glia con se— mi gui-do, Non trat - ten - ne Pè - re - da al-cun
vil - la our way— we did wend; Toil and hard-ship ne'er trou - bled Pe-

f
da - no, Per— l'a - mi-co il suo co - re par - lo.
re - da, For—his— heart— e'er was faith-ful to his friend.

Della suora, un amante straniero,
Colà il padre gli avea trucidato,
Onde il figlio, da pro' cavaliero,
La vendetta ne aveva giurato.
Gl' inseguimmo di Cadice in riva,
Nè la coppia fatal si trovò.
Per l' amico Pereda soffriva,
Chè l suo core per esso parlò.
Là e dovunque narrar che del pari
La sedotta col vecchio peria,

Chè a una zuffa di servi e sicari,
Solo il vil seduttore sfuggia,
Io da Vargas allor mi staccava ;
Ei seguir l' assassino giurò.
Verso America il mare solcava,
E Pereda a' suoi studi torno.

Coro.
Truce storia Pereda narrava,
Generoso il suo cor si mostrò.

Alcade.
Sta bene.

Preziosilla
(Con finezza.)
Ucciso fu quel Marchese ?

Studente.
Ebben ?

Preziosilla.
L'amante rapia sua figlia ?

Studente.
Si.

Preziosilla.
E voi l'amico fido, cortese,
Andaste a Cadice, dopo Siviglia ?
Ah, gnaffe, a me non se la fa,
No, per mia fè—tra la la là !

Alcade
(S' alza, e guardato l' oriuolo dice.)
Figliuoli, è tardi ; poichè abbiam cenato
Si rendan grazie a Dio, e partiam

Tutti.
Partiamo.

Alcade.
Or buona notte !

A stranger, the lover of his sister,
Had there his father slain,
Wherefore his son, as true knight
Had sworn to be avenged.
We followed to the shores of Cadiz.
But ne'er o'ertook the guilty pair.
Pereda felt for his friend's distress,
Whom he most truly loved.
Here it is needful to inform you,
That the seduced one perished with her
sire:
In a struggle 'twixt servants and assassins
The vile seducer fled alone.
From Vargas then I parted ;
For he swore to follow the assassin:
He crosses the ocean to America,
And Pereda to his studies returns.

Chorus.
A dismal story Pereda has related,
Which shows a generous soul.

Alcade.
It is well.

Preziosilla
(Slyly.)
Slain was the Marquis ?

Studente.
What then ?

Preziosilla.
The lover carried off his daughter ?

Studente.
Yes.

Preziosilla.
And you, the friend, faithful, chivalrous
Went to Cadiz, afterwards to Seville ?
Ah, truly, such tales to me
Carry no weight, tra la !

Alcade
(Rising and looking at the clock.)
My children, it is late, and we have supped:
Let us give thanks and go.

All.
Let us go.

Alcade.
Now good night !

Coro.

Buona notte !

Tutti.

Andiamo.

(Partono.)

SCENA V. Una piccola spianata sul declivio di scoscesa Montagna. A sinistra precipizii e rupi; di fronte la facciata della chiesa della Madonna delgi Angeli, di povera ed umile architettura, a destra la porta del Convento, in mezzo alla quale una fine strella, da un lato la corda del companello. Sopra vi e una piccola tettoia sporgente. Al di la della chiesa alti monti col villaggio d' Horna-chuelos. La porta della chiesa e chiusa, ma larga, sopra dessa una finestra semicircolare lasciera vedere la luce interna. A mezza scene, un po' a sinistra, sopra quattro gradini s' erge una rozza croce ei pietra, corrosa dal tempo. La scena sara illuminata da luna chiarissima.

DONNA LEONORA giunge, ascendendo dalla destra, stanca, vestita da uomo, con pastrano a larghe maniche, largo capello e stivali.

Leonora.

Son giunta—grazie, o Dio !
Estremo asil quest' è per me—son giunta !
Io tremo !　La mia orrenda storia è nota
In quell' albergo—e mio fratel narrolla !
Se Scoperta m'avesse !　Cielo !　Ei disse
Naviga verso occaso Don Alvaro !
Nè morto cadde quella notte in cui
Io, io del sangue di mio padre intrisa,
L' ho seguito, e il perdei !　ed or mi lascia,
Mi fugge ! ohimè, non reggo a tanta am-
　　bascia !

(Cade inginocchio.)

Chorus.

Good night !

All.

Let us go.

(They depart.)

SCENE V. A small level space, on the side of a steep Mountain. On the left, precipices and rocks; facing the audience, the facade of the Church of the "Madonna degli Angeli," of simple architecture: on the right, the door of the Convent in the middle of which is a small window, on one side the cord of the bell, above which is a small projecting roof. On the other side of the church are high mountains, and the village of Hornachuelos. The door of the church is closed, but spacious; above it a semicircular window shows the light within. Half way down the stage, a little to the left, on four steps, is a rough stone cross, corroded by time. There is a bright moonlight over the whole scene.

DONNA LEONORA arrives, in male attire, ascending from the right, wearing a cloak with large sleeves, a large hat, and boots

Leonora.

I have arrived—thank Heaven !
This is my last refuge—I am here !
I tremble !　My dreadful story is known :
In that inn my brother did recount it.
Oh Heavens ! had he discovered me !
He said Don Alvaro was sailing westward,
And fell not on that fearful night
When, steeped in my father's blood,
I followed and lost him !　Now he leaves
　　me—
Flies from me !—Ah me, I cannot bear it !

(Falls on her knees.)

MADRE, MADRE — O HOLY MOTHER (Leonora and Chorus)

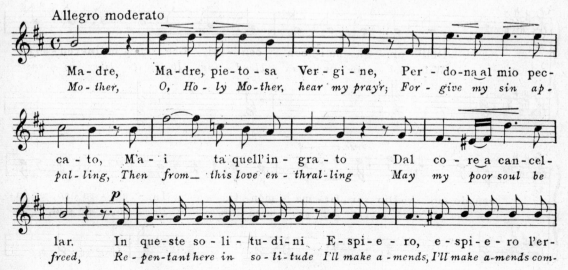

Allegro moderato

Ma-dre,　Ma-dre, pie-to-sa　Ver-gi-ne,　Per-do-na al mio pec-
Mo-ther,　O, Ho-ly Mo-ther,　hear my pray'r;　For-give my sin ap-

ca-to,　M'a-i　ta quell'in-gra-to　Dal co-re a can-cel-
pal-ling,　Then from— this love en-thral-ling　May my poor soul be

lar.　In que-ste so-li-tu-di-ni　E-spi-e-ro, e-spi-e-ro l'er-
freed,　Re-pen-tant here in so-li-tude I'll make a-mends, I'll make a-mends com-

spi-ra-no a quest' al - ma   Fe - de,   Con - for-to e cal - ma!
to my soul 'tis bring - ing   Calm - ness,   and faith un - sha - ken.

co - ram   Do-mi-no   co-rum, Do-mi-no qui fe - cit nos.

Al santo asilo accorrasi.

(S' avvia.)

E l'oserò a quest' ora ?

(Arrestandosi.)

Ma si potria sorprendermi !
Oh, misera Leonora,
Tremi ?—il pio frate accoglierti
No, non ricuserà.
Non mi lasciar, soccorrimi,
Pietà, Signor, pietà.

(Va a suonare il campanello del Convento.)

SCENA VI. Si apre la finestrella della porta, e n'esce la luce d' una lanterna. Che riverbera sul volto di DONNA LEONORA, la quale si arretra speventata. FRA MELITONE parla sempre all' interno.

Melitone.

Chi siete ?

Leonora.

Chiedo il Superiore,

Melitone.

S' apre
Alle cinque la chiesa,
Se al giubileo venite.

Leonora.

Il Superiore—
Per carità !

Melitone.

Che carità a quest' ora !

Leonora.

Mi manda il Padre Cleto.

Melitone.

Quel sant' uomo ? Il motivo ?

Leonora.

Urgente.

Let me to the sacred asylum haste.

(Going.)

But dare I, at this hour ?

(Stopping.)

Yet I may be o'ertaken !
Oh, wretched Leonora,
Dost fear ?—the holy friar
To receive thee will not refuse.
Have mercy, Heaven, mercy !
Aid me, desert me not !

(Rings the convent-bell.)

SCENE VI. The little window in the door opens, through which is seen a light, which is reflected in DONNA LEONORA'S face, who starts back alarmed. BROTHER MELITONE speaks from within.

Melitone.

Who is it ?

Leonora.

I seek the Superior.

Melitone.

At five o'clock
The church will open,
If to the jubilee you come.

Leonora.

The Superior—
For charity's sake !

Melitone.

Charity at this hour !

Leonora.

I am sent by Father Cleto.

Melitone.

By that holy man ? The reason ?

Leonora.

Most urgent.

Melitone.

Perchè mai ?

Leonora.

Un infelice !

Melitone.

Brutta solfa—perè v' apro ond' entriate.

Leonora.

Nol posso.

Melitone.

No ? Scomunicicato siete ?
Chè strano fia aspettar a ciel sereno.
V' annuncio—e se non torno,
Buona notte.

        (Chiude la finestrella.)

SCENA VII. DONNA LEONORA, sola.

Leonora.

Ma s' ei mi respingesse !
Fama pietoso il dice,
Ei mi proteggerà;—Vergin, m'assisti !

SCENA VIII. DONNA LONORA, il PADRE GUARDIANO. fra
MELITONE.

Guardiano.

Chi mi cerca ?

Leonora.

Son io.

Guardiano.

Dite.

Leonora.

Un segreto—

Guardiano.

Andate Melitone.

Melitone

        (Partendo.)

(Sempre segreti !
E questi santi soi han da saperli !
Noi siamo tanti cavoli.)

Guardiano.

Gratello
Mormorate ?

Melitone.

Oibò, dico ch' è pesante
La porte, e fa romore.

Guardiano.

Obbedite.

Melitone.

Why so ?

Leonora.

An unfortunate creature !

Melitone.

A likely tale—however, I will let you in.

Leonora.

I cannot enter.

Melitone.

No ? Are you excommunicated ?
'Tis strange you should prefer the open air,
I will announce you—and if I don't return,
Good night.

        (Shuts the window)

SCENE VII. DONNA LEONORA, alone.

Leonora.

But if he should repulse me ?
He is reputed merciful.
He will protect me ;—Holy Virgin, aid me !

SCENE VIII. DONNA LEONORA, the FATHER GUARDIANO
BROTHER MELITONE.

Guardiano.

Who asks for me ?

Leonora.

'Tis I.

Guardiano.

Speak on.

Leonora.

A secret—

Guardiano.

Go, Melitone.

Melitone

        (Going.)

(Always secrets !
And these saints only know them !
We are nobodies !)

Guardiano.

Brother,
Are you grumbling ?

Melitone.

Oh no, I said the door
Was heavy, and creaked,

Guardiano.

Obey.

Melitone.

(Che tuon da Superiore !)

(Rientra in Convento socchiudendone la porta.)

SCENA IX.   DONNA LEONORA e il PADRE GUARDIANO.

Guardiano.

Or siam soli.

Leonora.

Una donna son io.

Guardiano.

Una donna a quest' ora !—gran Dio !

Leonora.

Infelice, dulusa, rejetta,
Dalla terra, e dal ciel maledetta,
Che nel pianto prostratavi al piede,
Di sottrarla all' inferno vi chiede.

Guardiano.

Come un povero frate lo può ?

Leonora.

Padre Cleto un suo foglio v'inviò ?

Guardiano.

Ei vi manda ?

Leonora.

Sì.

Guardiano

(Sorpreso.)

Dunque voi siete
Leonora di Varges ?

Leonora.

Fremete !

Guardiano.

No: venite fidente alla croce,
Là del Cielo v' inspiri la voce.

Leonora

(S' inginocchia presso la croce, la bacia, quindi torna meno agitata
al PADRE GUARDIANO.)

Ah, tranquilla l' alma sento
Dacchè premo questa terra ;
De' fantasmi lo spavento
Più non provo farmi guerra ;
Più non sorge sanguinante
Di mio padre l' ombra innante,
Nè terribile l' ascolto
La sua figlia maledir.

Melitone.

(Quite the voice of the Superior !)

(Re-enters the Convent, half-closing the door.)

SCENE IX.   DONNA LEONORA and the FATHER GUARDIANO.

Guardiano.

Now, we are alone.

Leonora.

I am a woman.

Guardiano.

A woman at this hour !—good heavens !

Leonora.

Unhappy, deluded, rejected
On earth, and cursed by Heaven !
Who, prostrate at your feet, with tears
Implores you to save her from destruction.

Guardiano.

How can a poor friar do so ?

Leonora.

Father Cleto sent you a letter ?

Guardiano.

He sent you ?

Leonora.

Yes.

Guardiano

(Surprised.)

Then you must be
Leonora di Vargas ?

Leonora.

You shudder !

Guardiano.

No: in confidence approach the cross,
There may Heaven inspire you.

Leonora

(Kneeling close to the cross, kisses it, then turning with less
agitation to FATHER GUARDIANO.)

Ah, my soul is calm
Now I tread this soil;
The dread forebodings
I no longer feel within me ;
Nor does there rise before me
The bleeding shade of my sire;
I do not hear with horror
His curses on his child.

Guardiano.

Sempre indarno qui rivolto
Fu di Satana l' ardir.

Leonora.

Perciò tomba qui desio,
Fa le rupi ov' altra visse.

Guardiano.

Che !—sapete —

Leonora.

Cleto il disse.

Guardiano.

E volete—

Leonora.

Darmi a Dio !

Guardiano.

Guai per chi si lascia illudere
Dal delirio d'un momento !
Più fatal per voi, si giovane,
Sorgerebbe il pentimento.
Nel futuro chi può leggere,
Chi immutabil farvi il cor.
E l' amante ?

Leonora.

Involontario
Di mio padre è l' uccisor.

Guardiano.

Il fratello ?

Leonora.

La mia morte
Di sua mano egli giurò.

Guardiano.

Meglio a voi la sante porte.
Schiuda un chiostro.

Leonora.

Un chiostro ? No.
Se voi scacciate questa pentita,
Andrò per balze gridando aita.
Ricovro ai monti ciba, alle selve,
E fin le belve ne avran pietà.
Qui, qui del cielo udii la voce:
Salvati all' ombra di questa croce—
Voi mi scacciate ? E questo il porto;
Chi tal conforto mi toglierà ?

(Corre ad abbracciar la croce.)

Guardiano.

Never has Satan dared
These precincts to approach,

Leonora.

Therefore a tomb I seek
Among the rocks where one other lived.

Guardiano.

What !—do you know—

Leonora.

Cleto mentioned it,

Guardiano.

And you wish—

Leonora.

To devote myself to Heaven !

Guardiano.

Woe unto those who delude themselves
In the wild frenzy of a moment !
More wretched for you, so young,
Would repentance hereafter become.
Who can read the future,
Or make the heart steadfast ?
And thy lover ?

Leonora.

He by mischance
My father killed.

Guardiano.

Thy brother ?

Leonora.

My death he has sworn
By his own hand.

Guardiano.

For you 'twere best to seek
A cloister's holy shelter.

Leonora.

A cloister ? No.
If you reject the penitent,
Aid will I shrieking ask the rocks,
Shelter the mountains, food the woods ;
The savage beasts at least will pity me.
Here, where heaven's voice is heard
Salvation in the shadow of the Cross I seek.
You cast me out ? This is the haven
Of solace—you will tear me from it ?

(Runs and clings to the cross.)

Guardiano.

  (A te sia gloria, o Dio clemente,
  Padre dei miseri onnipossente,
  A qui sgabello sono le sfere !
  Il tuo volere—si compirà !)
  E fermo il voto ?

Leonora.

  E fermo,

Guardiano.

  V' accolga dunque Iddio !

Leonora.

  Bontà divina ?

Guardiano.

  Sol io saprò chi siate.
  Tra le rupi è uno speco ; ivi starete.
  Presso una fonte, al settimo, di scarso
  Cibo porrovvi io stesso.

Leonora.

  V' andiamo.

Guardiano

            (Versa la porta.)

  Melitone !

        (A MELITONE chi comparisce.)

  Tutti i fratelli con ardenti ceri,
  Dov' è l' ara maggiore,
  Nel tempio si raccolgan del Signore.

              (MELITONE rientra.)

Guardiano.

  (Thine be the glory, O merciful Heaven !
  Father of sinners, omnipotent,
  Who o'er all worlds reigns,
  Let Thy will be accomplished.)
  Thou art resolved ?

Leonora.

  I am.

Guardiano.

  Heaven accept thee !

Leonora.

  Oh, clemency divine !

Guardiano.

  I alone shall know who thou art.
  Among the rocks is a cave, thy future abode:
  Beside a spring, every seven days,
  Thy scanty food I myself will bring.

Leonora.

  Let us go.

Guardiano

            (Turning to the door.)

  Melitone !

        (To MELITONE who enters.)

  Let all the brothers, with lighted torches,
  Before the high altar assemble,
  In the temple of our Lord.

              (MELITONE withdraws.)

SULL' ALBA IL PIEDE — *TO SEEK THE LONELY HERMITAGE* Duet. (Guardiano and Leonora)

GUARDIANO

Allegro moderato

Sull' al-ba il pie-de all' e - re-mo So - lin-ga_ vol-ge - re-te, Ma
To seek the low-ly her-mit-age At dawn you_ must be stir-ring But

pria dal pa-ne an - ge-li-co Di - vin con-for-to a - vre-te, Le
first take of the sa-cra-ment, God's grace on_ you con - fer - ring, Em-

san-te la-ne a cin ge-re I - te, sia fer-mo il cor. Sul nuo-vo cal-le a
brace the cross with sim-ple faith To set your mind at rest, And Heav'n will not de-

LEONORA

Tua gra - zia, o Di - o, Sor-
My   pray'rs and thanks - giv - ing To

reg-ger-vi___ V'as-sis-te-ra il Si - gnor.
ny you aid,___ You will be rich-ly__ blest.

LEONORA

ri-de-al-la__ re - jet - ta!   Oh, gau - dio in - so-li-to! Io
Thee on   high are__ wing-ing,   And hap-pi-ness un - mer-it-ed Thy

son,__ Io son ri-be-ne-det-ta! Gia sen-to in me ri - na-sce-re A
peace. to my poor heart is bring-ing, New hope once more with-in I feel, New

nuo-va vi-ta il cor; Plau - di-te, o co-ri an-ge - li-ci, Mi per-do-no il Si-
cour-age in my breast; Me - thinks an-gel-ic songs I hear And par - don makes me

gnor, Mi per-do - no il Si - gnor_____ Mi per-do-no il Si - gnor.
blest, And par-don, par-don makes me blest,_____ Thy par-don makes me blest.

[Enters the Convent, but returns immediately with the dress of the Franciscan order, and gives it to Leonora.

SCENA X. La gran porta della Chiesa si apre. Di fronte vedesi l' altar maggiore, illuminato. L' organo suona. Dai lati del coro procedono due lunghe file di FRATI, con cerei ardenti. Piu tardi il PADRE GUARDIANO precede LEONORA in abito da FRATE. Egli la conduce fuor della chiesa, FRATI che gli si schierano intorno. LEONORA si prostra innanzi a lui, che stendendo solennemente le mani sopra il suo capo intuona.

SCENE X. The great door of the Church opens. In front is seen the high altar, illuminated. The organ is sounded. From the sides of the choir proceed two long rows of FRIARS, with lighted tapers. A little later, the FATHER GUARDIANO, followed by LEO-NORA, in the FRIAR'S dress. He leads her out of the church, followed by the FRIARS, who range themselves around. LEONORA pro-strates herself before him. he solemnly spreads his hands over her head, and chants.

Guardiano.
Il santo nome di Dio Signore
Sia benedetto.

Tutti.
Sia benedetto.

Guardiano.
The holy name of the Lord
Be blessed.

All.
Be blessed.

Guardiano.

    Un' alma a piangere viene l' errore,
    I queste balze chiede ricetto.
    Il santo speco noi la schiudiamo—
    V' è noto il loco ?

Tutti.

    Lo conosciamo.

Guardiano.

    A quell' asilo sacro inviolato
    Nessun si appressi.

Tutti.

    Obbediremo.

Guardiano.

    Il cinto umile non sia varcato.
    Che nel divide.

Tutti.

    Nol varcheremo.

Guardiano.

    A chi il divieto frangere osasse,
    O di quest' anima scoprir tentasse
    Nome o mistero, maledizione !

Tutti.

    Maledizione ! maledizione !
    Il cielo fulmini incenercisa
    L' empio mortale se tanto ardisca ;
    Su lui scatenisi ogni elemento,
    L' immonda cenere ne sperda il vento.

Guardiano
            (A LEONORA.)

    Alzatevi, e partite.
    Alcun vivente più non vedrete.
    Dello speco il bronzo
    Ne avverta se periglio vi sovrasti,
    O per voi giunto s'a l' estremo giorno—
    A confortarvi l' alma
    Volerem, pria ch' a Dio faccia ritorno.
    La Vergine degli angeli
    Vo copra del suo manto,
    E voi protegga vigile
    Di Dio l' angelo santo.

Tutti.

    La Vergine, ec.

(LEONORA bacia la mano del PADRE GUARDIANO s' avvia all' eremo sola. Il GUARDIANO stendendo le braccia verso di lei, la benedice. Cade la tela.)

FINE DELLA' ATTO SECONDO.

Guardiano.

    A penitent soul, to atone for errors,
    Demands a shelter in these rocks.
    The holy cave we will open—
    Do you know the place ?

All.

    We know the place.

Guardiano.

    The sacred holy asylum
    Let none approach.

All.

    We will obey.

Guardiano.

    The low boundary enclosing **it**
    Let none pass,

All.

    We will not.

Guardiano.

    To him who dares this rule to break,
    Or of this poor soul seeks to discover
    The name or story, malediction !

All.

    Malediction ! malediction !
    May the thunderbolt reduce to ashes
    The impious mortal who dares attempt it ;
    May all the elements be loosed upon him,
    And his impure ashes be scattered by the
        wind.

Guardiano
            (To LEONORA.)

    Rise and depart. No living soul
    Will see you more. The bell in the cave
    Will give us notice if you are in danger :
    If your last hour be at hand,
    We will haste to bring absolution
    Ere thy soul to God returns.
    The Virgin of the heavenly host
    Cover you with her holy mantle,
    And the holy angels of God
    Be to you watchful guardians.

All.

    The Virgin, etc.

(LEONORA kisses the hand of FATHER GUARDIANO, and sets out alone for the hermitage. GUARDIANO, extending his arms towards her, blesses her. The curtain falls.)

END OF THE SECOND ACT.

ATTO III	ACT III
In Italia. presso Velletri.	*In Italy, near Villeteri.*

SCENA I. Bosco. Notte oscurissima. DON ALVARO in uniforme di Capitano Spagnuolo de' Granatieri del Re, si avanza lentamente dal fondo. Si sentono voci interno a destra.

1a Voce.

Attenti, gioco.—Un asso a destra.

2a Voce.

Ho vinto.

1a Voce.

Un tre alla destra—cinque a manca.

2a Voce.

Perdo !

Alvaro
      (Che si sara innoltrato.)

La vita e inferno all infelice invano
Morte desio !—Siviglia !—Leonora !
Oh, rimembranze !—Oh notte !
Ch' ogni mio ben rapisti !
Sarò infelice eternamente è scritto.

Della natal sua terra il padre volle
Spezzar l' estranio giogo, el coll', unirsi ;
All' ultima degli Incas la corona
Cingerne confidò—fallì l' impresa,
In un carcere nacqui ; m' educava
Il deserto ; sol vivo per chè ignota
E mia regale stirpe. I miei parenti
Sognaro un trono e, li destò la scure !

Oh, quando fine avran le mie sventure ?

SCENE I. A wood. A dark night. DON ALVARO, in the uniform of a Captain of Royal Spanish Grenadiers, advances slowly from the back. Voices are heard on the right, from within.

1st Voice.

Attention, I play.   An ace to the right.

2nd Voice.

I have won.

1st Voice.

A three to the right—five to the left.

2nd Voice.

I have lost.

Alvaro
      (Who has come forward.)

Life has no charms for unhappy souls.
In vain I seek to die !—Seville !—Leonora !
Oh, sad memories !—Fatal night,
Which of every good deprived me !
It is decreed that I shall ever be unfortunate.
My father sought to free his native land
From foreign rule ;
United to the last of the Incas,
He hoped to obtain the crown.
He failed—and in prison I was born,
In the desert reared, and only live because
My royal birth is unknown.   My parents
Dreamt of thrones, and suffered by the scaffold.
Ah, when will my sorrows end ?

OH, TU CHE IN SENO — *O SAINTED SOUL* Air. Alvaro

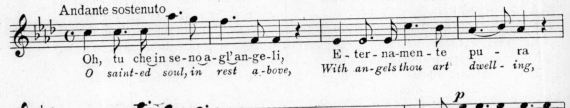

Andante sostenuto

Oh, tu che in se-no a-gl'an-ge-li,   E - ter - na-men - te   pu - ra
O   saint-ed soul, in   rest a-bove,   With an-gels thou art   dwell - ing,

Sa - li-sti bel - la, in-co - lu-me   Dal la mor-tal jat - tu-ra. Oh, tu che in se-no a-
There, in the bless-ed   realm of love,   Joy thou hast found past tell-ing. O saint-ed soul in

gl' an-ge-li, Sa - li - sti bel-la e pu - ra, Non i-scor-dar di
rest a-bove, With an-gels thou art dwell-ing, In pi - ty turn thy

vol - ger. Lo sguar-do a me ta - pi - no, Che sen - za no - me ed
glan - ces up-on my soul in sor - row, Who wan-der here in

e - su - le, In o - dio del de - sti - no, Che sen - za no - me ed
ex - ile And dread each com - ing mor - row, Who wan-der here in

e - sul, In o - dio del de - sti - no, Chie - do a-ne - lan - do, ahi
ex - ile, And dread each com - ing mor - row, Yes, in this war and

mi - se - ro, Chie - do a-ne - lan-do, ahi mi - se - ro, La mor - te d'in-con-
mi - se - ry, For ev - er seek-ing, ev - er seek-ing death a - mid the

trar, Leo-no - ra mia, soc-cor-ri - mi, Leo-no - ra mi - a, soc-cor - ri,
foe, Oh, Le - o - no-ra, pi - ty me, Oh, Le - o - no-ra, pi-ty, pi - ty

mi, Pie - ta, pie - ta,_____ pie-ta del mi - o pe-nar; Leo-no - ra, soc-cor-ri
me, And give me help,_____ And give me help to bear my woe; Leo-no - ra, oh, pi - ty

mi, pie - ta, del mi - o pe - nar;_ Leo-no - ra, mi - a, pie -
me, And give me help to bear my woe;_ Oh, Le - o - no - ra, give

ta,— pie - ta del mi - o, pe-nar, soc-cor-ri mi, pie-ta di me!—
help, give help to bear, to bear my woe, give help to bear, to bear my woe!—

Voce (Dall' interno a destra.)	*Voice* (From within.)
Al tradimento !	Treachery !
Voci.	*Voices.*
Muoia !	Down with him !
Alvaro.	*Alvaro.*
Quali grida ?	What cries are these ?
Voce.	*A Voice.*
Aita !	Help !
Alvaro.	*Alvaro.*
Si soccorra !	To your aid !

(Accorre al luogo onde si udivano le grida. Si sente un picchiare di spade. Alcuni Ufficiali attraversano la scena, fuggendo in disordine da destra a sinistra.)

SCENA II.   DON ALVARO ritorna con DON CARLO.

(Runs to the place from whence the sounds proceed. A clashing of swords is heard. Some Officers cross the stage in disorder flying right and left.

SCENE II.   DON ALVARO returns with DON CARLOS.

Alvaro.	*Alvaro.*
Fuggir ! Ferito siete ?	They are fled ! Are you wounded ?
Carlo.	*Carlos.*
No, vi debbo La vita.	No : but I owe to you my life.
Alvaro.	*Alvaro.*
Chi erano ?	Who are they ?
Carlo.	*Carlos.*
Assassini.	Assassins.
Alvaro.	*Alvaro.*
Presso ! Alcampo così ?	What so near the camp ?
Carlo.	*Carlos.*
Franco Dirè : fu alterco al gioco.	Frankly, it was a gambling quarrel.
Alvaro.	*Alvaro.*
Comprendo, colà, a destra ?	I understand ; there on the right ?
Carlo.	*Carlos.*
Sì.	Yes.
Alvaro.	*Alvaro.*
Ma come, Si nobile d' aspetto, a quella bisca Scendeste ?	But, how, seeming so noble, Descend to such low **company** ?

Carlo.

Nuovo sono.
Del general con ordini sol jeri
Giunsi ; senza voi morto
Sarei.   Or dite a chi miei giorni debbo ?

Alvaro.

Al caso.

Carlo.

Pria il mio nome
Dirò—(non sappia il vero)—
Don Felice de Bornos, ajutante
Del Duce.

Alvaro.

Io Capitan de' Granatieri
Don Federico Herreros !

Carlo.

La gloria dell' esercito !

Alvaro.

Signore—

Carlo.

Io l' amistà ne ambia, la chiedo, e spero.

Alvaro.

Io pure della vostra sarò fiero.

(Si stringono le destre.)

Voci

(Interne, a sinistra, e squillo di trombe.)

All' armi !

A 2.

Andiamo—all' armi !

Carlo.

Ah più gradito questo suono or parmi !
Con voi scendere al campo d' onore,
Emularne l' esempio potrò.

Alvaro.

Testimone del vostro valore,
Ammirarne le prove saprò.

SCENA III. E il Mattino. Salotto nell' abitazione d' un ufficiale superiore dell' esercito Spagnuolo in Italia non lungi da Velletri. Nel fondo sonvi due porte, quella a sinistra mette ad una stanza da letto, l' altra e la comune. A sinistra presso il proscenio a una finestra. Si sente il romore della vicina battaglia.

Un Chirurgo Militare, ed alcuni Soldati, ordinanze dalla comune corrono alla finestra.

Soldati.

Arde la mischia !

Carlos.

I am a stranger, with orders from the general.
I yesterday arrived, and but for you I had
  died.
Say, to whom do I owe my life ?

Alvaro.

To chance.

Carlos.

I will first tell my name—
(Not my true one)—
Don Felice de Bornos,
Adjutant to the Duke.

Alvaro.

I Captain of the Grenadiers,
Don Federico Herreros !

Carlos.

The pride of the army !

Alvaro.

Signor—

Carlos.

I desire and would obtain your friendship.

Alvaro.

I shall be proud to have yours.

(They shake hands.)

Voices

(Within, to the left, with sound of a trumpet.)

To arms !

Together.

Let us go—to arms !

Carlos.

Ah, that sound is more agreeable now !
With you I will go to the field of honor,
And seek to emulate your bright example.

Alvaro.

Witness of your valor,
In future I shall know how to admire it.

SCENE III. Morning. A small room in the house of a superior officer in the Spanish army, in Italy, not far from Velletri. At the back are two doors, one on the left leads to a bedroom, the other is the common door.   On the left, near the proscenium, is a window.   The noise is heard of the neighboring battle.

A Military Surgeon, and some common Soldiers, run to the window.

Soldiers.

The   battle   rages !

Chirurgo

(Guardando con cannocchiale.)

Prodi i granatiere !

Soldati.

Li guida Herreros.

Chirurgo

(Guardando con cannocchiale.)

Ciel ! ferito o spento
Ei cadde ! Piegano i suoi ! l'Ajutante
Li raccozza alla carica li guida !
Già fuggono i Tedeschi ! I nostril han vinto
Portan qui il Capitano.

Soldati.

Ferito !

(Corrono ad incontrarlo.)

Voci

(Fuori.)

A Spagna gloria !

Altre.

Viva l' Italia !

Tutti.

E nostra la vittoria !

SCENA IV   DON ALVARO, ferito e svenuto e portato in una lettiga da quattro Granatieri. Da un lato e il Chirurgo, dall' altro DON CARLO, coperto di polvere ed assai afflitto. Un Soldato depone una valigia sopra un tavolino. La lettiga e collocata quasi nel mezzo della scena.

Carlo.

Piano—qui posi—approntisi il mio letto.

Chirurgo.

Silenzio.

Carlo.

V' ha periglio ?

Chirurgo.

La palla che ha nel petto mi spaventa.

Carlo.

Deh, il salvate.

Alvaro

(Rinviene.)

Ove son ?

Carlo.

Presso l' amico.

Alvaro.

Lasciatemi morire.

Surgeon

(Looking through a telescope.)

Brave   grenadiers !

Soldier.

Herreros leads them.

Surgeon

(Looking through a telescope.)

Heavens ! he falls
Wounded or dead ! His men give way !
The Adjutant rallies and leads them to
   the charge !
The Germans fly ! Our troops conquer !
They bring hither the Captain.

Soldier.

Wounded !

(They run to meet him.)

Voices

(Without.)

Glory to Spain !

Others.

Long live Italy !

All.

Ours is the victory !

SCENE IV. DON ALVARO, wounded and insensible, is borne in on a litter by four Grenadiers. On one side the Surgeon, on the other DON CARLOS, covered with dust and sorrowful. A Soldier places a traveling-bag on a small table. The litter is placed nearly in the middle of the scene.

Carlos.

Gently—lay him here—get ready my bed.

Surgeon.

Silence !

Carlos.

Is there danger ?

Surgeon.

The bullet in his chest alarms me.

Carlos.

Ah, try to save him !

Alvaro

(Recovering his senses.)

Where am I ?

Carlos.

With your friend.

Alvaro.

Leave me to die.

Carlo.

Vi salveran le nostra cure premio
L' ordine vè sarà di Calatrava.

Alvaro

(Trasalendo.)

Di Calatrava ! No—mai !

Chirurgo.

Siate calmo.

Carlo.

(Ch, ! inorridi di Calatrava al nome !)

Alvaro.

Amico—

Chirurgo.

Se parlate—

Alvaro.

Un detto sol.

Carlo

(Al Chirurgo.)

Ven prefo ne, lasciate.

(Chirurgo si ritrae al fonde.)

Carlos.

Our cares will save you.
The Order of Calatrava will be conferred
upon you.

Alvaro

(Shuddering.)

Of Calatrava ! No—never !

Surgeon.

Be calm.

Carlos.

(He shuddered at the name of Calatrava !)

Alvaro.

My friend—

Surgeon.

If you speak—

Alvaro.

Only one word.

Carlos

(To the Surgeon.)

Leave us, I pray you.

(The Surgeon retires to the back.)

SOLENNE IN QUEST' ORA -- *IN THIS SOLEMN HOUR*-Duet (Don Alvaro and Don Carlo)

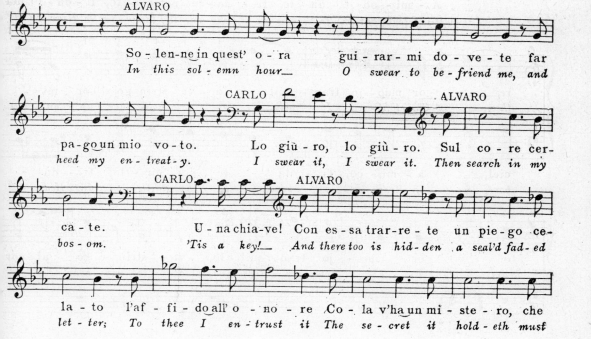

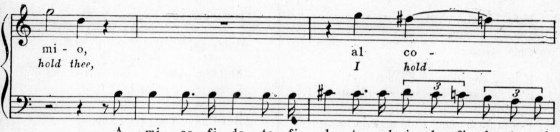

mi - o,   al   co -
hold thee,   I   hold_____

A - mi - co, fi - da - te, fi - da - te nel cie - lo, fi - da - te nel
My friend, put thy faith now in Heav-en, thy faith now in Heav-en a -

re,_____ or muo-jo tran-quil - lo vi strin-go al cor mi - o!   Ad -
thee,_____ Con-tent-ed I die___ as I hold thee up-on my heart.   Fare-

ciel;_____ a - mi-co, fi - da - te nel cie - lo, fi - da - te.
bove,_____ in Heav-en a - bove, put thy faith now in Heav - en.

di - .o,   ad - di - o, ad - di - o!
well____ now.   fare - well__ now . for ev - er!

Ad - di - o, ad - di - o, ad - di - o!
[Fare - well now, fare - well now for ev - er!

(Il Chirurgo e le Ordinanze trasportano il ferito nella stanza la letto.)	(The Surgeon and Soldiers carry the wounded man into the bedroom)
S ENA V. DON CARLOS, poi il Chirurgo.	SCENE V. DON CARLOS, afterwards the Surgeon.
Carlo.	*Carlos.*
Morir ! Tremenda cosa !	Die ! How terrible !
Sì intrepido, sì prode,	So fearless, so brave.
Ei pur morrà ! Uom singolar costui !	Yet he must die ! What a strange man !
Tremò di Calatrava !	He shuddered at the name of Calatrava !
Al nome ! A lui palese	Does he know it has been disgraced ?
N' è forse il disonor ? Cielo ! qual lampo !	Heavens ! a thought strikes me !
S' ei fosse il seduttore ?	What if he were the vile seducer ?
Desso in mia mano, e vive !	In my hands, and yet alive !
Se m' ingannassi ? Questa chiave il dica.	But if I should mistake ? This key will tell.
(Apre convulso la valigia, e ne trae un plicco suggellato.)	(He hastily opens the bag, and draws out a sealed packet.)

Ecco i fogli.
(Fa per aprirlo.)

Che tento ?
(S' arresta.)

E la fè che giurai ? e questa vita
Che debbo al suo valor ? Anch' io l' ho
   salvo !
E s' ei fosse quell' Indo maledetto
Che macchiò il sangue mio ?

(Risoluto.)

Il suggello si franga.
(Sta per eseguire.)

Niun qui mi vede ; No !
(S' arresta.)

Ben mi vegg' io ?
(Getta il plicco, e se ne allontana con raccapriccio.)

Urna fatale del mio destino,
Va, t' allontana, mi tenti insano ;
L' onor a tergere qui venni, e insano
D' un onta nuova nol brutterò.
Un giuro è sacro per l' uom d' onore ;
Que' fogli chiudano il lor mistero—
Disperso vada il mal pensiero ;
Che all' atto indegno mi concitò.
E s' altra provar invenir potessi ? Vediam.

(Torna a frugare nella valigia e vi trova un astuccio.)

Qui v' ha un ritratto.
(Lo esamina.)

Suggel non v' e'—nulla ei ne disse—nulla—
Promisi—s' apra dunque.
(Eseguisce.)

Ciel ! Leonora !
(Con estaltazione.)

Don Alvaro e' il ferito !
Ora egli viva—
Edi mai man poi mueoia.

Chirurgo
(Si presenta lieto sulla porta della stanza.)

Lieta novella è salvo.
(Rientra.)

Carlo.
Oh gioia ! oh gioia !

Here are the papers.
(About to open them.)

What am I doing ?
(Stops.)

And the oath I swore ?   And the life
I owe to his valor ?

But I have also saved him.
Yet if he were this vile Indian
Who has my named disgraced ?
(Resolutely.)

The seal shall be broken.
(Is about to do it.)

None see me ! No. !
(Stops.)

Do I not see myself ?
(Throws away the packet, and turns from it with horror.)

Fatal urn of my destiny,
Away, in vain you tempt me ;
Hither I came to clear my honor,
And will not stain it with a new disgrace.
An oath is sacred to a man of honor ;
Those papers contain their own secret—
Away with the evil thought
That urged me to the base attempt.
But if other proof I might obtain ;
Let me see.
(Looks into the bag, and finds a case.)

Here is a portrait.
(Examines it.)

Here is no seal—he spoke not of it—
Nothing did I promise.
(Opens it.)

Heavens ! Leonora !
(Excitedly.)

The wounded man is then Alvaro !
Let him live—then, later die by my hands

Surgeon
(Appearing at the door of the room.)

Here is the ball: he is saved !
(Retires.)

Carlos.
Oh, happiness ! oh, joy !

AH! EGLI E SALVO — *OH, WHAT A JOY* Air. (Don Carlos)

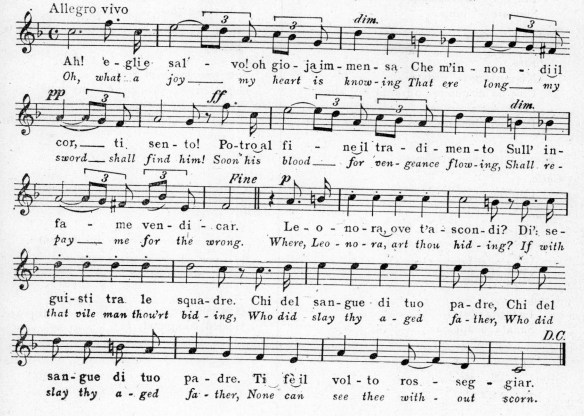

Allegro vivo

Ah! 'e - glie sal - vo! oh gio - ja im - men - sa Che m'in - non - di il
Oh, what a joy___ my heart is know-ing That ere long___ my

cor, ___ ti sen - to! Po-tro al fi - ne il tra - di - men - to Sull' in -
sword___ shall find him! Soon his blood___ for ven-geance flow-ing, Shall re-

Fine

fa - me ven - di - car. Le - o - no - ra, ove t'a - scon - di? Di': se -
pay___ me for the wrong. Where, Leo - no - ra, art thou hid - ing? If with

gui - sti tra le squa - dre. Chi del san - gue di tuo pa - dre, Chi del
that vile man thou'rt bid - ing, Who did slay thy a - ged fa - ther, Who did

D.C.

san - gue di tuo pa - dre. Ti fe il vol - to ros - seg - giar.
slay thy a - ged fa - ther, None can see thee with - out scorn.

Ah, felice appien sarei
Se potesse il brando mio,
Amendue d' averno al Dio,
D' un sol colpo consacrar.
(Parte rapidamente.)

Ah, I should be truly happy
If with my own sword,
And with the selfsame blow
I might send both to realms below.
(Exit.)

SCE A VI. Accampamento Militare presso elletri. Sul davanti a sinistra e una bottega da rigattiere; a destra altra ove si vendono cibi, bevande, frutta. All' ingiro tende militari, baracche di rivenduglioli, ecc. E notte, la scena e deserta. Una Patt glia entra cautamente in scena, esplorando il campo.

SCENE VI. Millitary Encampment, near Velletri. In front is a sutler's booth. To the right, others with food, fruits, bottles. Around are soldiers' tents, huxter's stalls etc. Night. he scene is vacant. The watch-guard enter cautiously, and search the camp

Coro.

Compagni, sostiamo,
Il campo esploriamo ;
Non s' ode rumore,
Non brilla un chiarore ;
In sonno profondo
Sepolto ognun sta.
Compagni, inoltriamo.
(Allontonandosi a poco a poco.)

Chorus.

Comrades, halt !
The camp explore.
No sound is heard,
No light is seen,
In sleep profound
Now all repose.
Comrades, forward !
(Go off gradually.)

Fra poco la sveglia
Suonare s' udrà.

SCENA VII.   Spunta l' alba lentamente.   Entra DON ALVARO pensoso.

Alvaro.
Nè gustare m' è dato
Un'.ora di quiete ; affranta è l' alma
Dalla lotta crudel.
Pace ed oblio indarno io chieggo al Cielo.

SCENA. VIII.   Detto e DON CARLO.

Carlo.
Capitan.

Alvaro.
Chi mi chiama ?
(Avvicinandosi e riconoscendo CARLO gli dice con affetto.)

Voi che sì larghe cure
Mi prodigaste ?

Carlo.
La ferita vostra
Sanata è appieno ?

Alvaro.
Sì.

Carlo.
Forte ?

Alvaro.
Qual prima.

Carlo.
Sosterreste un duello ?

Alvaro.
E con chi mai ?

Carlo.
Nemici non avete ?

Alvaro.
Tutti ne abbian—ma a stento
Comprendo—

Carlo.
No ?—Messaggio non v' inviava
Don Alvaro l' Indiano ?

Alvaro.
Oh tradimento !
Sleale ? il segreto fu dunque violato ?

Ere long the morning call
Will rouse them.

SCENE VII.   The day slowly dawns.   Enter DON ALVARO, in deep thought.

Alvaro.
Not one hour of rest
Can I enjoy. Tortured is **my** soul
With the cruel struggle.
Peace and oblivion I ask of Heaven in vain.

SCENE VIII.   Enter DON CARLOS.

Carlos.
Captain.

Alvaro.
Who calls me?
(Advancing recognizes CARLOS with gladness.)

Is it you who such great care
Upon me lavished ?

Carlos.
Has your wound
Healed completely ?

Alvaro.
Yes.

Carlos.
Strong ?

Alvaro.
As ever.

Carlos.
Could you fight a duel ?

Alvaro.
And with whom ?

Carlos.
Have you no enemy ?

Alvaro.
All have some—but I hardly
Understand—

Carlos.
No ?—Don Alvaro the Indian,
Did he not send you a message?

Alvaro.
Oh, treachery ! disloyal man?
The secret has been there disclosed ?

Carlo

    Fu illeso quel piego, l' effigie ha parlato ;

    Don Carlo di Vargas, tremate, io sono.

Alvaro.

    D' ardite, minaccie non m' agito al suono.

Carlo.

    Usciamo, all' istante un di noi dee morire.

Alvaro.

    La morte disprezzo, ma duolmi inveire

    Contr' uom che per primo amistade m' offria.

Carlo.

    No, no profanato tal nome non sia.

Alvaro.

    Non io, fu il destino, che il padre v' ha ucciso ;

    Non io che sedussi quell' angiol d' amore—

    Ne guardano entrambi, e dal paradiso

    Ch' io sono innocente vi dicono al core—

Carlo.

    Adunque colei ?

Alvaro.

    La notte fatale

    Io caddi per doppia ferita mortale ;

    Guaritone, un anno in traccia ne andai—

    Ahimè, ch' era spenta Leonora trovai.

Carlo.

    Menzogna, menzogna !

    La suora—ospitavala antica parente ;

    Vi giunsi, ma tardi—

Alvaro

        (Con ansia.)

    Ed ella—

Carlo.

    E fuggente.

Alvaro

        (Trasalendo.)

    E vive ! o amico, il fremito

    Ch' ogni mia fibra scuote,

    Vi dica che quest' anima

    Infame esser non puote—

    Vive ! gran Dio, quell' angelo !

Carlos.

    Unopened was the packet, **but the** portrait spoke ;

    Tremble, for I am Don Calros di **Vargas.**

Alvaro.

    Threats disturb me not.

Carlos.

    Come, on the instant one of us must die !

Alvaro.

    Death I despise, but it grieves me to injure

    Him who first offered me friendship.

Carlos.

    Profane not the word.

Alvaro.

    Not I, but fate, your father slew ;

    I ne'er seduced that lovely angel ;

    Both look on us, and from heaven

    Tell your heart I am innocent.

Carlos.

    And she ?

Alvaro.

    That fatal night I fell,

    Through many mortal wounds ;

    Then, cured, I sought her for a year.

    And found Leonora dead.

Carlos.

    False, false !

    My sister found refuge with a relative ;

    I arrived too late.

Alvaro

        (With anxiety.)

    And she ?

Carlos.

    Has fled.

Alvaro

        (Joyously.)

    She lives ! Ah, my friend.

    The trembling which my frame pervades

    Will tell you that my soul

    Cannot be so debased.

    She lives ! thank **God** !

Carlo.

    Ma in breve morirà.

Alvaro.

    No, d' un imene il vincolo
    Stringa fra noi la speme ;
    E s'ella vive, insieme
    Cerchiamo ove fuggì.
    Giuro che illustre origine
    Eguale a voi mi rende,
    E che il mio stemma splende
    Come rifulge il dì.

Carlo.

    Stolto ! fra noi dischiudesi
    Insanguinato avello ;
    Come chiamar fratello
    Chi tutto mi rapì ?
    D' eccelsa o vile origine,
    E duopo ch' io vio spegna,
    E dopo voi l' indegna
    Che il sangue suo tradì.

Alvaro.

    Che dite ?

Carlo.

    Ella morrà.

Alvaro.

    Tacete !

Carlo.

    Il giuoro
    A Dio ; cadrà l' infame.

Alvaro.

    Voi pria cadretc nel fatal certame.

Carlo.

    Morte ! ov 'io non cada esangue
    Leonora giungerò.
    Tinto àncor del vostro sangue
    Questo acciar le immergerò.

Alvaro.

    Morte, sì !—col drando mio.
    Un sicario ucciderò ;
    Il pensier volgete a Dio,
    L' ora vostra alfin suonò.

      (Sguainano le spade e si battono furiosamente.)

Carlos.

    But she will shortly die.

Alvaro.

    No, by the fond nuptial tie
    Soon may we be united ;
    If yet she lives, together
    Let us seek her abode.
    I swear that rank as noble
    Even as thine, I own,
    And that my birth is pure,
    Unstained, as light of day.

Carlos.

    Madman ! rising between us
    A river of blood is flowing ;
    How can I call him brother,
    Who did my hopes efface ?
    Whate'er may be thy origin,
    I live but to destroy thee ;
    Then too shall die the unworthy one
    Who did her race betray.

Alvaro.

    What sayest thou ?

Carlos.

    She shall die !

Alvaro.

    Hold !

Carlos.

    I swear to heaven
    The infamous wretch shall die !

Alvaro.

    Thou shalt first die thyself in mortal combat.

Carlos.

    But ere I fall, Leonora shall perish!
    This sword, with your blood dyed red
    Will I plunge into her heart.

Alvaro.

    Die thou ! with my steel
    Will I slay the assassin ;
    Turn your thoughts to heaven,
    For your last hour is nigh.

      (They draw swords an l fight furiously.)

SCENA IX. *Accore la Pattuglia del campo per separati.)*

Coro.

Fermi, arrestate !

Carlo

(Furente.)

No. La sua vita.

Coro.

Lunge di qua si tragga.

Alvaro.

(Forse—del ciel l' aita a me soccorre.)

Carlo.

Colui morrà !

Coro

(A CARLO che cerca svincolarsi.)

Vieni

Carlo.

Carnefice del padre mio !

(A DON ALVARO viene trascinato altrove dalla pattuglia.)

Alvaro.

Or che mi resta ! Pietoso Iddio

Tu inspira, illumina il mio pensier.

(Gettando la spada.)

Al chiostro, all' eremo, ai santi altari

L'obblio, la pace chiegga il guerrier.

(Esce.)

SCENA X. *Spunta il sole.—il rullo dei tamburi e lo squillo delle trombe danno il segnale della sveglia. La scena va animandosi a poco a poco. Soldati Spagnuoli ed Italiani di tutte le armi sortono dalle tende ripulendo schioppi, spade, uniformi, ecc., ecc. Ragazzi militari giuocano ai dadi sui tamburi. Vivandiere che vendono liquori, frutta, pane, ecc., PREZIOSILLA dall' alto d' una baracca predice la buona ventura. Scena animatissima.*

Coro.

Lorchè pifferi e tamburi

Par che assordino la terra,

Siam felici, ch' è la guerra

Gioja e vita al militar.

Vita gaia, avventurosa,

Cui non cal doman nè jeri,

Ch' ama tutti i suoi pensieri

Sol nell' oggi concentrar.

Preziosilla

(Alle Donne.)

Venìte all' indovina.

Ch' è giunta di lontano,

E puote a voi l' arcano.

SCENE IX. *The Sentries of the Camp run to part them*

Chorus.

Hold ! stay !

Carlos

(Raging.)

No : his life !

Chorus.

Drag him hence !

Alvaro.

(Heaven has sent me aid.)

Carlos.

He shall die.

Chorus

(To DON CARLOS, who tries to fight him.)

Come away.

Carlos.

Murderer of my father !

(To DON ALVARO, as he is dragged off by the Sentries.)

Alvaro.

What now remains for me ? Merciful Heaven,

A thought from above inspires me.

(Throws down the sword.)

To the cloister I go and at the holy altar,

Peace and oblivion will the warrior seek.

(Exit.)

SCENE X. *Sunrise.   The roll of drums and call of trumpets give the signal for waking. The scene gradually becomes full of life. Spanish and Italian soldiers emerge from their tents, cleaning muskets, swords, uniforms, etc. etc. Young recruits play at dice on the drum heads. Vivandiers sell liquors, fruit, bread, etc. PREZIOSILLA, mounted on a stand, tells fortunes. Great animation*

Chorus.

When fife and drums

Deafen the world,

We rejoice, for war to the soldier

Is life and full delight.

A life of joy and adventure

To him who cares naught for the morrow;

Who loves in his thoughts to dwell

On the bright hopes of to-day,

Preziosilla

(To the Women.)

Come to the fortune-teller,

Who has come from distant parts ;

She to you can reveal

Futuro decifrar.

(Ai Soldati.)

Corrette a lei d' intorno,
La mano le porgete.
Le amanti apprenderete
Se fide vi restar.

Coro.

Corriamo all' indovina
La mano le porgiamo,
Le belle udir possiamo
Se fide vi restar.

Preziosilla.

Chi vuole il paradiso
Si accendo di valore,
E il barbaro invasore
S' accenga a debellar.
Avanti, avanti, avanti.
Predirvi sentirete
Qual premio coglierete
Dal vostro battagliar.

(Molti la circondano.)

Coro.

Avanti, ec.

Soldati.

Qua, vivandiere, un sorso.

(La Vivandiere versano loro.)

Uno.

Alla salute nostra !

Tutti

(Bevendo.)

Viva !

Altro.

A Spagna ! ed all' Italia unite !

Tutti.

Evviva !

Preziosilla.

Al nostro eroe, Don Federico Herreros.

Tutti.

Viva ! Viva !

Uno.

Ed al suo degno amico
Don Felice de Bornos.

Tutti.

Viva ! viva !

What the future will bring.

(To the Soldiers.)

Come around her,
And hold out your hands ;
So all you can learn
If your maidens be true.

Chorus.

Let us haste to the teller of fortunes,
And show her our hands,
Thus we all can learn
If our fair ones are true.

Preziosilla.

He who longs for Paradise
Must show himself brave,
Prepare to subdue
The savage horde of invaders,
Come on, come on, come on,
And you shall hear foretold
What the prize you shall win
In the war that you wage.

(Many surround her.)

Chorus.

Come on, etc.

Soldiers.

Here, vivandiers, give us to drink.

(The vivandiers give them drink.)

A Soldier.

To our own health we drink !

All

(Drinking.)

Hurrah !

Another.

To Spain and Italy united !

All.

Hurrah !

Preziosilla.

To our hero, Don Federico Herreros !

All.

Hurrah ! hurrah !

A Soldier.

And to his noble friend,
Don Felice de Bornos !

All.

Hurrah ! Hurrah !

SCENA XI L' attenzione e attirata da TRABUCO. rivendugio-lo, che dalla bottega a sinistra viene con una cassetta al colla portante vari oggetti di meschino valore?.

Trabuco.

A buon mercato chi vuol comprare ?
Forbici, spille, sapon perfetto !
(Lo attorniano.)
Io vendo e compero qualunque oggetto,
Concludo a pronti qualunque affare.

Soldato 1.

Ho qui un monile, quanto mi dai ?
(Lo mostra.)

Soldato 2.

Ve' una collana ? Se vuoi la vendo.
(Lo mostra.)

Soldato 3.

Questi orecchini li pagherai ?
(Lo mostra.)

Coro.

Vogliamo vendere ?
(Mostrando orologi, anelli, ecc.)

Trabuco.

Ma quanto vedo
Tutto è robaccia, brutta robaccia !

Coro.

Tale, o furfante, è la tua faccia.

Trabuco.

Pure aggiustiamoci ; per ogni pezzo
Do trenta soldi.

Tutti
(Tumultuando.)

Da ladro è il prezzo.

Trabuco.

Ih ! quanta furia ! c' intenderemo,
Qualch' altro soldo v' aggiungeremo—
Date qua, subito !

Coro.

Purchè all' istante
Venga il danaro bello e sonante.

Trabuco.

Prima la merce—qua—colle buone.

Soldati.

A te.
(Dandogli gli affetti.)

Altri.

A te.
(Dandogli gli affetti.)

SCENE XI. TRABUCO, the Pedlar, attracts their attention, who, from the shop on the left, comes with a box at his waist, carrying various objects of small value.

Trabuco.

Who will buy at a bargain?
Scissors, pins, scented soap !
(They surround him.)
I buy and sell all sorts of things
And quickly conclude my bargains.

1st Soldier.

Here is a necklace—what will you give ?
(Showing it.)

2nd Soldier.

Here is another—I will sell it.
(Showing it.)

3rd Soldier.

Wilt pay the price of these earrings ?
(Showing them.)

Chorus.

We'll sell ?
(Showing watches, rings, etc.)

Trabuco.

But what you show me
Is all rubbish, mere rubbish !

Chorus.

Just like yourself, you rogue !

Trabuco.

However, we may agree: for each article
I will give thirty soldi.

All
(Enraged.)

'Tis the price of a thief !

Trabuco.

Eh ! what a fuss ! we shall agree,—
Another soldo we will add:
Give them here—quick.!

Chorus.

Provided on the instant
We see the money sound and shining.

Trabuco.

The merchandise first—here—fair play.

Soldiers.

There's for thee.
(Giving the things.)

Others.

For thee.
(Giving things.)

Altri.

A te.

(Dandogli gli affetti.)

Trabuco

(Ritira le robe e paga.)

A voi, a voi, benone !

Coro.

Al diavol vattene !

(Cacciandolo.)

Trabuco

(Da se contento.)

(Che buon affare !)

A buon mercato chi vuol comprare ?

(Avviandosi ad altro lato del compo.)

SCENA XII. Detti, e Contadini questuanti, con Ragazzi a mano

Contadini.

Pane, pan per caritò!
Tetti e campi devastati
N' ha la guerra, ed affamati,
Cerchiam pane per pietà.

SCENA XIII. Detti, ed alcuni RECLUTE, piangenti, che giungono scortate.

Reclute.

Povere madri deserte nel pianto !

Per dura forza dovemmo lasciar.
Della beltà n' han rapiti all' incanto,
A' nostre case vogliamo tornar.

Vivandiere

(Accostandosi gaiamente alle RECLUTE. e offerendo loro da here.)

Non piangete, giovanotti,
Per le madri e per la belle ;
V' ameremo quai sorelle,
Vi sapremo confortar.
Certo il diavolo non siamo ;
Quelle lacrime tergette.
Al passato, ben vedete,
Ora è inutile pensar.

Preziosilla

(Entrando fra le RECLUTE. ne prende alcune pel braccio, e dice loro burlescamente.)

Che vergogna !—Su coraggio !
Bei figliuoli, siete pazzi ?
Sè piangete quai ragazzi,
Vi farete corbellar.

Others.

For thee.

(Giving things.)

Trabuco

(Taking the things and paying.)

To you, to you, very good !

Chorus.

Go to the devil !

(They drive him away.)

Trabuco

(Highly pleased.)

(What good luck !)

Who will buy everything cheap ?

(Goes to the other side of the camp.)

SCENE XII. The same, and PEASANTS begging and leading Children

Peasants.

Bread, for charity's sake !
The war has destroyed
Our homes and our fields ;
Starving we ask for bread !

SCENE XIII. The same, and some RECRUITS, weeping, with an escort.

Recruits.

Our poor mothers are deserted in their grief !

By force we were made to leave,
And from our lovers' arms torn away.
To our homes we wish to return.

Vivandiers

(Approaching gaily the RECRUITS, and offering them drink.)

Do not repine, O young men,
For your mothers and your lovers ;
Like sisters we will love you,
And seek to console you.
Truly fiends we are not,
Then dry your tears
And cease to think
Upon the happy past.

Preziosilla

(Mixing with the RECRUITS, takes some of them by the arm, and says, jeeringly.)

Shame on you !—Show more courage !
Great babies, are you mad ?
If you wail like little children
You will be jeered and hooted.

Un' occhiata a voi d' intorno,
E scommetto che indovino ;
Ci sarà più d' un visino,
Che sapravvi consolar.

Tutti.

Nella guerra è la follia
Che dee il campo rallegrar.
Viva ! viva la pazzia,
Che qui sola ha da regnar !

(Le Vivandiere prendono francamente le RECLUTE pel braccio,
c s' incominicà vivacissima danza generale. Ben presto la con-
fusione e lo schiamazzo giungono al como.)

SCENA XIV. Detti e Fra MELITONE, che preso nel vortice
della danza, e per un momento costretto a ballare colle Vivandiere.
Finalmente, riuscito a fermarsi, esclama:

Melitone.

Toh, toh ! poffare il mondo ! oh che tem-
pone !
Corre ben l'aventura !—Anch' io ci sono !
Venni di Spagna a medicar ferite,
Ed alme a medicar. Che vedo ! è questo
Un campo di Christiani, o siete Turchi ?
Dove s' è visto berteggiar la santa
Domenica cosi ? Ben più faccenda

Le *bottiglie* vi dan che le *battaglie* !
E invece di vestir *cenere* e *sacco*
Qui si tresca con *Venere*, con *Bacco* ?
Il mondo è fatto una casa di pianto ;
Ogni convento, o qual profanazione !
Or è *covo del vento* ! I *Santuari*
Spelonche diventàr di sanguinari
E perfino i *tabernacoli di Cristo*
Fatti son *ricettacoli del tristo*.
Tutto è soqquadro.
E la ragion ? pe' vostri
Peccati

Soldati.

Ah, frate ! frate !

Melitone.

Voi le feste
Calpestate, rubate, bestemmiate—

Soldati Italiano.

Togone infame !

Soldato Spag.

Segui pur, padruccio.

All.

Cast your eyes around,
And I'll wager you can find
More than one face here
To console your vain regrets.

All.

In war it is folly only
That makes the camp resound.
Hurrah ! long life to folly.
That alone has a right to reign !

(The Vivandiers boldly sieze the RECRUITS by the arm, and commence a dance all around. Soon the noise and confusion reach
its height.)

SCENE XIV. The same, and BROTHER MELITONE, who,
seized in the whirl of the dance, is obliged to dance with the
Vivandiers. At last, managing to release himself, he exclaims:

Melitone.

Oh, oh ! good heaven ! what a wild life !
Adventures are coming fast !—I am in
for it !
I came from Spain wounds to heal,
And souls to cure. What do I see ?
Is this a camp of Christians or of Turks ?
Where do people make such a mockery
Of the holy Sabbath ? You have more
to do
With bottles than with battles !
And instead of putting on sackcloth and
ashes,
You play tricks with Venus and Bacchus.
The world is made a place of tears ;
Every convent—oh, what profanation—
Is open to the winds. The sanctuaries
Are become dens of murderers !
And, to crown all, the most sainted shrines
Made refugees for rascals.
All is upset ; and wherefore ?
Through your sins.

Soldiers.

Ah, friar ! friar !

Melitone.

You despise the feasts of the Church,
You rob, you swear—

Italian Soldier.

Infernal friar !

Spanish Soldier.

Go on, old fellow.

Melitone.

E membra e capi siete d' una stampa ;
Tutti eretici.

Italiano.

Or or l' aggiustiam noi.

Melitone.

Tutti, tutti, cloaca di peccati,
E finchè il mondo puzzi di tal *pece*
Non isperi mai la terra alcuna *pace*.

Italiano.

Dàlle, dàlli !
(Serrandolo intorno)

Spagno
(Difendendolo.)

Scappa ! scappa !

Italiano.

Dàlli, dàlli sulla cappa !

(Cercano picchiarlo, ma egli se la svigna, declamando sempre.)

Preziosilla

(Ai Soldati che lo inseguono uscendo di scena.)

Lasciatelo, ch' ei vada.

Far guerra ad un cappuccio!—bella impresa !

Non m' odon?—sia il tamburo sua difesa.

(Prende a caso un tamburo, e imitata da qualche Tamburino, lo suona. I Soldati accorrono tosto a circondarla seguiti da tutta la turba.)

Melitone.

And chiefs and soldiers all of a stamp,
All heretics.

Italian.

We will soon settle you.

Melitone.

All, all, sinks of iniquity ;
And until the world is smothered with tar,
The earth cannot hope for peace.

Italian.

Give it him!
(Crowding round him)

Spanish
(Defending him)

Escape ! be off !

Italian.

Give it him—knock him on the head !

(They try to beat him, but he avoids them, continuing to exclaim.)

Preziosilla.

(To the Soldiers, who follow him off the stage.)

Let him alone, let him go.

Make war upon a friar !—a fine affair !

They hear me not—the drum shall defend him.

(Takes up a drum, and, imitated by a little Drummer, sounds it.) The Soldiers immediately surround her, followed by the whole throng.)

RATAPLAN, DELLA GLORIA — *RATAPLAN, SONGS OF GLORY* (Preziosilla and Chorus)

Allegro vivo

Ra - ta - plan, ra - ta - plan, del - la glo - ria Nel sol - da - to ri -
Ra - ta - plan, ra - ta - plan, songs of glo - ry Make the sol - dier's heart

tem - pra l'ar - dor; Ra - ta - plan, ra - ta - plan, di vit - to - ria Que - sto
thrill with de - light; Ra - ta - plan, ra - ta - plan, in a sto - ry All their

suo - no e se - gnal pre - cur - sor! Ra - ta - plan, ra - ta - plan, ra - ta -
val - or - ous deeds we re - cite. Ra - ta - plan, ra - ta - plan, ra - ta -

plan, ra - ta - plan, ra - ta - plan, ra - ta - plan, ra - ta -
plan, ra - ta - plan, ra - ta - plan, ra - ta - plan, ra - ta -

plan, ra - ta - plan, plan, plan, ra - ta - plan, ra - ta - plan, plan, plan.
plan, ra - ta - plan, plan, plan, ra - ta - plan, ra - ta - plan, plan, plan.

Rataplan, si raccolgon le schiere,	Rataplan, the troops assemble,
Rataplan, son guidate a pugnar.	Rataplan, are led to the fight,
Rataplan, rataplan, le bandiere	Rataplan, rataplan, the banners
Del nemico si veggon piegar !	Of the enemy give way before us.
Rataplan, pim, pum, pam, inseguite	Rataplan, pim, pum, pam, pursue
Chi le terga, fuggendo, voltò.	The coward who flees from the foe.
Rataplan, le gloriose ferite	Rataplan, the wounds of the brave
Col trionfo il destin coronò.	Are with triumph crowned by fate.
Rataplan, della patria la gloria,	Rataplan, the glory of the country
Più rifulge de' fili al valor !	Shines forth in the valor of her sons
Rataplan, rataplan, la vittoria	Rataplan, rataplan, victory
Al guerriero conquista ogni cor.	Has won each warrior's heart.
FINE DELL' ATTO TERZO.	END OF THE THIRD ACT.

ATTO IV

SCENA I. Vicinanze d' Hornachuelos. Interno del Convento della Madonna degli Angeli. Meschino porticato circonda una Corticella con aranci, oleandri, gelsomini. Alla sinistra dello spettatore, e la porta che mette alla via; a destra altra porta, sopra la quale si legge 'Clausura.'

Il PADRE GUARDIANO passeggia gravemente leggendo il breviario. Dalla sinistra entrano molt Pezzenti, d' ogni eta e sesso, con rozze scodelle, alla mano pignatte o piatti.

Coro.

> Fate la carità,
> E un' ora che aspettiamo !
> Andarcene dobbiamo,
> Fate la carità.

SCENA II. Detti e FRA MELITONE, che viene dalla destra, caperto il ventre d' ampio grembiale bianco ed ajutato da altro Laico, porta una grande caldaja a due manichi, che depongono nel centro; il Laico riparte.

Melitone.

> Che ! siete all' osteria ! Quieti.

(Incomincia a distribuire col ramaiuolo la ministra.)

Donne
>> (Spingendosi fra loro.)
> Qui, presto a me.

Vecchi.

> Quante porzioni a loro.

Altri.

> Tutti vorrian per sè.

Tutti.

> N' ebbe già tre Maria.

Una
>> (A MELITONE.)
> Quattro a me.

Tutti.

> Quattro a lei !

Detti.

> Sì, perchè ho sei figliuolì.

Melitone.

> Perchè ne avete sei ?

Detta.

> Perchè li mandò Iddio.

Melitone.

> Sì, sì, Dio—non li avreste
> Se al par di me voi pure la schiena percoteste
> Con aspra disciplina, e più le notti intere
> Passaste recitando rosari e miserere.

ACT IV

SCENE I. The neighborhood of Hornachuelos. Interior of the Convent of the 'Madonna degli Angeli.' A simple Colonnade surrounds a small Court, filled with orange trees, oleanders, and jessamines. On left of the spectator, a door opening on the road; on the right another door, on which is written 'Clausura.'

The FATHER GUARDIANO walks about, seriously reading his breviary. From the left enter many Beggars, of each sex, with rough porringers, pipkins, or plates in their hands.

Chorus.

> Alms we beg of you.
> An hour we have waited,
> And soon we must go.
> Alms ! Alms !

SCENE II. The above and BROTHER MELITONE, who comes from the right, with a large white apron in front, and, aided by another Lay-brother, carries a great cauldron with two handles, which they place in the middle; the Lay-brother goes away.

Melitone.

> What ! do you take this for an inn ? Be silent.

(Begins to distribute the minestra with a ladle.)

Women
>> (Pushing forward.)
> Quick, give me some.

Old Men.

> What a quantity for them.

Others.

> Each wants for it himself.

All.

> Maria has already had three.

A Woman
>> (To MELITONE.)
> Four for me.

All.

> Four for her !

Woman.

> Yes, for I have six children.

Melitone.

> Why have you six ?

Woman.

> Because Heaven sent them to me.

Melitone.

> Ay, ay, Heaven—you would not have them
> If, like me, you scourged your back
> With a sharp scourge, and spent the night
> In reciting rosaries and misereres.

Guardiano.

Fratel—

Melitone.

Ma tai pezzenti son di fecondità.

Davvero spaventosa.

Guardiano.

Abbiate carità.

Vecchi.

Un po' di quel fondaccio ancora ne donate.

Melitone.

Il ben di Dio, bricconi, fondaccio voi chiamate ?

Alcuni.

A me padre !

(Presentando le scodelle.)

Altri.

A me.

(Presentando le scodelle.)

Melitone.

Oh andatene in malora,

O il ramajuol sul capo v' aggiusto bene or ora !

Io perdo la pazienza !

Guardiano.

Oh, carità, fratello !

Donne.

Più carità ne usava il padre Raffaello.

Melitone.

Sì, sì ma in otto giorni, avutone abbastanza.

Di poveri e ministra, restò nella sua stanza.

E scaricò la soma sul dosso a Melitone,

E poi con tal canaglia usar dovrò le buone ?

Guardiano.

Soffrono tanto i poveri : la carità è un dovere.

Melitone.

Carità con costoro che il fanno per mestiere ?

Che un campanile abbattere co' pugni sarien buoni,

Che dicono fondaccio il ben di Dio ?

Bricconi !

Alcuni.

Oh, il padre Raffaele—

Guardiano.

Brother—

Melitone.

But these beggars are prolific

To such a wonderful degree.

Guardiano.

Be merciful.

Old Men.

Give us a little more of these dregs.

Melitone.

A godsend, you rogues, and you call it dregs !

Some.

To me, Father !

(Presenting their porringers.)

Others.

To me?

(Presenting theirs.)

Melitone.

Go to Jericho,

Or I will lay the ladle about your heads !

I lose all patience !

Guardiano.

Be merciful, brother !

Women.

Father Raffaello was more kind.

Melitone.

True, true, but after a week of soup and beggars

He had enough and took to his bed.

He left his burden on the back of Melitone.

And how can I be gentle with such rabble ?

Guardiano.

They suffer much : charity toward them is a duty.

Melitone.

Charity to those who make it their trade ?

Who could fell a steeple with their fists ?

Who call this godsend dregs ? The rogues !

Some.

Oh, Father Raffaello—

Altri.

Era un angelo.

Altri.

Un santo !

Tutti.

Se il padre Raffaele—

Melitone.

Non m'annoiate tanto !

(*Distribuisce in fretta il residuo, dicendo—*)

Il resto, a voi, prendetevi,
Non voglio più parole !

(*Fa rotolare la caldaia con un calcio.*)

Fuori di qua, lasciatemi,
Sì fuori, al sole, al sole :
Pezzenti più di Lazzaro,
Sacchi di pravità,
Via, via, bricconi, al diavolo !
Toglietevi di qua !

(*Indispettito le scaccia, confusamente, percuotendoli col grembiale che si sara tolto, e chiude la porta, restandone assai adirato e stanco.*)

SCENA III. Il padre guardaino e melitone.

Melitone

(*Asciugandosi il sudore con un fazzoletto bianco che avara cavato da una manica.*)

Auf ! pazienza non v'ha che basti !

Guardiano.

Troppa
Dal Signor non ne aveste :
Facendo carità un dover s' adempie
Da render fiero un angiol.

Melitone

(*Prendendo tabacco.*)

Che al mio posto
In tre dì finerebbe
Col ministrar de' schiaffi.

Guardiano.

Tacete ; umil sia Meliton, nè soffra
Se veda preferirsi Raffaele.

Melitone.

Io? no—amico gli son, ma ha certi gesti.
Parla da sè—ha cert' occhi.

Others.

Was an angel !

Others.

A saint !

All.

Yes, Father Raffaello—

Melitone.

Don't bother me so !

(*Hastily distributing what remains, saying—*)

Take what is left.

(*Makes the cauldron roll over with a kick.*)

I will have no more words—go ?
Out of here—leave me !
Yes, go and warm yourselves in the sun ;
Beggars greater than Lazarus.
Bags of depravity,
Go, rascals, go to the devil !
Be off from here !

(*He angrily drives them out, striking them with the apron he has taken off, and shuts the door, remaining very angry and tired.*)

SCENE III. Father guardiano and melitone.

Melitone

(*Wiping off the perspiration with a white handkerchief, which he takes from his sleeve.*)

Ouf ! I have no more patience !

Guardiano.

Truly Heaven has not
Blessed you with over much ;
Giving charity is fulfilling a duty
Which might rejoice an angel.

Melitone

(*Taking snuff.*)

Who would be done for in my place
In three days.

Guardiano.

Silence : be humble, Melitone, not be vexed.
Though Raffaello be preferred.

Melitone.

I? no—I am his friend : but he has such ways.
He talks to himself—has such looks.

Guardiano.

    Son le preci,
    Il digiun.

Melitone.

    Jer nell' orto lavorava
    Cotanto stralunato, che scherzando,

    Dissi : Padre, un mulatto
    Parmi–Guardommi bieco,
    Strinse le pugna, e—

Guardiano.

    Ebbene ?

Melitone.

    Quando cadde
    Sul campanil la fulgore, ed usciva
    Fra la tempesta gli gridai : Mi sembra
    Indo selvaggio un urlo
    Cacciò che mi gelava.

Guardiano.

    Che v' ha a ridir ?

Melitone.

    Nulla, ma il guardo e penso
    Che il demonio, narraste,
    Qui stette un tempo in abito da frate,
    Gli fosse il padre Raffael parente ?

Guardiano.

    Giudizzii temerarii. Il ver narrai ;
    Ma n' ebbe il superior revilazione
    Allora. Io, no.

Melitone.

    Ciò è vero !
    Ma strano è molto il padre ! La ragione ?

Guardiano.

    Del mondo i disinganni,
    L' assidua penitenza.
    Le veglie, l' astinenza
    Quell' anima turbar.

Melitone.

    Saranno i disinganni
    Adunque e l'astinenza.
    L' assidua penitenza,
    Che il capo gli guastar !

    (suona con forza il campanello alla porta.)

Guardiano.

    It is through his praying
    And fasting.

Melitone.

    Yesterday, as he worked in the orchard.
    His eyes seemed so starting out, that
      jestingly
    I said, 'Father, you look like a mulatto !'
    He turned an angry glance on me,
    Clenched his fist, and—

Guardiano.

    What then ?

Melitone.

    When the lightning struck the steeple,
    As he went out into the storm, I cried,
    'You look to me like a wild Indian !'
    Whereupon he uttered a howl
    That froze my blood.

Guardiano.

    What followed ?

Melitone.

    Nothing ; but I looked at him, and thought
    That the demon you told us of,
    Who once lived here in a friar's dress,
    Might be a relative of Father Raffaello.

Guardiano.

    A rash judgment. I told the tale ;
    But to the superior 'twas revealed,
    And not to me.

Melitone.

    That is true ;
    But the father is most strange ! What is
      the cause ?

Guardiano.

    Finding out the deceit of the world,
    Constantly performing penance,
    Vigils and abstinence,
    Have disturbed his mind.

Melitone.

    Discovering the world's deceit,
    The various abstinences,
    And the frequent penances,
    Have upset his brain !

    (The bell at the door is rung violently.)

204   LA FORZA DEL DESTINO—THE FORCE OF DESTINY.

Guardiano.
>Giunge qualcuno—aprite.
>>(Parte.)

SCENA IV. FRA MELITONE e DON CARLO, che avviluppato in un grande mantello, entra francamente.

Carlo
>(Alteramente.)
>Siete voi il portiere ?

Melitone.
>(E goffo ben costui !)
>S' ora v' apersi, parmi.

Carlo.
>Il padre Raffaele ?

Melitone.
>(Un altro !) Due ne abbiamo ;
>L' un di Porcuna, grasso,
>Sordo come una talpa, l' altro scarno,
>Bruno, occhi (ciel quali occhi !) voi chiedete ?

Carlo.
>Quell dell' inferno.

Melitone.
>(E desso !) E chi gli annuncio ?

Carlo.
>Un cavalier.

Melitone.
>(Qual boria ! è un mal arnese.)
>>(Parte.)

SCENA V. DON CARLOS, poi DON ALVARO in abito da frate.

Carlo.
>Invano Alvaro ti celasti al mondo
>
>E d'ipocrita veste
>Scudo fecesti alla viltà. Del chiostro
>
>Ove t' ascondi m' additàr la via
>L'odio e la sete di vendetta ; alcuno
>Qui non sarà che ne divida ;
>Solo il tuo sangue può lavar l' oltraggio
>Che macchiò l' onor mio ;
>E tutto il verserò, lo giuro a Dio.

Guardiano.
>Someone has arrived—open.
>>(Exit.)

SCENE IV.—FATHER MELITONE, and DON CARLOS, who enters boldly, wrapped in a great cloak.

Carlos
>(Haughtily.)
>Are you the porter ?

Melitone.
>(The man must be a fool !)
>It appears to me I just let you in.

Carlos.
>Father Raffaello?

Melitone.
>(Another !) We have two of them ;
>One from Porcuna, fat,
>Deaf as a post ; the other lean, dark eyes,
>(Heavens, what eyes !) Which do you want ?

Carlos.
>The fiend.

Melitone.
>('Tis he !) And whom shall I announce ?

Carlos.
>A cavalier.

Melitone.
>(What arrogance ! an ill-bred fellow.)
>>(Exit.)

SCENE V. DON CARLOS, after him DON ALVARO, in a monk's habit.

Carlos.
>In vain, Alvaro, from the world thou hidest,
>And with hypocrite's garb
>Wouldst shield thy villainy. To the cloister
>Which concealed thee, hate
>And vengeance pointed out the way.
>None here shall hold me from thee ;
>Thy blood alone can cleanse the stain
>From my outraged honour :
>And before heaven I swear to shed it !

Alvaro.

Fratello—

Carlo.

Riconoscimi.

Alvaro.

Don Carlo ! Voi vivente !

Carlo.

Da un lustro ne vo' in traccia,
Ti trovo finalmente :
Col sangue sol cancellasi
L' infamia ed il delitto.
Ch' io ti punisca è scritto
Sul libro del destin.
Tu prode fosti, or monaco,
Un' arma qui non hai ;
Deggio il tuo sangue spargere,
Scegli, due ne portai.

Alvaro.

Vissi nel mondo—intendo ;
Or queste vesti l' eremo,
Dicon che i falli ammendo,
Ah ! cessi il sangue alfin !
Lasciateme.

Carlo.

Difendere
Quel sajo, nè il deserto.
Codardo, non ti possono.

Alvaro

(Trasalendo.)

Codardo ! tale asserto—

(Poi frenandosi.)

(Ah no !—assistima, Signore !)

(A DON CARLO.)

La minaccie, i fieri accenti,
Portin seco in preda i venti;
Perdonatemi, pietà.
A che offendere cotanto
Chi fu solo sventurato !
Deh chiniam la fronte al fato :
O fratel, pietà, pietà !

Carlo.

Tu contamini tal nome.
Una suora mi lasciasti
Chi tradita abbandonasti
All' infamia, al disonor.

Alvaro.

Brother—

Carlos.

Behold and know me.

Alvaro.

Don Carlos ! Alive !

Carlos.

For five years I have been on thy track,
At length I find thee :
With blood alone can thy imfamy
And misdeeds be blotted out.
'Tis written in the book of fate
That I shall punish thee.
Thou wert then valiant, now a monk ;
Thou hast no weapon here ;
As I must shed thy blood,
Two have I brought : choose.

Alvaro.

In the world I have lived—I understand ;
The garments I wear, this desert place,
Proclaim my errors reformed,
Ah ! at least cease this strife ;—
Leave me.

Carlos.

Coward,
Neither the cassock, or the desert,
Can protect thee !

Alvaro

(Shrinking.)

Coward ! that assertion—

(Restraining himself.)

(Ah no !—help me, Heaven !)

(To DON CARLOS.)

Threats, fierce and angry tones
Are cast to the winds ;
Pardon and pity me.
Wherefore goad so far
Him who was only unfortunate ?
Let us yield to fate :
Brother, mercy, mercy !

Carlos.

Thou dost contaminate the name.
Thou hast left me a sister
Whom thou didst betray, and then abandon
To infamy and dishonour !

Alvaro.

No, non fu disonorata,
Ve lo giura un sacerdote !
Sulla terra l'.ho adorata
Come in cielo amar si puote.
L'amo ancora, e s' ella m' ama
Più non brama questo cor.

Carlo.

Non si placa il mio furore
Per mendace e vile accento ;
L' arme impugna, ed al cimento
Scendi meco, o traditor.

Alvaro.

Se i rimorsi, il pianto omni.
Non vi parlano per me,
Qual nessun mi vide mai,
Io mi prostoro al vostro piè !
(Eseguisce.)

Carlo.

Ah, la macchia del tuo stemma
Or provasti con quest' atto !

Alvaro
(Balzando in piedi furente.)

Desso splende piucchè gemma.

Carlo.

Sangue il tinge di mulatto.

Alvaro
(Non potendo piu frenarsi.)

Per la gola voi mentite !
A me un brando .
(Glielo strappa di mano.)
Un brando—uscite !

Carlo
(Avviandosi.)

Finalmente !

Alvaro
(Ricomponendosi.)

No; l' inferno
Non trionfi. Va—riparti.
(Getta la spada.)

Carlo.

Ti fai dunque di me scherno ?
S' ora meco misurarti,
O vigliacco, non hai core,
Ti consacro al disonore !
(Gli da uno schiaffo.)

Alvaro.

No, she was not dishonoured,
It is a priest who swears it !
On earth I have adored her.
As only in Heaven they can love.
I love her still, and if she love me,
My heart has no other wish.

Carlos.

My rage will not be quelled
By base and lying words ;
Take the weapon, and to the combat
I challenge thee, O villain.

Alvaro.

If my remorse and tears
Speak not to you in my favour,
I will do what none have ever seen—
Prostrate myself at your feet !
(Kneels.)

Carlos.

Ah, the baseness of thy birth
Thou hast now proved by this act !

Alvaro
(Rising up furiously.)

That is more than jewels resplendent.

Carlos.

It is tinged with the blood of the mulatt?

Alvaro
(No longer able to restrain himself.)

I cast the lie in your teeth !
Give me a sword !
(Snatches one from his hand.)
A weapon—lead on !

Carlos
(Moving on.)

Al last !

Alvaro
(Recovering himself.)

No ; the fiend shall not
Prevail. Go—away !
(Throws away the sword.)

Carlos.

What, dost thou make a jest of me ?
If to measure weapons with me
Thou hast not courage, coward,
Thus I disgrace thee !
(Gives him a blow.)

Alvaro

(Furente.)

Ah, seguasti la tua sorte !

Morte a entrambi !

(Raccogliendo la spada.)

Carlo.

A entrambi morte !

A 2.

Paga l' ira alfin sarà.

Te l' inferno ingoierà !

(Escono currendo dalla sinistra.)

SCENA VI. Valle tra rupi inaccessibili, attraversata da un ruscello. Nel fondo, a sinistra dello spetattore, e una Grotta con porta practicabile, e sopra una campana che si potra suonare dall' interno. E il tramonto. La scena si oscura lentamente; la luna apparisce splendidissima.

DONNA LEONORA pallida, sfigurata, esce dalla grotta agitatissima

Leonora.

Pace, pace, mio Dio ! cruda sventura

M' astringe, ahimè, a languir ;

Come il dì primo da tant' anni dura

Profondo il mio soffrir.

L'amai, gli è ver ! ma di beltà e valore

Cotando Iddio l' ornò.

Che l' amo ancor, nè togliermi dal core

L' imagine saprò.

Fatalità ! fatalità !—un delitto

Disgiunti n' ha quaggiù !

Alvaro, io t' amo, e su mel cielo è scritto ;

Non ti vedrò mai più !

Oh, Dio, Dio fa ch' io muoja ; chè la calma

Può darmi morte sol.

Invan la pace qui sperò quest' alma

In preda a lungo duol.

(Va ad un sasso, ove sono alcune provigione deposte da lPADRE GUARDIANO.)

Misero pane, a prolungarmi vieni

La sconsolata vita—ma chi giunge ?

Profanare che ardisce il sacro loco ?

Maledizione ! maledizione !

(Torna rapidamente alla Grotta, e vi si rinchiude)

SCENA VII. Si ode dentro la scena un cozzar di spade.

Carlo

(Dal' interno.)

Io muojo !—Confession !—

Alvaro

(Furiously.)

Thy death warrant is sealed !

Death to both !

(Picks up the sword.)

Carlos.

Death to both !

Both.

Wrong shall at last be avenged,

And hell shall receive thee !

(They rush out towards the left.)

SCENE VI. A valley amongst inaccessible rocks, traversed by a stream. At the back, on the left of the spectator, is a Grotto with a practicable door, and above it a bell, which can be sounded from within. The sun has set. The scene darkens gradually; The moon rises brightiy.

DONNA LEONORA, pale, wan, enters agitated from the grotto.

Leonora.

Peace, grant me peace, O Lord ;

By dire misfortune I'm condemned to languish ;

As on the first day, during so many years,

Profound has been my grief.

I loved him ! with beauty and courage

Heaven had so endowed him.

I love him still, nor can I from my heart

Banish his image.

O cruel fate !—a crime

Has parted us forever here below !

Alvaro, I love thee, and in heaven 'tis decreed

That I shall never see thee more !

O Lord, suffer me to die, for peace

To my soul comes only in death.

Here in vain I hope for peace,

A prey to lingering woe.

(She goes to a stone, on which are some provisions, placed there by FATHER GUARDIANO.)

Miserable food, thou comest to prolong

A wretched life—but who approaches ?

Who dares profane this sacred spot ?

Malediction ! malediction !

(Returns quickly to the Grotto and shuts herself in.)

SCENE VII. A clashing of swords is heard close at hand.

Carlos

(Without.)

I am slain !—Absolution !

L'alma salvate.

(ALVARO entra in scena colla spada sguainata.)

E questo ancor sangue d'un Vargas.

Carlo

(Sempre dall' interno.)

Padre.   Confession.

Alvaro

(Getta la spada.)

Maledetto io son ; ma è presso
Un eremita.

(Corre alla grotta e batte alla porto.)

A confortar correte
Un uom che muor.

Leonora

(Dall' interno)

Nol posso.

Alvaro.

Fratello ! in nome del Signor.

Leonora.

Nol posso.

Alvaro

(Batte con piu forza.)

E d' uopo.

Leonora

(Dall' interno suonando la campana.)

Ajuto !   Ajuto !

Alvaro.

Deh venite.

SCENA VIII.   Detto e LEONORA che si presenta sulla porta.

Leonora.

Temerarii, del ciel l' ira fuggite !

Alvaro.

Una   donna !   qual   voce—ah   no—uno
spettro.

Leonora

(Riconoscendo DON ALVARO.)

Che miro ?

Alvaro.

Tu—Leonora !

Leonora.

Egli è ben desso.

(Avvicinandosi ad ALVARO.)

Io ti riveggo ancora.

Save my soul.

(ALVARO enters, with unsheathed sword.)

Again is the blood of Vargas shed.

Carlos

(Still without.)

A priest—absolution.

Alvaro

(Throwing down the sword.)

I am accursed :
But here dwells a hermit.

(Runs to cave, and beats at the door.)

Hasten to aid.
A dying man.

Leonora

(From the cave.)

I cannot.

Alvaro.

Brother, in the name of heaven !

Leonora.

I cannot come.

Alvaro

(Beating furiously.)

His last moments are near.

Leonora

(Ringing the bell in the cave.)

Help ! help !

Alvaro.

Come quickly !

SCENE VIII.   LEONORA appears at the door of the cave.

Leonora.

Rash one, fly from the wrath of heaven !

Alvaro.

A woman ! that voice ! ah, no—'tis a
vision !

Leonora

(Recognizing DON ALVARO.)

What do I see !

Alvaro.

Leonora !

Leonora.

'Tis he.

(Advancing to ALVARO)

Again I see thee !

Alvaro.

Lungi—lungi da me— queste mie mani
Grondano sangue. Indietro !

Leonora.

Che mai parli ?

Alvaro

(Accennando.)

Là giace spento un uom.

Leonora.

Tu l'uccidesti ?

Alvaro.

Tutto tentai per evitar la pugna.
Chiusi i meie dì nel chiostro.

Ei mi raggiunse—m' insultò—l'uccisi.

Leonora.

Ed era ?

Alvaro.

Tuo fratello !

Leonora.

Gran Dio ?

(Corre ansante verso il bosco.)

Alvaro.

Destino avverso
Come a scherno mi prendi !
Vive Leonora e ritrovarla deggio
Or che versai di suo fratello il sangue !

Leonora

(Dall' interno, mette un grido.)

Ah !

Alvaro.

Qual grido !—che avvenne ?

SCENA IX. LEONORA ferita entra sostenuta dal GUARDIANO
e detto.

Alvaro.

Ella—ferita !

Leonora

(Morente.)

Nell' ora estrema perdonar non seppe.
E l'onta vendicò nel sangue mio.

Alvaro.

E tu paga non eri
O vendetta di Dio !—Maledizione !

Alvaro.

Away, away from me, my hands
Are stained with blood. Look yonder.

Leonora.

What meanest thou ?

Alvaro

(Pointing.)

See, there lies a dying man.

Leonora.

Thou has killed him ?

Alvaro.

Vainly I tried to evade this fray.
Within the cloister's shelter passed my
life !
He sought me out there—insulted me,—
I slew him.

Leonora.

And he was ?

Alvaro.

Thy brother !

Leonora.

Great heaven !

(Runs breathlessly towards the wood.)

Alvaro.

Relentless destiny
Thus mocks me ever !
Leonora lives, and I meet her
With her brother's blood upon me.

Leonora

(Shrieks without.)

Ah !

Alvaro.

That cry ! what has happened.

SCENE IX. LEONORA enters, wounded, supported by GUARD-
IANO.

Alvaro.

'Tis she—wounded !

Leonora

(Dying)

In his last hour he pardoned not ;
And with my blood revenged his shame.

Alvaro.

And thou art thus repaid,
Oh, vengeance of heaven ! malediction !

Guardiano
                    (Solenne.)
    Non imprecare ; umiliati
    A lui ch'è giusto e santo—
    Che adduce a eterni gaudii
    Per una via di pianto.
    D'ira e furor sacrilego.
    Non profferir parola,
    Mentre quest' angiol vola
    Al trono del Signor.

Leonora
                    (Con voce morente.)
    Si, piangi— e prega.

Alvaro.
    Un reprobe, un maledetto io sono.
    Flutto di sangue inalzasi.
    Fra noi.

Leonora.
    Di Dio il perdono io ti prometto.

Guardiano.
    Prostrati !

Leonora.
    Alvaro.

Alvaro.
    A quell' accento
    Più non poss' io resistere.
        (Gettandosi ai piedi di LEONORA.)
    Leonora, io son redento,
    Dal ciel son perdonato !

Leonora e Guardiano.
    Sia lode a te Signor.

Leonora.
                    (Ad ALVARO.)
    Lieta or poss' io precederti.
    Alla promessa terra.
    Là cesserà guerra.
    Santo l'amor sarà.

Alvaro.
    Tu mi condanni a vivere,
    E mi abbandoni intanto !
    Il reo, il reo soltanto.
    Dunque impunito andrà !

Guardiano
                    (Solemnly.)
    Curse thou not. Humble thyself
    Before Him who is just and holy ;
    Who by a path of tears
    To eternal joys conducts thee.
    Pour not forth words.
    Of ire and sacrilegious fury.
    While this angel ascends
    To the heavenly throne.

Leonora
                    (With dying accents.)
    Yes,—weep and pray.

Alvaro.
    Reprobate, accursed am I.
    Barriers of blood between us
    Have arisen.

Leonora.
    Heaven grants me power to pardon thee.

Guardiano.
    Kneel.

Leonora.
    Alvaro—

Alvaro.
    Those loved tones
    No more can I resist.
        (Throwing himself at LEONORA'S feet.)
    Leonora, I am saved,
    Heaven has forgiven my sins.

Leonora & Guardiano.
    Power eternal, praise be to **Thy name** !

Leonora
                    (To ALVARO.)
    Gladly now can I precede thee
    To the promised land ;
    There strife shall cease.
    And holy love shall reign.

Alvaro.
    Thou condemnest me to live
    While thus forsaking me ;
    I, the guilty one,
    Alone go unpunished.

Guardiano.

    Santa del suo màrtirio
    Ella al Signore ascenda.
    E il suo morir ti apprenda
    La fede e la pieta !

Leonora.

    O Ciel ti attendo, addio !
    Io ti precedo Alvaro.

Alvaro.

    Morta !

Guardiano.

    Salita a Dio.

        (Cala lentamente la tela.)

        FINE DELL' OPERA.

Guardiano.

    Holy in her martyrdom,
    She now departs to heaven ;
    And piety and faith
    Her death will teach thee.

Leonora.

    Oh, heaven, I await thee ; farewell,
    I do but precede thee, Alvaro.

Alvaro.

    Dead !

Guardiano.

    Ascended to heaven !

        (Curtain slowly falls.)

        END OF THE OPERA.

AÏDA

by

GIUSEPPE VERDI

LIBRETTO BY ANTONIO GHISLANZONI

THE STORY OF THE ACTION

Aïda, daughter of Amonasro, King of Ethiopia, has been led into captivity by the Egyptians. While in bondage sne conceives a tender passion for Radames, a young Egyptian warrior, who warmly responds to her affection. The opening incidents of the opera disclose these facts, and set forth, besides, the choice of Radames as leader of an expedition against the invading forces of Ethiopia, and the love, still unrevealed, of Amneris, daughter of Egypt's sovereign, for the fortune-favored chieftain. Amneris suspects the existence of a rival, but does not learn the truth until Radames returns victorious. The second act commences with a scene between the Princess and the slave. Amneris wrests from Aïda the secret she longs and yet dreads to fathom, and dire hate at once possesses her. Radames comes back, laden with spoils. Among his prisoners—his rank being unknown to his captors—is Amonasro, father of Aïda. Radames asks of his sovereign that the captives be freed. The King consents to releasing all of them except Aïda and Amonasro. The monarch then bestows upon the unwilling Radames the hand of Amneris, and amid songs of jubilation the act terminates. In the third act the marriage of Amneris and Radames is on the eve of celebration. Radames, however, is devotedly attached to Aïda, and the maiden, urged thereunto by Amonasro, seeks to persuade the soldier to flee to Ethiopia and turn his sword against his native land. Without resolving upon the act of treachery, Radames lends an ear to her supplications. The party is about to take to flight, when the High Priest, Ramphis, and Amneris, both of whom have overheard the lovers, appear. Aïda and Amonasro, on the advice of Radames, escape. Radames remains to await his fate. This is speedily decided. Radames, in act the fourth, is tried on a charge of treason. Amneris, repentant, vainly endeavors to save his life,—for the lover of Aïda scorns to renounce her,—and he is deaf to the entreaties of the daughter of the King, whose jealousy, as Amneris herself is aware, has brought about his downfall. The dénouement is not long delayed. The final picture shows the interior of the Temple of Vulcan. Above is the hall of worship; below, the vault in which Radames, doomed to die, is interred alive by the priests. As the stone is sealed over his head, Aïda, who has awaited Radames in the tomb, rises before him. The lovers are locked in a last embrace as Amneris, heart-broken, kneels in prayer on the marble which parts from the living the couple now united in death.

AÏDA

ACT I.

SCENE I.—Hall in the Palace of the King at Memphis; to the right and left a colonnade with statues and flowering shrubs; at the back a grand gate, from which may be seen the temples and palaces of Memphis and the Pyramids.

(RADAMES and RAMPHIS.)

Ramphis.

Yes, a report runs that the Ethiopian dares
Again defy us, and the Valley of the Nile
And Thebes to threaten.—A messenger shortly
Will bring the truth.

Radames.

The sacred Isis
Didst thou consult?

Ramphis.

She has named
Of the Egyptian phalanxes
The supreme leader.

Radames.

Oh! happy man!

Ramphis

(with meaning, gazing at RADAMES).

Young and brave is he. Now to the king
I convey the decrees of the goddess.

(Exit.)

Radames

(alone).

If that warrior I were! If my dream
Should be verified! An army of brave men
Led by me—victory—the applause
Of all Memphis! And to thee, my sweet Aïda,
To return, crowned with laurels!
To say to thee,—for thee I have fought, and for thee conquered!

ATTO I.

SCENA I.—Sala nel Palazza del Re a Menfi. A destra e a sinistra una colonnata con statue e arbusti in flori—Grande porta nel fondo, de cui appariccone i tempii, i palazzi di Menfi e le Piramidi.

(RADAMES e RAMFIS.)

Ramfis.

Sì: corre voce che l'Etiope ardisca
Sfidarci ancora, e del Nilo la valle
E Tebe miniacciar—Fra breve un messo
Recherà il ver.

Radames.

La sacra
Iside consultasti?

Ramfis.

Ella ha nomato
Delle Egizie falangi
El condottier supremo.

Radames.

Oh lui felice!

Ramfis

(con intenzione, fissando RADAMES).

Giovine e prode è desso—Ora, del Nume
Reco i decreti al Re.

(Esce.)

Radames

(solo).

Se quel guerrier
Io fossi! se il mio sogno
Si avverasse!... Un esercito di prodi
Da me guidato... e la vittoria... e il plauso
Di Menfi tutta!—E a te, mia dolce Aïda,
Tornar di lauri cinto...
Dirti: per te ho pugnato e per te ho vinto!

CELESTE AÏDA—*RADIANT AÏDA*   Air (Radames)

Ce - les-te A - i - da,   for - ma di - vi - na,   Mi - sti - co ser - to
Heav'n-ly_ A - i - da,   beau - ty_ re - splen-dent,   Mys - te - rious blend - ing

di lu - ce e fior,   del mio pen - sie - ro,   tu sei re - gi - na, tu di mia
of flow'rs and light,   Queen of_ my   soul thou   reign-est tran-scen-dent, Thou of my

vi - ta sei lo splen-dor,   Il tuo bel   cie - lo vor-rei ri -
life art the splen-dor bright.)   To thy bright   skies once more I'd re -

dar - ti, le dol-ci brez-ze del pa - tria suol, un re-gal ser - to sul crin po-
store thee, To the soft air of thy na - tive land, Gar-lands im - pe - rial I would wreathe

sar - ti, er - ger-ti un tro - no vi-ci-no al sol, ah!_   Ce - les-te A - i - da,
o'er thee, Raise thee a throne_ near the sun to stand! ah!_   Heav'n - ly_ A - i - da,_

for - ma di - vi - na,_   mi - sti - co rag-gio   di lu - ce e fior;
beau - ty_ re - splen - dent,_   Mys - te - rious blend-ing   of flow'rs and light;

del mio pen-sie - ro   tu sei re - gi - na, tu di mia vi - ta sei lo splen-dor.
Queen of_ my soul thou reign-est tran-scen-dent, Thou of my life art the splen-dor bright.

Il tuo bel cie - lo vor-rei ri - dar-ti; le dol-ci brez-ze del pa-tria
To thy bright skies once more I'd re - store thee, To the soft air of thy na-tive

suol; un re - gal ser - to sul crin po - sar - ti, er - ger-ti un tro - no vi-ci-no al
land, Gar-lands im - pe - rial I would wreathe o'er thee, Raise thee a throne e -ter-nal to

ppp

sol, un tro - no vi - ci-no al sol, un tro - no vi - ci-no al sol.
stand; A throne near the sun to stand, A throne near the sun to stand.

Amneris. (Enter AMNERIS.)

What unwonted fire in thy glance!
With what noble pride glows thy face.
Worthy of envy—oh, how much—
Would be the woman whose beloved aspect
Should awaken in thee this light of joy!

Radames.

With an adventurous dream
My heart was blessed. To-day the goddess
Declared the name of the warrior who to the
    field
The Egyptian troops shall lead. If I were
To such honor destined!

Amneris.

Has not another dream
More gentle, more sweet,
Spoken to thy heart? Hast thou not in
    Memphis
Desires—hopes?

Radames.

I! (What a question!
Perhaps—the hidden love
Which burns my heart she has discovered—
The name of her slave
She reads in my thoughts!)

Amneris.

(Oh! woe if another love
Should burn in his heart;
Woe, if my search should penetrate
This fatal mystery!)

Radames (Enter AÏDA.) (seeing AÏDA).

She!

Amneris. (AMNERIS e detto.)

Quale insolita givia
Nel tuo sguardo! Di quale
Nobil fierezza ti balena il volto!
Degna di invidia oh! quanto
Saria la donna il cui bramato aspetto
Tanta luce di gaudio in te destasse!

Radames.

D'un sogno avventuroso
Si beava il mio cuore—Oggi, la diva
Profferse il nome del guerrier che al campo
Le schìere Egizie condurrà... S'io fossi
A tale onor prescelto...

Amneris.

Nè un altro sogno mai
Più gentil... più soave...
Al cuore ti parlò?... Non hai tu in Menfi
Desiderii... speranze?

Radames.

Io!... (quale inchiesta!)
Forse... l'arcano amore
Scoprì che m' arde in core...
Della sua schiava il nome
Mi lesse nel pensier!)

Amneris.

(Oh! guai se un altro amore
Ardesse a lui nel core!...
Guai se il mio sguardo penetra
Questo fatal mister!)

Radames (AÏDA e detto.) (vedendo AÏDA).

Dessa!

Amneris.

(He is moved! And what
A glance he turns to her!
Aïda!—My rival—
Perhaps is she?)

(After a short silence turning to AïDA.)

Amneris.

(Ei si turba... e quale
Sguardo rivolse a lei!
Aïda!... a me rivale...
Forse saria costei?)

(Dopo breve silenzio volgendois ad AïDA.)

VIENI, O DILETTA—*COME, DEAREST FRIEND*　Trio (Amneris, Aïda and Radames)

Andante mosso　　　　　AMNERIS

Vie — ni o di - let - ta ap-pres-sa-ti　　schia - va non sei ne an-
Come, dear-est friend, come near to me,　　Slave I no long- er

cel - la,　　Qui do-ve in dol - ce fa - sci-no　　Io ti chia-mai so -
name thee;　　Here in af-fec - tion's ten - der bonds,　My sis-ter I pro-

rel - la,　　　Pian - gi?　　del - le tue la - cri-me sve - la il se -
claim thee,　　Weep'st thou?　　Why are these tears flow-ing, tell me thy

AIDA *Più mosso*

gre - to,　sve-la il se - gre-to a me.　Ohi-mè!　di guer-ra fre-me-re　l'a-
se - cret,　thy se-cret tell to me.　A-las!　the din of strife re-sounds,　The

tro - ce gri-do io sen - to　Per l'in-fe-li - ce pa-tri-a,　per me,　per voi pa-
war- like hosts as - sem-ble,　For my un-hap-py na-tive land,　For me,　for thee, I

AMN

ven - to.　Fa-vel-li il ver?　nè s'a-gi-ta più gra-ve cu-ra in te?
trem- ble.　Dost tru-ly speak?　no grav-er care dis-turbs thy gen-tle heart?

Allegro　　　　　　　　　　　　　　　RADAMES

Tre-ma,　　o re - a schia-va,　　　Nel vel-
Trem-ble,　　O slave dis- sem-bling!　　Up - on

ra - to a-mor è___ pian-to di___ sven-tu - ra - - - to a-mor.
hap - py smart, Are   flow-ing from love's un - hap - - - py smart!

(Enter the KING, preceded by his Guards and followed by RAMPHIS, his Ministers, Priests, Captains, etc., etc. An Officer of the Palace, and afterwards a Messenger.)

King.

Great cause summons you,
O faithful Egyptians, around your king.
From the confines of Ethiopia a Messenger
Just now arrived—grave news he brings.
Be pleased to hear him.
(To an Officer.)
Let the messenger come forward.

Messenger.

The sacred soil of Egypt is invaded
By the barbarous Ethiopians! Our fields
Are devastated! The crops burned!
And emboldened by the easy victory, the
    depredators
Already march on Thebes.

All.

They dare so much!

Messenger.

A warrior indomitable and fierce
Conducts them—Amonasro.

All.

The King!

Aïda.

(My father!)

Messenger.

Already Thebes is in arms, and from the
    hundred gates
Breaks forth upon the invading barbarian,
Carrying war and death.

King.

Yes, be war and death our cry!

All.

War! War!

King.

Tremendous! inexorable!
(Addressing RADAMES.)
Of our unconquered legions
Venerated Isis

(Il RE, preceduto dalle sue guardie e seguito da RAMFIS da Ministri, Sacerdoti, Capitani, ecc., ecc. Un Uffiziale di Palazzo, indi un Messaggiero.)

Il Re.

Alta cagion vi aduna,
O fidi Egizii, al vostro Re d'intorno.
Dal confin d'Etiópia un Messaggiero
Dianzi giungea—gravi novelle ei reca...
Vi piaccia udirlo...
(Ad un Ufficiale.)
Il Messaggier si avanzi!

Messaggiero.

Il sacro suolo dell' Egitto è invaso
Dai barbari Etiope—i nostri campi
Fur devastati... arse le messi... e baldi
Della facil vittoria, i predatori
Già marciano su Tebe...

Tutti.

Ed osan tanto!

Messaggiero.

Un guerriero indomabile, feroce,
Li conduce—Amonasro.

Tutti.

Il Re!

Aïda.

(Mio padre!)

Messaggiero.

Già Tebe è in armi e dalle cento porte
Sul barbaro invasore
Proromperà, guerra recando e morte.

Il Re.

Si: guerra e morte il nostro grido sia.

Tutti.

Guerra! guerra!

Il Re.

Tramenda, inesorata...
(Accostandosi a RADAMES.)
Iside venerata
Di nostre schiere invitte

Has already designated the supreme leader—
Radames.

All.

Radames!

Radames.

Thanks be to the gods!
My prayers are answered.

Amneris.

(He leader!)

Aïda.

(I tremble!)

King.

Now move, O warrior,
To the temple of Vulcan. Gird thee
With the sacred arms, and fly to victory.
Up! To the sacred bank of the Nile
Hasten, Egyptian heroes;
From every heart let burst the cry,
War and death to the foreigner!

Ramphis and Priests.

Glory to the gods! Remember all
That they rule events;
That in the power of the gods alone
Lies the fate of warriors.

Ministers and Captains.

Up! Of the Nile's sacred shore
Be our breasts the barrier;
Let but one cry resound:
War and death to the foreigner!

Radames.

Holy rage of glory
Fills all my soul.
Up! Let us rush to victory:
War and death to the foreigner!

Amneris
(bringing a banner and consigning it to RADAMES).
From my hand receive, O leader,
The glorious standard.
Be it thy guide, be it thy light,
On the path of glory.

Aïda.

(For whom do I weep? For whom pray?
What power binds me to him!
I must love him! And this man
Is an enemy—an alien!)

Già designava il condottier supremo:
Radames.

Tutti.

Radames.

Radames.

Sien grazie ai Numi!
I miei voti fur paghi.

Amneris.

(Ei duce!)

Aïda.

(Io tremo!)

Il Re.

Or, di Vulcano al tempio
Muovi, o guerrier—Le sacre
Armi ti cingi e alla vittoria vola.
Su! del Nilo al sacro lido
Accorrete, Egizii eroi;
Da ogni cor prorompa il grido.
Guerra e morte allo stranier!

Ramfis e Sacerdoti.

Gloria ai Numi! ognun rammenti
Ch'essi reggono gli eventi—
Che in poter d'e Numi solo
Stan le sorti guerrier.

Ministri e Capitani.

Su! del Nilo al sacro lido
Sien barriera i nostri petti;
Non echeggi che un sol grido:
Guerra e morte allo stranier!

Radames.

Sacro fremito di gloria
Tutta l'anima mi investe—
Su! corriamo alla vittoria!
Guerra e morte allo stranier!

Amneris
(recando una bandiera e consegnandota a RADAMES).
Di mia man ricevi, o duce,
Il vessillo glorioso;
Ti sia guida, ti sia luce
Della gloria sul sentier.

Aïda.

(Per chi piango? per chi prego?...
Qual poter m'avvince a lui!
Deggio amarlo... ed è costui
Un nemico... uno stranier!)

Ill.

War! War! Extermination to the invader!
Go, Radames, return conqueror!

(Exeunt all but AÏDA.)

Aïda.

Return victorious! And from thy lips
Went forth the impious word! Conqueror
Of my father—of him who takes arms
For me—to give me again
A country, a kingdom; and the illustrious
name
Which here I am forced to conceal! Con-
queror
Of my brothers, with whose dear blood
I see him stained, triumphant in the ap-
plause
Of the Egyptian hosts; and behind the
chariot
A king!—my father—bound with chains!
The insane word
Forget, O gods!
Return the daughter
To the bosom of her father;
Destroy the squadrons
Of our oppressors!
Unhappy one! What did I say?—And my
love
Can I ever forget,
This fervid love which oppresses and en-
slaves,
As the sun's ray which now blesses me?
Shall I call death
On Radames?—On him whom I love so
much?
Ah! Never on earth was heart torn
By more cruel agonies.
The sacred names of father, of lover,
I can neither utter, nor remember—
For the one—for the other—confused—
trembling—
I would weep—I would pray;
But my prayer changes to blasphemy.
My tears are a crime—my sighs a wrong—
In dense night the mind is lost—
And in the cruel anguish I would die.

Tutti.

Guerra! guerra! sterminio all' invasor!
Va, Radames, ritorna vincitor!

(Escono tutti meno AÏDA.)

Aïda.

Ritorna vincitor!... E dal mio labbro
Uscì liempi parola!—Vincitore
Del padre mio... di lui che impugna l'armi
Per me... per ridonarmi
Una patria, una reggia! e il nome illustre
Che qui celar mie è forza—Vincitore
De' miei fratelli... ond' io lol vegga, tinto
Del sangue amato, trionfar nel plauso
Dell' Egizie coorti!... E dietro il carro,
Un Re... mio padre... di catene avvinto!...

L'insana parola,
O Numi, sperdete!
Al seno d'un padre
La figlia rendete;
Struggete le squadre
Dei nostri oppressor!
Sventurata! che dissi?... e l'amor mio?...
Dunque scordar poss' io
Questo fervido amor che oppressa e schiava
Come raggio di sol qui mi beava?
Imprecherò la morte
A Radames... a lui che amo pur tanto!
Ah! non fu in terra mai
Da più crudeli angoscie un cor affranto.
I sacri nomi di padre... di amante
Nè profferir poss' lo, nè ricordar...
Per l'un... per l'altro... confusa... tremante..
Io piangere vorrei... vorrei pregar.
Ma la mia prece inbestemmia si muta...
Delitto è il pianto a me... colna il sospir...
In notte cupa la mente è perduta...
E nell' ansia crudel vorrei morir.

NUMI, PIETÀ!—*PITY, KIND HEAVEN*   Air (Aïda)

Nu-mi, pie-tà— Del mio sof-frir! Spe-me-non v'ha pel mio do-lor. A-mor fa-tal, Tre-men-do a-mor Spez-za— mi il cor,— fam-mi mo-rir! Nu-mi, pie-tà del mio— sof-frir, Ah! pie-tà, Nu-mi, pie-tà,— del mio— sof-frir,— Nu-mi, pie-tà del mio— sof-frir, pie-tà, pie-tà, del mio sof-frir

Pi-ty, kind Heav'n, To Thee I fly; Hope there is none in this my woe. Oh! fa-tal love, Thy pow'r I know, Break thou, my heart,— cause me to die. Pi-ty,— kind Heav'n, Thy pow'r I know. Oh,— kind Heav'n, pi-ty my woe, Thy mer-cy show,— pi-ty, kind Heav'n, re-lieve— my— woe: re-lieve my woe, re-lieve my woe.

SCENE II.—Interior of the Temple of Vulcan at Memphis. A mysterious light descends from above; a long row of columns one behind another is lost in the darkness; Statues of various deities; in the middle of the scene, above a platform covered with carpet, rises the altar, surmounted by sacred emblems; from golden tripods rises the smoke of incense.	SCENA II.—Interno del Tempio di Vulcano a Menfi. Una luce misteriosa scende dal' alto.—Uno lunga fila di colonne l'una all' altra addossate, si perde fra le tenebre. Statue di varie Divinità. Nel mezzo della scena, sovra un palco coperto da tappeti, sorge l'altare sormontato da emblemi sacri. Dai tripedi d'oro si innalza il fumo degli incensi.
PRIESTS and PRIESTESSES—RAMPHIS at the foot of the altar, afterwards RADAMES—The song of the PRIESTESSES accompanied by harps, is heard from the interior.	SACERDOTI e SACERDOTESSE—RAMFIS ai piedi dell' altare—A suo tempo, RADAMES—Si sente dall' interno il canto delle SACERDOTESSE accompagnato dalle arpe.

Priestesses   (in the interior).

Infinite Phthah, of the world
Animating spirit,
We invoke thee!

Infinite Phthah, of the world
The fructifying spirit,
We invoke thee!

Sacerdotesse   (nell' interno).

Immenso Fthà, del mondo
Spirito animator,
Noi ti invochiamo!

Immenso Fthà, del mondo
Spirito fecondator,
Noi ti invochiamo!

Fire uncreate, eternal,
Whence the sun has light,
We invoke thee!

Priests.

Thou who from nothing hast made
The waters, the earth and the heavens,
We invoke thee!

God, who of thy spirit
Art son and father,
We invoke thee!

Life of the Universe
Gift of eternal love,
We invoke thee.

(Enter RADAMES, introduced unarmed—While he goes to
the altar the PRIESTESSES execute the sacred dance—On the
head of RADAMES is placed a silver veil.)

Ramphis.

Mortal, beloved of the gods, to thee
Is confided the fate of Egypt. Let the holy
    sword
Tempered by the gods, in thy hand become
To the enemy, terror—a thunderbolt—
    death.
        (Turning himself to the gods.)
God, guardian and avenger
Of this sacred land,
Spread thy hand
Over the Egyptian soil.

Radames.

God, who art leader and arbiter
Of every human war,
Protect thou and defend
The sacred soil of Egypt.

(While RADAMES is being invested with the consecrated
armor, the PRIESTS and PRIESTESSES resume the religious
hymn and mystic dance.)

END OF THE FIRST ACT.

Fuoco increato, eterno,
Onde ebbe luce il sol,
Noi ti invochiamo!

Sacerdoti.

Tu che dal nulla hai tratto
L'onde, la terra e il ciel,
Noi ti invochiamo!

Nume che del tuo spirito
Sei figlio e genitor,
Noi ti invochiamo!

Vita dell' Universo,
Mito di eterno amor,
Noi ti invochiamo!

(RADAMES viene introdotto senz' armi—Montre va all'
altare, le SACERDOTESSE eseguiscono la danza sacra—Sul capo
di RADAMES vien steso un velo d'argento.)

Ramfis.

Mortal, diletto ai Numi—A te fidate
Son d'Egitto le sorti,—Il sacro brando
Dal Dio temprato, per tua man diventi
Ai nemici terror, folgore, morte.
        (Volgendozi al Nume.)
Nume, custode e vindice
Di questa sacra terra,
La mano tua distendi
Sovra l'Egizio suol.

Radames.

Nume, che duce ed arbitro
Sei d'ogni umana guerra,
Proteggi tu, difendi
D'Egitto il sacro suol!

(Mentre RADAMES viene investito delle armi sacre, le
SACERDOTESSE e SACERDOTI riprendono l'inno religioso e la
mistica danza.)

FINE DELL' ATTO PRIMO.

I PAGLIACCI
(Punchinello)

by

RUGGIERO LEONCAVALLO

PREFATORY NOTE.

RUGGIERO LEONCAVALLO, who wrote both the book and music of *Pagliacci*, belongs to the feverish neo-Italian school of composers for the theatre, whose other leading lights are his contemporaries, Puccini, Mascagni, and Giordano. *Pagliacci* was written at about the same time as Mascagni's *Cavalleria Rusticana*, and was likewise submitted to the prize competition of the publisher Sonzogno, in which Mascagni's opera was the successful work; but there is a credible story that *Pagliacci* would have received the award, but for the fact of its being in two acts instead of one, which placed it outside the conditions. The astute publisher, however, secured and issued both operas; and *Pagliacci* made a sensation only second to that of the triumphant *Cavalleria*. It was first produced, May 21, 1892, at the Dal Verme Theatre, Milan, with the following cast:

CANIO	GIRAUD.
TONIO	MAUREL.
SILVIO	ANCONA.
BEPPE	DODDI.
NEDDA	MME. STEHLE.

It soon made its way into the leading Italian and German theatres, scored a season's success in London, and was heard the following year in New York. Now the work holds a permanent place in the repertory of the great opera-houses.

Leoncavallo asserts that the tragedy on which he founded his libretto actually took place in the mountains of Calabria at a given date; but the idea is not a new one in stage-literature, having been previously used in somewhat similar form by both Spanish and French dramatists. The nearest approach to the opera is found in "La Femme du Tabarin," a tragi-parade by Catulle Mendès, which was performed, in 1887, at the *Theatre Libre* in Paris.[1] In fact, Mendès attempted to enjoin the performance of *Pagliacci* at Brussels, on the ground that Leoncavallo had stolen his plot; but the latter was able to demonstrate that the same story had been used long before.

In his treatment of the tragedy, Leoncavallo has made both text and music poignantly effective. The one purpose of the music is to vivify the dramatic significance of the text in every detail; the raw passions and brute impulses of a crude people are dealt with swiftly and directly, and the ironic contrasts which the action invites are seized and brought surely home to the spectator.

THE ARGUMENT.

THE scene of the story is laid in Calabria at the time of the Feast of the Virgin di Mezzagosto. During the prelude Tonio comes forward, as in the Prologue of ancient Greek tragedy, and explains that the subject of the play is taken from real life, and that the composer has devoted himself to expressing the sentiment, good or bad, but always human, of the characters he introduces, without commenting on their social condition. He then makes a sign for the curtain to rise.

The first act shows the meeting of two roads at the entrance of a village; at the right a travelling theatre. Villagers greet the arrival of a troupe of strolling players. Canio, the *Punchinello*, and chief of the little troupe, invites the crowd to attend the performance at seven o'clock, and then goes off with Beppe (the *Harlequin*) and several peasants to drink at the tavern. Tonio the *Clown* remains behind to care for the donkey, but takes advantage of Canio's absence to declare his love to Nedda, who is the *Columbine* of the troupe, and also Canio's wife. Upon being pressed for a kiss, she strikes Tonio with a whip, and he goes off vowing to be revenged. Then Silvio, a rich young villager, joins Nedda and tries to induce her to leave her husband, and the forlorn life of a stroller, which she loathes, to run away with him. Tonio espies

[1] The play has had at least one performance in New York, in which George Fawcett played the part of Tabarin.